TUSCANY

LANDSCAPE HISTORY ART

Text by

Franco Cardini

with sections on thirty-one towns and cities

BARNES & NOBLE

NEW YORK

S. ET BIBATIS SVPER MENSAM

Contents

STATO DI LVCCA
LVNI
SARZANA
PIETRA PANA
LVCCA
PISA
LIVORNO
PRATO
Campi
Fiesoli
FIORENZA
Barberino
Scarparia
Pratolino
S.Donato
Regello
SIENA
Staggia
COLLE
Poggibonsi
Chianti
Populonia
Piombino
Lago di Castigl
GORGONA
CAPRAIA
MARE TYRRHEN
Tombolo
SIENA
FIORENZA
ETRVRIA
CAELI TEMPERIE
AGRORVM CVLTV
VRBIVM ET OPPIDORVM
CELEBRITATE
VILLAR·ET SVBSTRVCTIONVM
FREQVENTIA
FLVMINVM AC PONTIVM
COMMODITATE
PISCOSIS LACVBVS
SALVBRIB·AQVAR·REMEDIIS
MERCATVRAE VSV
MILITVM ROBORE
LIBERAL·ARTIVM STVDIIS
INGENIORVM PRAESTANTIA
INCOLARVM DENIQVE
IN PONTIFICES ROMANOS
OBSERVANTIA
ET PIETATE ERGA D·O·M·
INSIGNIS

INTRODUCTION
TO THE JOURNEY

The Name and the Territory

When we speak of Tuscany we must first of all understand what we are talking about: a certain area with certain boundaries, a historical region the confines of which may coincide with those of the present political and administrative region, though not entirely and not necessarily. All the same, we would be doing an injustice to its landscape, to its people, to its various modes of speech, to the traditions still flourishing there, if our appreciation of the basic unity within the region did not also do justice to the profound differences, the particulars, and in short all the very diverse, though harmonizing, voices that go to make up the chorus.

We often say "Tuscany" while thinking simply of Florence. It is for the most part non-Tuscans who fall into this trap, to the great indignation of the Tuscans (Florentines included), since the historical, linguistic and cultural structure of the region – in spite of the exceptional importance of the "capital," which in any case exceeds the confines of the region itself – is eminently polycentric. Someone attempted to define it, rather delightfully, as a "thousand-year-old city-culture." Yet even today, in the era of the megalopolis, between the folds of its hills and mountains, and on the carpets of its few restricted plains, this region of cities still preserves broad areas that are en-

tirely or prevalently rural, or even uninhabited. It is often said that the Tuscans are absolutely unmistakable amongst the Italians, but by so saying we underestimate the fact that the region has many "frontier" areas, where this uniqueness is toned down, and where a Tuscan takes on something of Liguria, Emilia, Romagna, Umbria or Lazio.

The region contains a wealth of small differences, and even more or less evident internal divisions. From the basic point of view of climate, altitude and economy, there are in fact at least three Tuscanys: the region of the Apennines; the hilly areas which, from the rolling country of the "Lucchesia" across the gentle hills of Chianti and the Val d'Elsa, extend as far as the Colline Metallifere and Monte Amiata; and finally the coastal areas and the narrow river valleys wedged between hills and mountains. And this apart from the Tuscan islands, similar only in part to the coastal areas.

Gentile da Fabriano, *Adoration of the Magi*, detail of the predella. Uffizi, Florence; bottom, the ancient village of Monteriggioni (Siena)

pp. 4-5, Ignazio Danti, *Etruria*. Galleria delle Carte Geografiche, Vatican

But the region also changes a great deal from north to south. To the north of the Arno, where Tuscany starts to climb into the Apennines, which press it closer and closer to the sea as one goes northwards, approaching Liguria and Emilia, the characteristics of the region are at-

tenuated, and we have what we might call a "less Tuscan Tuscany." From the southern bank of the great river, almost as far as the gates of Siena, we find what may be the most specific and characteristic nucleus of the region (but to which, we repeat, the region itself cannot be entirely reduced, except at the price of unacceptable distortions). From Siena down we have the "Deep South" of Tuscany, with its treeless miles, with its Maremma, its sparser population, its different human and agricultural landscape.

Our Tuscany – the Tuscany we are about to speak of in these pages – is by no means a kind of magic triangle neatly outlined between the mountains and the Tyrrhenian Sea, clearly and precisely cut off from the rest of Italy. On the contrary, in one respect it is inextricably linked to the neighbouring regions, while in another it has within it so many diversities and nuances that any theory prejudicially in favour of unity would not hold water.

Ought one then to speak of "le Toscane," as we speak of "le Marche," "gli Abruzzi," and as until a short while ago we used to speak of "le Puglie" and "le Calabrie?" Well, no. And this denial is by no means emotional, but based on at least three valid reasons, one geographical, one historical, and the third linguistic and cultural. Geographically speaking the lines drawn by the Tyrrhenian, the Apennines and the Tiber mark out a pretty clear border, even if it is anything but "closed." Historically, after the organization provided by the Romans for the *regio* of Tuscia-Etruria, and the Late Mediaeval rise of a Longobard duchy (later a Frankish "march") of Tuscia, the leadership assumed by Florence in the process of transformation from a Commune to a regional State in the 14th and 15th cent. (in spite of considerable resistance from Siena and Lucca), and the establishment of the Grand Duchy under the houses of Medici and Lorraine, impressed an indelible stamp upon the region. Finally, Tuscan speech, in all its many varieties, has from the 13th cent. onwards, and in particular during the 19th cent., asserted itself as the literary language of United Italy, while even for this very reason confirming its original character as a regional tongue. This last aspect of the matter is the very one which makes it difficult to talk about Tuscany to Italians other than Tuscans; on account of a linguistic and literary involvement, it is hard for any Italian today not

The Apuan Alps with the city of Carrara in the background

The harmony of the Tuscan landscape in the environs of Siena, in the Val d'Orcia and in the Florentine part of Chianti

to think of Tuscany as just a little bit his own. It is hard, that is, to think of it as a "foreign" region.

Having said this, we must add that this very feeling can give rise to the most dangerous misunderstandings, for beneath a surface that is clear, simple, rational, serene and polished, the Tuscan landscape and people can occasionally be intractable, harsh, closed and mysterious. It is no coincidence that the peoples who left the deepest marks on the region (although, in part, the least visible), and who made the greatest contribution to its unitary character, were two enigmatic and defeated peoples, two protagonists of vanished civilizations: the Etruscans and the Longobards.

The similarity between the Etruscans and the Longobards, historically rather implausible, nevertheless comes

and federal ties, and in short on "horizontal" relationships. The antipathy shown by the Tuscans, from the 14th cent. onwards, towards the growing dominance of Florence, may be explained not only by the rivalry between cities and parties typical of the era of the Communes during the Middle Ages, but also perhaps by this ancient tendency towards a federal equilibrium that did not tolerate dominant powers. From the Etruscan *poleis* to the mediaeval Communes there runs the golden thread of a preference for a "little homeland" and for an independence that is almost never chauvinistic or exclusive, but rather (except for times of bitter conflict, which there certainly were) inclined naturally towards alliance and exchange with the neighbouring "little homelands." Meanwhile within any type of settlement or small area, there grew up a multiplicity of local characteristics, with their various traditions, and maybe even rivalries, pride and obstinacies.

Many cities, historically hostile to one another; a changing, irregular landscape marked by ranges of hills and no lack of really mountainous areas; many valleys, usually narrow, and frequently only in quite recent times reclaimed from the marshes. If this lie of a land, everywhere uneven and at times rugged, may at least in part be the cause of the closed, argumentative and aggressive character of many Tuscan people, or at least of that rather

spontaneously to mind whenever we compare their histories to those of their respective victors, who in both cases brought with them a supra-regional and supra-national culture that was destined to found empires: the Romans and the Franks. In comparison with their hierarchical, co-ordinating and "vertical" spirit, both the Etruscans and the Longobards appear to have been endowed with a quite different genius. Though destined to lose out in immediate historical circumstances, it was based on local liberties

pleasing roughness that is the basis of their common character, we should certainly add that a close look at its geological-historical features forces us to identify a number of sub-regional areas, each endowed with a robust character of his own.

With a few exceptions these areas correspond to the valleys of the most important rivers which cut through Tuscany. To start from the north-west of the region as defined for administrative purposes today, we first meet the basin of the river Magra, occupying the province of Massa-Carrara, which historically speaking looks towards Liguria, and was only assigned to Tuscany in 1871. This is the Lunigiana, the territory of the ancient city and diocese of Luni. Immediately to the south-east is the Garfagnana, which is the narrow valley of the river Serchio between the Apuan Alps and the watershed formed by the Apennines. To the south-west, there is the somewhat flat, sandy coastal area of the Versilia, with its pinewoods and its beaches, once fashionable and to some extent still so. With its centre at Viareggio, historically speaking this area is linked to one of the three great "capitals" of the region, Lucca. This same city is the centre for the lower valley of the Serchio – the Lucchesia – and the Valdinievole which includes the towns of Pescia and Collodi. Between Lucca and Pistoia the horizon is without any outstanding features until we get to Monte Albano and the middle Arno valley. This was a vast marshy area until it was reclaimed in the 18th cent. by order of Grand Duke Pietro Leopoldo. From it emerge only the "islands" formed by small hills such as that of Montecatini Alto. Further north the landscape once more becomes rugged, with the mountains towering above Pistoia (Montagna Pistoiese) which act as the watershed between this territory and that of Bologna. Travelling eastwards, after the narrow Val di Bisenzio, we enter the valley of the Sieve and its tributaries, corresponding to the historical area of the Mugello. From here, once we cross the Futa Pass, 930 metres up in the Apennines, we leave the geographical but not the historical area of Tuscany. We have in fact arrived in "Tosco-Romagna," occupying the upper basins of the Santerno, the Senio and the Lamone, with their chief centres at Firenzuola, Palazzuolo sul Senio and Marradi.

Horses grazing in the Maremma near Grosseto

Casa Ximenes in the marshland of Diaccia-Botrona at Castiglione della Pescaia (Grosseto)

If to the north the Mugello crosses the Apennines into Romagna, to the south it shades off into the lower Val di Sieve. Here it meets the mid-valley of the Arno (Medio Valdarno) at Pontassieve, which stands at the meeting of the waters.

Pontassieve is in fact a key-point. The Arno, which begins life by flowing south, having rounded the massif of the Pratomagno turns sharply north, and makes a broad curve just before Pontassieve. Here it collects the tributary waters from the Mugello, and heads westward past Empoli to Pisa and the sea. From Pontassieve we can cross the wooded bulk of the Pratomagno by way of the Passo della Consuma and thereby reach the Casentino. This is the upper valley of the Arno, marked at its northernmost limits by the mountains of Falterona and Fumaiolo, the sources respectively of the Arno and the Tiber. Immediately to the east of the Casentino we come to the Val Tiberina, which borders on Umbria, as in fact does the Val-

sandy and low-lying. This is the Maremma, the ancient *Maritima* now almost completely reclaimed, though it has not yet entirely lost the wonder of its great pinewoods, its pasturelands, its marshes abounding in wildfowl. The Maremma is divided into three parts: the "pisana" (between Cecina and the estuary of the Cornia), the "grossetana" (the coast between Cornia, Albegna and the lower reaches of the Ombrone), and the "senese" (upper reaches of the Ombrone), but it also extends as far as Monte Amiata, the Val d'Orcia, the Colline Metallifere and the so-called "Crete" (the bare, clay landscape south of Siena).

In the mid-valley of the Arno, between Empoli and San Miniato, we turn south into the broadest and most interesting valley in central Tuscany, the Val d'Elsa, along which ran the famous mediaeval road, the Via Francigena. From this valley to the south-west we may cross the hills around Volterra and reach the Val di Cecina and the sea. Going eastward we pass through the Chianti hills on our way to the upper Arno Valley with its chief centres at San Giovanni and Terranuova.

So here we have mountains, hills, valleys, marshes; woods of oak, chestnut and beech, with firs in the Apennines and vast pinewoods along the seashores; traces of a volcanic past visible here and there throughout the region, from Monte Morello to Monte Amiata, and which particularly in the centre and south of the region explain the presence of thermal springs of some importance; considerable deposits of metal ore, especially in the triangle between Massa Marittima, Amiata and the island of Elba; areas such as the middle and lower Arno valley, in which a vast population growth linked with an often unharmonious industrial development appear to have forever ruined the landscape and the balance of the environment, cheek by jowl with areas of apparently incontaminated beauty. These are the contradictions and contrasts which make Tuscany so full of surprises, and at the same time an explosive mixture of problems.

dichiana, the neighbouring basin of the river Chiana.

But let us return to the Arno and look at the area to the south of its left bank. Between Pisa and the river Cecina the coast around Livorno towers high above the sea. This little river rises in the Colline Metallifere, and abounds in echoes of Etruscan culture. It flows into the sea almost as soon as it has passed the small town that is called after it, and to the south of this the coast once again becomes

Benozzo Gozzoli, *Angels in Adoration*, detail with the city. Palazzo Medici-Riccardi, Florence

The pristine medieval charm of San Gimignano

"The Most Touching Landscape in the World"

As we drive along the Autostrada del Sole, or else the hair-raising but nonetheless picturesque Via Aurelia, in spite of a wealth of wonderful glimpses and sudden, breathtaking sights, we may not always be aware that we are passing through what Fernand Braudel thought was "the most touching landscape in the world." If it is true that the Maremma ought to be seen in the scorching midsummer sun, and Chianti when the first vine-leaves begin to redden; and if the forest of Camaldoli is at its most bewitching in the early-morning mists, and the "Balza" at Volterra in the sunset, it stands to reason that we cannot always be at the right place at the right time of day or season of the year. All the same, the reputation for being "modern" and "dynamic" which

Tuscany enjoys (and, let it be said, with ample justification) should not lead us to forget that it is one of the most densely wooded regions in the whole of Italy, and that it can boast a coastline 300 kilometers long.

Woods and sea shores, moreover, subject to decay and exposed to ecological death. From the outskirts of the Megalopolis that now stretches from Florence to Prato and Pistoia, and from Pisa to Livorno, or from the desolate stretches of the Apennines and the Garfagnana where emigration and the decline of population have created scores of abandoned villages, the traces of the landscape that inspired Benozzo Gozzoli, Leonardo and (later) Fattori

are not always very clearly discernible. Tourism itself is a notorious factor in the ruin of the environment, and yet (this appears paradoxical only at first sight) it constitutes one of the strongest reasons for arresting this ruination, while at the same time proving that so far it has not succeeded in despoiling Tuscany of its fame not only as a land of art and culture, but also of unique "natural" beauties.

The adjective "natural" is a magical one; so why do I provoke the reader by putting it in inverted commas? History can perhaps suggest an answer, for when it comes down to it almost no landscape is natural. If the Tuscan landscape is really as "touching" as Braudel would have us believe, the fact is that such feeling never arises spontaneously and without reflection. Both landscape and feeling are the products of centuries of cultural evolution, of choices made, of co-existence between man and his environment.

Bulldozers and avalanches of cement, acres of rubble and rubbish and the smoking factory chimneys, all these change the face of city and country alike, and blur their colours. Yet, together with historical memory there is a geographical memory which resides in place-names and takes us back to a quite different set of images, to the land-

Top, the landscape of the Crete Senesi; left, view of the countryside around Volterra

Facing page, top, Giovanni di Paolo, *Madonna dell'Umiltà*, detail. Pinacoteca Nazionale, Siena; bottom, Ambrogio Lorenzetti, *Effects of Good Government in the Countryside*, detail. Palazzo Pubblico, Siena

scape as it once was. Examples are the names of places in which we find such elements as "bosco" (wood), "macchia" (thicket), "prato" (meadow) – and the reader will have no difficulty in thinking of countless equivalents in English. Any territory is in fact a palimpsest. Nothing in it is really and truly "natural," unless we are content with an Arcadian and properly speaking phoney concept of nature; nothing is really in an aboriginal state.

By the beginning of the first millennium BC the region had more or less taken on the appearance it has today, at least on the level of large-scale morphology. Lakes and marshes had already shrunk back from the plains, with the exception of the large basins of the lower Valdarno, the Maremma and the Valdichiana, while the volcanoes in the southern parts of the area – including Monte Amiata – were already extinct. Only the coastline, due to the constant accumulation of alluvial soil at the estuaries of the rivers, had a different profile, though not as different as all that. By the 7th to 6th centuries BC the sand-bars now forming the lagoon of Orbetello had already joined the Argentario to the mainland, while it was during those same centuries that Greek influence introduced both the vine and the olive. These two "timeless" spirits at work in the magic landscape of Tuscany are actually not timeless at all. There

was, believe it or not, a time when wine and oil did not yet gladden the tables of our forebears (unless, of course, they were imported ...). The cypress-tree, which only in this part of the world succeeds in being something other than a *memento mori,* was introduced here only in Etruscan-Roman times, when the reorganization of the network of roads and a new measurement and distribution of territory (known as "centuriation") gave the region a really new look. But we have to wait for the late Middle Ages and the dawn of the modern era before seeing the Tuscan landscape take on that unique balance between man and nature in which man lives in scattered farms covering the hills as if with a network of dwellings, close enough to each other but not too close. One might call it the ideal osmosis between a town immersed in nature's verdure and a densely populated countryside.

This admittedly is true above all in the upper Valdarno, in Chianti and in Val d'Elsa, areas often taken as the one and only model of the "Tuscan countryside," which in fact also has its share of harshness and desolation. Both the harmoniousness, which is largely one of yesterday's myths, and the pollution which is widespread though not total, must come to terms with the dynamics of history. This is true also of the climate, which changes like everything else in the process of time, and here as elsewhere is affected by the cutting down of the woods, and modifications in the flow of water, and the general pollution of the environment. On the whole we now have a temperate Mediterranean climate, with the highest mean annual temperature in the Maremma (16° C) and the lowest in the valleys of the Appennines (12° C). Winters are often visited by the sun, but

Facing page, road with cypresses
in the Sienese countryside

Top, Leonardo da Vinci,
Annunciation, detail. Uffizi,
Florence; left, Fra Angelico,
Deposition from the Cross, detail.
Museo di San Marco, Florence

Wine and Oil

M ention Tuscan wine and the name that springs immediately to mind is Chianti. In fact, the esteem that it has enjoyed since ancient times has resulted in the extension of the name to include wine produced in marginal areas that are not really part of the hilly region between Siena, Florence and Valdarno known as Chianti. But fear not: the good Chianti, the real Chianti, is still there. How does one recognize it? Well, in the first place, of course, by the certified label with a black cockerel on a gold disk. But even more important is to know one's stuff. As with mushroom hunting, the first rule is to be competent.

Wine has a lot of serious and almost religious devotees, and it also has its own history. In Florence, the economic historian Federigo Melis

Top, Bartolomeo Bimbi, *Grapes*. Villa di Poggio a Caiano; above, Duccio di Buoninsegna, *Maestà*, detail of the *Entry into Jerusalem*. Museo dell'Opera, Siena

Guido Reni, *The Boy Bacchus*. Galleria Palatina, Florence

was a great expert on it, and described it in studies which are still famous. But if Tuscan wine was famous even in the Middle Ages, Chianti Classico as it is today is a relatively new product. The historic, mediaeval area of Chianti consists of the three communes of Radda, Gaiole and Castellina, but the "classic" wine-producing zone was more than doubled in 1933, bringing in the communes of Greve, and small parts of those of Castelnuovo Berardenga, Tavarnelle Val di Pesa, Barberino Val d'Elsa and even a few hectares in Poggibonsi. But the area remains extremely small.

Baron Bettino Ricasoli, an austere landowner of the region, laid down the proportions of various kinds of grapes to be used in the making of Chianti Classico. These proportions have been changed somewhat, but still involve a majority (65-70%) of Sangiovese (to give the wine body and colour) and some

10 or 15% of Canaiolo to give it softness and aroma. The remainder is made up of two white varieties of grape, the Trebbiano Bianco and the Malvasia, which give it "finesse" and a touch of acidity (needed for aging). Although Chianti's capacity for aging is still much vaunted, nowadays there are many people who like to drink it when it is new. Tastes change, especially through the influence of a part of the American market that prefers a fresher and lighter drink.

But there are other great wines, whose history is not as long as that of Chianti. These are the Brunello di Montalcino, the Vino Nobile di Montepulciano, and the wines from Bolgheri and Val di Cornia. Other excellent red wines are the "Chianti" from the hills of Siena and Arezzo, that of Val di Sieve (Rufina, Pomino, Nipozzano), and the wine of the Lower Valdarno (Montalbano, Carmignano). We should not forget the so-called "Supertuscans", red wines aged

Bernardino Poccetti, *The Marriage at Cana*, detail. Badia di Ripoli, Florence

for a long time that have been produced by many estates since the eighties using vines different from the native ones.

Less well known are the white wines, though they include fine products such as the "virgin" white wines of the Val di Chiana, the gilded Vernaccia of San Gimignano, and the "Galestro," which appeals to the modern palate because of its light fresh taste and slight effervescence. There are also good dessert wines, "passiti" (made from dried grapes), Muscatel and Vin Santo. In the last few years leading wine producers such as Antinori and Frescobaldi have begun to make a dry sparkling wine by the méthode champenoise, and with considerable success.

The question of olive oil is a more tricky one. The Tuscans consider the famous oil from Liguria to be too thin, and the oil from Puglia, on the contrary, to be too dense and heavy. Until a year or two ago the oils from Lucca were very much appreciated. They are light, and golden, and full of flavour. In these times of "natural" flavours, perhaps people will prefer the denser oil from Chianti or around Siena, which (when fresh) is green and peppery. But the great freeze of February 1985 somewhat compromised things, rendering inevitable a certain rise in prices and opening the way, for less demanding consumers, for oils of Mediterranean origin (Spanish, Greek and Turkish) or from Puglia.

can also be fairly severe (especially when the northern "tramontana" wind blows), with a certain amount of snow, though (except in high mountain areas) fitful and seldom very deep. These alternate with a spring and autumn that are mild, though (especially spring) often rainy. The fact that the Apuan Alps are so close to the sea, and that therefore the warm sea- winds come up against an immediate obstacle, makes Versilia an area of frequent rainfall. The coasts are also exposed to strong south-westerly gales, while the mid-August storms – to be feared the whole length of the coastline – disrupt the bathers on the beach in a way that has practically become a local tradition.

In geological terms the region of Tuscany is not all that ancient, and for the most part it cannot be placed earlier than the Tertiary Age. A metamorphosis taking place in the Tertiary Age does appear, in point of fact, to have produced the particularly crystalline quality of the marble from the Apuan Alps, while another example of prized marble is that of the so-called "Giallo di Siena," which comes from the Montagnola district. However, the most widespread stone in Tuscany is without doubt what is known as "macigno," a quartzose sandstone, while in the Apuan Alps and the Garfagnana a vast karstic area gives rise to numerous caves abounding in remains of palaeontological and prehistoric times. Geother-

The Camaldoli Forest and the Canale del Lupo in the Apennines near Lucca

The western slope of Monte Corchia in the Apuan Alps

mic phenomena in the region are many and various, and thermal baths are to be found all over the region, from the Lucchesia to the Sienese Maremma, as well as unusual phenomena such as the jets of hot air (known as "soffioni") in the region between the Cecina and the Cornia; discharges of gas (carbon dioxide, hydrogen sulphide), and the springs of hot water frequent in the territory of Lucca and of Siena.

With respect to its hills and mountains, everyone agrees that the first thing that strikes one about the beau-

we find the beginnings of the central Italian Apennines, which are calcareous, usually bare, and rounded in outline. Between this range and the coast is a series of irregularly alligned ridges, usually between 600 and 1000 metres in height (say, 2-3 thousand feet), stretching north-west and south-east between Montecatini and Monte Amiata. This is the so-called Antiappennino, in the centre of which is the system usually known as the Colline Metallifere. The plains, other than those along the coast, occupy the basins of the rivers Arno, Chiana and Tiber.

ty of Tuscany is its variety. By this we mean the abundance of high ground, summits and crests arranged in no apparent order, with a prevalence of hilly or very hilly country, mountains which occasionally rise to about 2000 metres (well over 6000 ft.) but are generally far more modest, and plains along the rivers and near the coast, which cover a bare 10% of the total area of the region. In the Garfagnana, the Apennines and the Apuan Alps, the mountains can even resemble the Dolomites, and indeed they might be thought of as the "Tuscan Alps." Further south

In view of the usual ratio between plains and river basins, it is not surprising that a region with so little flat land is endowed with a rather modest network of rivers. Given both the moderate rainfall and the prevalence of impermeable soils, even the major water-courses have a meagre flow, and even this is very seasonal (an exception is the Serchio, which rises in the high Apennines south of the Cisa Pass, in an area with heavy rainfall and permeable limestone soils). Though liable to both drought and flood (as we saw during the great flood of 1966),

Fetovaia beach on the Island of Elba

Fucecchio marsh (Pistoia)

the Arno with its 241 kilometers in length and its tributaries from the left (Chiana, Pesa, Elsa, Era) and from the right (Sieve, Bisenzio) is the most impressive river in the region. Next comes the Ombrone (161 km.), with its tributary the Orcia, then the Serchio (103 km.). Following these, from north to south, are the Magra (65 km.), the Cecina (76 km.), the Cornia (50 km.), the Albegna (67 km.) and the Fiora (71 km.).

There once existed an extensive and intriguing Tuscany of lakes and marshlands. Between Florence, Pistoia and

square kilometers, the small marshes at Bientina and Fucecchio, the lakes of Montepulciano and Chiusi, as well as the coastal lake of Burano south of Orbetello. The little lakes in the Apennines are nothing but picturesque puddles. In exchange, we have a number of artificial lakes.

The islands of Tuscany, almost all of them within the stretch of sea between the promontory of Piombino and the Argentario (the exception being the more northerly Gorgona), are perhaps to be considered as an extension of the Antiapennines. They could well be the remains of

Lucca was the kingdom of the canebrakes, flat-bottomed barges and wildfowl, while the Valdichiana was a vast, shallow lake. The "Loggia del Pesce" which makes a fine, but faintly absurd, display of itself in the middle of Cortona – within sight of a Lake Trasimeno that has been irreversibly polluted – is a reminder of the times when lake-fish were abundant. The marshes provided Tuscans with their Lenten fare and plenty of game for their feast-days. Of all this, there is little left today: the lake of Massaciuccoli near Viareggio, with an area of some 7

the ancient land of *Tyrrbenis,* now long submerged, to which the Argentario itself belonged. The largest of the islands is Elba, which rises at its western end to over 1000 metres. Its iron deposits have been exploited since Etruscan times, while its rocky coasts – like those of the more southerly island of Giglio – are ideal for underwater fishing. We should also mention the craggy island of Montecristo, a granite rock now wisely protected as a reserve for flora and fauna, and the islet of Giannutri, with its ruined Roman villa.

**The nature reserve of Lake Burano
in the Maremma (Grosseto)**

Tuscany is not a bad place to go on a safari, at least if you are a palaeontologist. If we may judge from the remains, found mostly in the upper Valdarno, the region once abounded in elephant, hippopotamus, rhinoceros, antelope, deer and several kinds of large felines. What we have today is less exotic, but not without interest, with roe-deer and (above all) wild boar in the Maremma; red and fallow deer and – in the forest of Campigna – even

the mouflon or wild sheep, all these protected in the reserves of San Rossore, Migliarino and Alberese; badgers, foxes, porcupines and small carnivores (martens, polecats, otters) scattered all over the region. Bears, alas, disappeared about two hundred years ago, though in wintertime the occasional frightened wolf-cub may be glimpsed, on a visit from the Pratomagno or the Umbrian Apennines. To speak of birds, apart from the eagles which nest in the awe-inspiring scenery of the Orrido di Botri, in the Garfagnana, the most common denizen of the "maquis" is the partridge, whereas the pheasant is by now a mere mouthful for the dinner-table produced in the game reserves. Wild geese, mallard, snipe and coots are to be found at Massaciuccoli and in the little that is left of the marshes in Maremma. Amongst

Two views of the Parco dell'Uccellina
nature reserve (Grosseto)

reptiles, apart from the many kinds of snake, a special interest is attached to a species of lizard that is widespread in the islands and on the Argentario, but not on the mainland. This we may consider evidence in favour of the existence of the ancient land of *Tyrrbenis*.

From the point of view of the flora, in common with the rest of a country with such a long coastline as Italy, the most obvious thing is the difference between the coastal area, where the "Mediterranean maquis" is predominant, and the interior with its vegetation more typical of the Apennines. The coastal maquis is a mixture (often very dense) of arbutus, holm-oak, myrtle, juniper and bramble. Man has in many instances replaced this wilderness with the pinetree, but in the last few decades forest fires both great and small, recurring every summer, have once again changed the look of the coastal areas.

The moment we leave the coast the scene becomes what botanists describe as sub-Mediterranean, with small oak-trees, heather, juniper and a few patches of pines resulting from recent reforestation schemes. Between 300 and 600 metres this sub-Mediterranean flora gives place to mountain flora, and the scene is dominated by the chestnut up to heights of 800-1000 metres, above which is the kingdom of the beechtree.

Higher still the beech yields pride of place to the silver fir, which raises its stately head in the national forests of Abetone, Vallombrosa and Camaldoli. As the Apennines at this point are not all that lofty, there are relatively few and re-

Giovanni Fattori, *Herds in the Maremma*, detail. Museo Civico Giovanni Fattori, Livorno

Bottom, "modern cowboys" at Alberese (Grosseto)

stricted areas totally free of trees and therefore devoted to pasture. The fact is that cattle-rearing in Tuscany does not amount to much. The situation is different for sheep and goats, which are increasingly occupying the areas abandoned by the shrinking cultivation of the hilly areas, turning what once were fields into grazing lands. In the Maremma an effort has been made to increase the population not only of horses but of buffalo. The latter are few and extremely costly, but with the help of ecologists, "agritourism" and the present resurgent interest in these large, handsome beasts deserving to be saved from extinction, their numbers might possibly grow. In the summertime, around Punta Ala, you find a crowd of "dude" cowboys. They might make one scratch one's head from an anthropological point of view, but they also serve their purpose in the context of an "educated" type of tourism aware of the need to safeguard nature.

The People

An area of many populous cities, as well as a densely settled countryside, Tuscany has probably "always" been fairly well-populated, at least in historical times. All the same, we have nothing certain before the 14th-15th centuries, when surveys and land-registries provide us with a fair amount of information, in quantity if not in quality. It is hard to calculate the drop in population that doubtless struck the entire region in the first half of the 14th cent., reaching its climax in the wake of the Black Death. After this the population began to grow again, interrupted only by the plague of 1630. In the 16th cent. the Tuscans numbered about a million, and at the end of the 18th cent. about 1,200,000. In the 1860s (at the time of the unification of Italy) the number had grown to 2 million, and thence to about 3,540,785 according to the census of 2000. In recent years, the steep fall in the birthrate and the decline in the number of marriages have combined to create close to zero population growth, notwithstanding the massive influx of immigrants, chiefly from countries outside the European union, which has made Tuscany the region with the fifth largest number of foreign residents in the country. In comparison with immigrants entering Tuscany, the Tuscans who leave

Top right, Domenico
Ghirlandaio, *Nativity*, detail.
Santa Trinita, Florence

Facing page, the abandoned
village of Campocatino in
Garfagnana

their homeland are relatively few. If anything they leave their birthplace but stay in the region, though this phenomenon is nothing new. There has been an exodus from mountainous and other isolated districts towards more developed and populated areas, such as the lower Valdarno, and of course towards the big towns in general. It was not until the early years of this century, immediately before the First World War, that there was any conspicuous emigration from Tuscany (and even then mostly from the Lucchesia, the Lunigiana and the Garfagnana) to foreign countries, including the United States.

The density of population is greatest in the lower Valdarno and the areas of Pisa, Livorno, Prato and the southern district of Pistoia, and is sparser in Siena and Arezzo and above all in the vast province of Grosseto, where there are scarcely more than 200,000 inhabitants in an area of almost 4,500 square kilometers, which means less than 50 inhabitants per square kilometer. The regional average of roughly 150 inhabitants per square kilometer is some 20% lower than the Italian national average. But these are merely a few statistics, quoted in round numbers so as to give some idea of the scale of certain phenomena. Given the profound historical and geographical differences obtaining between the various zones of Tuscany, the "regional average" in itself means little or nothing. Far more important, and perhaps more serious in every way, is the tendency for the population to concentrate in certain areas. In the last few decades this has led to the annihilation of whole communities, especially in mountain areas, which have been replaced with "dormitory-towns" and the like, where relationships between individuals and different communities becomes a real problem. Let it be understood that this is true only up to a certain point in districts such as the Lunigiana, the Garfagnana or the Montagna Pistoiese, where there are plenty of small landowners and people still live on their farms or in tiny villages. Nor is it necessarily the case in Chianti or the Valdelsa, where the population is spread here and there, and the landscape has remained intensely "humanized," even though in many places we are dealing with a population of newcomers from the big cities of Tuscany, or even from other regions, and indeed

from abroad (Great Bretain, Germany, the United States). And at this point it is a question of the "weekend" or "holiday" house, of farming as a hobby, and producing wine and oil for family consumption or for the small-scale marketing of a very high-quality product.

What we have so far briefly outlined are those characteristics of the Tuscans which may be assessed from a quantitative point of view; nor can we afford to ignore them in these pages. But we have mentioned them chiefly

All too much has been said about the "native character" of the Tuscans. For example, from the 13th cent. on we have been told about a so-called Tuscan School of Poetry, which in point of fact was anything but a "unified" school of poetry or of thought, and included poets from Arezzo, Pisa, Lucca and Florence, none of whom worried their heads about "unity" of language, subject, or culture in general – and how could it have been otherwise? Or if there was some measure of unity, it had nothing to do

to serve as a background to another, perhaps more important, question, and one less open to quantitative analysis. Who are the Tuscans? Do they really exist? If so, what relation do they bear to their "forefathers" (or, to put it slightly less rhetorically, the people who lived in the region before them)? Who left such a copious and complex historical legacy that we moderns sometimes have no right to call it ours, and very often feel - and are called - unworthy of it.

with the common denominator of "Tuscan" to which we moderns are apt to give too much a posteriori importance. It is true that Curzio Malaparte in his novels managed to create the "type" of the "damned Tuscan," but his creation had the shortcomings of every other such "type." It does not apply to any one case in particular, and having been brought to life by words it dies with them.

It would therefore be ridiculous to say that the Tuscans have an ethnical, historical and cultural identity which

Domenico Ghirlandaio, *Head of Woman.* Gabinetto dei Disegni e delle Stampe degli Uffizi, Florence

School of Leonardo, *Head of Woman.* Gabinetto dei Disegni e delle Stampe degli Uffizi, Florence

distinguishes them from their neighbours and sets its stamp on them over the course of centuries. This would be to ignore the falsity of borders and distinctions in the actual being and becoming of things in this world, and the illusoriness of making neat outlines and compact blotches of colour (as on a political map) out of what is in reality part of a continuous process and a series of nuances.

A good example of all this is the dialect of the region – or rather, the "non-dialect." In a strict sense, there may

natives. This affirmation was based chiefly on the choice made by an élite in the context of a cultural development that ran parallel to the unifying political movement of the Risorgimento. Tuscan speech, or rather, educated Florentine, which Manzoni called "washing rinsed in the Arno," had a deep-rooted logic to recommend it, but it was by no means a necessary and compulsory solution. Indeed, it was a very deliberate choice, and one which (through state education) became actually imposed on the nation.

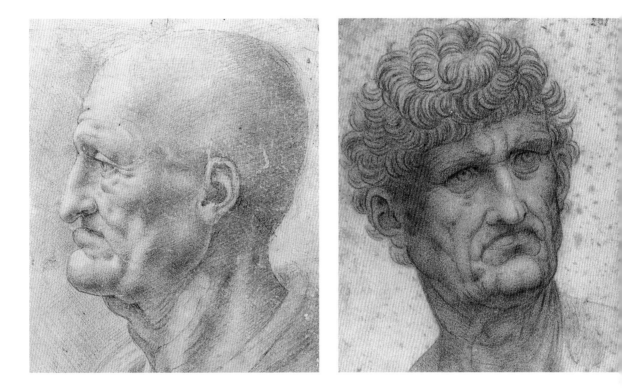

be a particular way of speaking, or more exactly a constellation of ways of speech. In short there is a "type of idiom" that we may call Tuscan.

As we all know, from the 13th cent. onward there was a "language problem" in Italy. In the course of a slow evolution over as much as six centuries, Tuscan – or rather, "educated Florentine" – asserted itself as the literary and "cultured" language throughout the nation, overcoming some fierce resistance and pretty weighty alter-

And this should be said as regards relations between Tuscans and non-Tuscans: that even within the Tuscan region the choice of Florentine was the result of a slow but constant historical movement, for from the 13th cent. on Florence gradually gained the political ascendency in Tuscany. This ascendency met with some strong resistance and some very worthy and reasonable alternatives, so that even at the end of the last century there were ringing challenges on the linguistic and literary plane. We need only mention

Leonardo, *Study of Profile of Old Man.* Gabinetto dei Disegni e delle Stampe degli Uffizi, Florence

Leonardo, *Study of Man's Head.* Accademia, Venice

"Peasant Culture"

Great and small, public and private, museums of "peasant culture" are now quite numerous, though not all of equal quality. We will confine ourselves to mentioning those at San Pellegrino and Villafranca in Val di Niagra. There are also quite a number of studies of Tuscan farmhouses (case coloniche) and manor houses. The most reliable approach to the peasant world of Tuscany, once we have set aside a somewhat ambiguous nostalgia for the country, is found in the study of materials and old techniques of labour and production. The Mugello, Alto Valdarno, Valdelsa, Valdorcia and the inland parts of the Maremma are the areas where the traditional style of building held out for longest. Among the more important objects that have fallen into disuse, a notable role is played not so much by worktools - which, in what in the broad sense is a "pre-industrial" environment, have a very long life and can still come in useful in a minor way - as by the weights and measures for both dry goods and liquids. The abandonment of these led to a real mental "revolution," especially around the time of the unification of Italy.

If it is difficult today to interpret the function of long discarded tools, and to reconstruct ancient methods of production with any degree of certainty, it is still more difficult to reconstruct a mental world connected with living conditions profoundly different from those obtaining today. We have to think of houses without running water or electricity, of the trouble of doing things that today we scarcely think about, of the darkness that plummets down on everything immediately after sunset, the uncertain, dangerous light from the fire, of candles and oil lamps. It was in such a context that people got together and sang songs and told stories, the latter (according to tradition) being either terrifying or magical.

Much of this everyday world can be found today in the oral tradition. There are songs of love, of nostalgia, but also, of political passion; there are ancient therapeutic recipes; ballads, satirical verses, traditional open-air performances known as "bruscelli" and so forth;

Cristiano Banti, *Meeting of Peasants*. Galleria d'Arte Moderna, Florence

An ancient olive press near Massa Marittima; right, the pressing of grapes

magical formulas and charms. All these are part of a culture made up of proverbs and sayings that seem never to change. From time to time in folk traditions there is an outcrop of ancestral memory, even going back beyond Christian times, as in the various cults in Chianti and the Aretino that have to do with water and with "galactoforous" stones, which help nursing mothers to produce more milk. Then there is the tradition of butchering an ox every year in honour of the Virgin of the Sanctuary of the Madonna del Sasso in Val di Sieci, which it seems occupies the site of an ancient pagan holy place.

This legacy of folklore has in the past been gleaned, but also re-interpreted and in part distorted by writers such as Renato Fucini, Vittorio Imbriani and Emma Perodi. More recently it has been examined with more care by such good anthropologists as Vittorio Dini, Pietro Clemente and Alessandro Falassi, while the songs have been once again re-interpreted by performers with a fine ear for genuine folkmusic, such as Caterina Bueno, Alfredo Bianchini and Riccardo Marasco.

Haymaking

Pietro Fanfani, a philologist from Collesalvetti, and his *Vocabolario* (1875), in which the "purist" definition is surrounded by a whole series of inducements aimed at safeguarding the non-Florentine "variants" of words and constructions.

However, the Tuscan "idiom," in its many variations which are the object of much reciprocal bickering, is clearly distinct from the Gallo-Italic dialects bordering on it to the north and east, both in vocabulary and in pronunciation; to such an extent that in certain districts in the Apennines the watershed of dialect is no less evident, clear-cut and drastic than that of geography. The special characteristics of Tuscan speech are less clear in comparison with dialects to the south. Between many areas of south-eastern Tuscany and the bordering districts of Umbria and Lazio there are many affinities, and of ancient date, therefore not to be explained away by exchanges which have taken place in recent years; indeed, there were even more of them in the past. Plural endings in -ora, for example, have now disappeared from Tuscan speech in all its many variations, whereas before the 16th cent. they were common enough: Someone like Franco Sacchetti could perfectly naturally use the word "*luogora*" instead of "*luoghi.*" In old Sienese the sounds -nd- and -mb- often became -nn- and -mm-, which is typical of Umbrian dialect, and then in the course of time dispensed with these assimilations, which in the 14th cent. were usual. The Arezzo district of the Valdichiana has been open to many influences, even to dialects from as far afield as Emilia. But the speech of Arezzo and Siena still retains some traces of Umbria and the Marche, such as the verb *vendare* instead of *vendere.*

In any case, the last thing we should do in dealing with Tuscan speech is to generalize. Tuscans other than Florentines, for example, are highly incensed when accused of using words or pronunciations typical of Florence. To mention one instance, it is by no means the case that throughout the region the diphthong -uo- becomes simply -o- (as in the word "*uomo- omo*"), and still less that weak inter-vocal

-k- and -t- sounds are always aspirated to -h-, according to a well-known phenomenon which has even been assigned an Etruscan origin. On the other hand, in all its many variations, the Tuscan speech does possess a certain cohesiveness, and is fairly widespread as well, since we should remember that even Corsican belongs to the west-Tuscan group of dialects.

If it is difficult to speak of the "idiom" without generalizations and rhetoric, it is even harder to talk of the "traditions," expecially today, when the word is abused and exploited and so-called authentic folk and peasant traditions seem to sprout from every crevice. Connected for the most part with feast-days and fairs, they are good fun in themselves but very dubious from a historical point of view.

Let us begin by resisting the temptation to use labels that appear on the surface to be applicable, but in fact explain nothing. That is, we must avoid the pretence that everything is perfectly clear and in its place, as long as we can scatter around a few labels such as "subordinate culture" or "submerged culture." The point is, what do we know about our ancestors? What legacies have come down to us from them? Are we today really able to recognize an authentic tradition passed on from generation to generation, and to distinguish this from things brought back by revivals?

A number of students of southern Italy have described the culture of the "Mezzogiorno" as a "peasant culture" – a gross generalization immediately contradicted by others. But Tuscan culture, luckily, is so varied as to discourage any attempt of this kind. All the same, to define it as a "city culture" makes sense. We do not of course mean that Tuscany is a territory composed entirely of cities. We only wish to point out that ever since Etruscan times the country districts, the pasturelands, even the marshes and mountains of the region, have gravitated towards an urban centre, towards a governing class of landowners and producer-consumers living in urban settlements, and towards sacred places (temples in early times, cathedrals

later) connected with the urban world. The refined way of life and the opulence of the manufactured products which we come across in Etruscan tombs is a result of this humanized and urbanized world. Even the Longobards, in spite of their nomadic and warlike past, adapted themselves to this mode of life. Without an appreciation of this "city-culture," in fact, we cannot understand the real character of the larger part of our landscape. Exception should be made, of course, for particular areas such as the Garfagnana, the Volterrano (area of Volterra), the Maremma, and the highest regions of the Apennines.

The legacy of language and dialect, archaeological discoveries, the layout of the territory, traditional tools and implements for both peasants and artisans, local festivals and saints' days: all these tend to divide Tuscany into areas analogous to those which emerge on the strictly linguistic level. There is a western region (around Lucca, Pisa and Livorno) which has certain characteristics in common with Liguria to the north and Emilia to the north-east; a central zone more or less contained in the triangle Florence, Siena-Volterra; an eastern area between the Arno and the Tiber and between Arezzo and Chiusi; and finally a southern area which includes the south of the province of Siena, Monte Amiata and the Maremma. For many years now the material evidence of these cultures has been collected in museums devoted to peasant culture and folk traditions, while (after a long stagnant period during which there was little or no interest in the tokens of past piety, and – especially after Vatican Council II – even indifference or scarcely-concealed intolerance) the dioceses and sanctuaries now frequently see to the preservation and cataloguing of relics, ex-votos and liturgical and devotional remains in their possession, even creating facilities for study. Much has also been done to collect and classify the oral culture of the region: stories, proverbs, songs, characteristic theatrical performances such as *contrasti* or *bruscelli*, ballads, ritualistic parodies such as *Sega-la-Vecchia*, types of urban folk-drama connected with

**Picking chestnuts in the Apennines
near Pistoia**

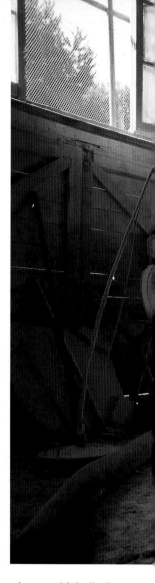

the *Commedia dell'arte,* and therefore with masques, rites and customs which may be traced back to a mythical and ritual substratum based on magic. All these have become the object of careful anthropological research.

The results of this quite rightly put paid to the commonplace according to which Tuscany, so rich in the monuments of a "great" cultural heritage, is on the other hand poor in respect to folk culture, and in any case little concerned to preserve what it has. This is a legend which in the past was lent the weight of legality by parties with an axe to grind, who thought of it as a healthy march towards progress, though today it is mentioned only as an accusation.

All that was a pretext, and still is, whatever the reasons for it. If anything, the fact is that folk-culture is by its very nature anchored firmly to the places and the rhythms of life, to whatever is characteristic of daily living, to the systems of production and the division of labour. A culture composed of actions, of the skilful use of certain implements, of respect for the seasons with regard to work in the fields and the phases of the liturgical year, of customs linked to agriculture and craftsmanship, of songs and stories passed around the fireside, could not help but wilt under the impact of urbanization, industrialization, and the mass-media which have convulsed life and customs not only on a social level, but also on the plane of personal relations and the family. In these circumstances the recovery of certain traditions (especially those connected with festivals) sometimes comes close to being an archaeological experiment, and at others a rather demagogical piece of mystification, or purely recreational. There are many anthropologists who maintain that when a tradition is dying because it no longer has the material conditions that sustained it, there is nothing to do but let it die, except possibly to give it a place on a few shelves in a museum,

Working of alabaster in Volterra

or in the pages of some learned volume. On the other hand, there are the people themselves; for, over the last few years, often in a muddled, rough-and-ready way, people have tried to re-establish contact with the past. All over the region such things as periodical markets, fairs in town and country alike and the celebration of local saints' days have been expanded in cases where they had survived and revived where they had fallen into disuse. Festivals and feast-days are celebrated once again as such, and not reduced to something purely recreational; and in the meantime the "health industry" is rediscovering the "natural" and "genuine" food of days of yore, and telling us how to prepare it. Our fashionable modern-day troubadours and cabaret artists rework our old ballads and (albeit at the piano-bar level) come up with new versions of our songs of sweat and toil and hardship, but also of love and joy. Agreed that this is an ambiguous phenomenon, and one not without an eye to the consumer market, rather on the level of the renovation of the old farmhouses by the scions of the prosperous, city-dwelling bourgeoisie. But this is also a way of saving what is left of a legacy that otherwise would be fated to disappear, or to survive only as an archaeological find. And it is also a way of keeping memories alive, of feeling that one is living in that flow of things without which there is neither a sense of history nor an awareness of communal identity.

Doing, Working, Producing

How well does one live in Tuscany? What the statistics say is "pretty well." It is true that there is a housing problem, but on the other hand there is no lack of weekend-houses. Nor do our industrial suburbs have any "new towns" or the like. Running water and central heating are now common features, and we are above the national average and therefore on a par with the northern regions. On the other hand (and this may seem strange), the Tuscans do not spend a lot of money on performances on a cultural level. This may be partly due to their proverbial stinginess (which does not hold good for the Sienese, who have a reputation for extravagance), and partly because they are up to their necks in culture at home, and are fairly convinced that they actually invented it. Behind the statistics we have the "standard of living," as they say; but in any case the statistics give us quantitative figures, and these are of little use in assessing quality.

As regards net product and income per head, Tuscany is between sixth and eighth among the regions of Italy, after the northern regions. Out of about 1,400,000 employed persons, one can say that in round figures

Sculpture workshop at Carrara

500,000 work in industry, 56,000 (less than 5% of the total) in agriculture, and the rest in various trades. What we have therefore, over and above the facts and figures, is a pretty dynamic picture with a number of disquieting elements. Until the end of the 1950s Tuscany was still a prevalently agricultural region. With the economic boom of the early 1960s a process of industrial development began, and in certain areas such as that of Prato and the middle and lower Valdarno quickly reached a considerable level of intensity. However, to a large extent this retained what appears to be the typical and "original" characteristic of the region, which is the tendency towards small but dynamic firms. This has brought with it a certain measure of economic weakness, but at the same time has provided a fair degree of elasticity that has often made it possible to deal with economic crisis.

It seems that in Tuscany there is a leaning towards the small-scale, independent business. If we put this together with the old share-cropping method of farming, the result is certainly not favourable to the demands of modern agriculture. Also unfavourable to this is the very physical structure of the region, full as it is of hills and mountains. A considerable amount of the potentially productive land in Tuscany is in fact occupied by woods and rough pastures. In the remaining areas there is still a tendency towards what until a few years ago was the norm, which is to say mixed farming in which vines, olives and wheat co-exist in the same field. Now, however, grain has declined in favour of vines and olives, and the hilly areas of Tuscany have been largely given over to the more profitable specialized production of "D.O.C" wines and olive oil, much of it for export. The great freeze of the winter of 1985, of course, reduced oil production to virtually nothing, forcing farmers to cut down or drastically prune almost all their trees; but on the other hand it is true that olives cultivated in the traditional manner gave a low yield, so that it has been often suggested that we should

A marble quarry in the Apuan Alps

make use of the disaster of the freeze by rationalizing our techniques of production. Wines are, of course, very much at home in the area, especially in the celebrated Chianti district. But other areas producing fine wines are the Colli Senesi (Sienese Hills), the Sieve valley, the valley between Florence and Pistoia (Carmignano wines), Bolgheri and the Cornia valley. Vegetable and fruit production does not exceed the requirements of the region, though some produce is of notably fine quality.

The woods are one of the glories of Tuscany, and also one of its problems. Its inhabitants do not always believe it, but Tuscany is the region of Italy most abounding in forests, with about 1,086,016 hectares of woodland, amounting to 47% of the total area of the region. From the economic point of view the woods are a great asset. The state-owned forests of Vallombrosa, Campigna and Camaldoli yield fine products for woodwork; the pinewoods along the coast and in the Valdarno give pine-nuts and resin; the chestnut woods yield not only their fruit (once a popular food and now after a long eclipse coming back into demand again) but also substances extracted from the bark and used in the tanning of leather; to the south of the Cecina we find an abundance of cork-oaks. Enormous stretches of territory have been reforested in the past few decades, while parts of

the region have been repopulated with certain species of animals. In spite of this, Tuscany will never again be the hunter's paradise that it once was. There is a certain amount of game throughout the region, including wild boar in the more densely wooded areas. But the hunting of game, like fishing, was once linked less to the woodlands than to the marshes, and these have all but vanished. Stock-raising is also in inevitable and irreversible decline. There are far fewer flocks of sheep migrating between the Apuan Alps and Apennines on the one hand and the coast of the Maremma on the other. At one time the festival of St. Luke (October 18th), at Impruneta near Florence, was a celebration of the return of the shepherds to the lowland pastures, but now, though retaining something of its nobility, has passed into the realm of folklore. On the other hand, especially in the districts of Siena and Grosseto, Sardinian shepherds have come in to fill the gap left by the peasants who have abandoned numerous farms. The most highly-prized product is "pecorino," a sheep's cheese that is mild when fresh but grows increasingly strong with age. The cattle population, both for meat and for work, is restricted, though the Tuscan genius for small-scale enterprise has made strides with the immensely prized "Chianina" breed of beef cattle. The real "Florentine" beefsteak comes from the Chianina, but

other traditional Tuscan breeds are the robust, attractive Maremmana and the Pisan, which gives good milk. An increasingly popular breed today is the Bruno-Alpina, which is imported. The pig is an old friend of the rural family economy, and at one time it was practically the only source of meat, either fresh or preserved. However, in the districts of Siena and Arezzo in particular we find pig-raising on a larger scale, and the production of high-quality ham, salame, etc.

It is very easy, and indeed a current intellectual affectation, to speak ill of the "return to the soil" as a kind of chic mystification, of luxury tourism draped with health-manias. The cowboys who once gave such a hard lesson to Colonel "Buffalo Bill" Cody have in turn become

a rarity, and their place has been taken by Sunday cowboys, those who patronize "agriturismo." All this may be rather irritating. All the same, there has been a revival of the glorious tradition of horse-breeding in the Maremma, while the "new romanticism" of looking for tiny patches of nature still intact or reconstituted at vast expense has here and there (also in the Maremma) led to the reappearance of the buffalo. A consumer's Garden of Eden? Even if it were so, our time has committed worse crimes. It is a pity, though, that no "agriturismo" thinks of saving the few poor donkeys, mules and hinnies. After giving valiant service for centuries, transporting people and things, these humble poor relations of the horse are now disappearing from the region: only a few thousand are

Facing page, top, bas-relief with *Meleager Hunting the Wild Boar.* Parish church of San Giovanni, Campiglia Marittima (Livorno); bottom left, Ambrogio Lorenzetti,

Effects of Good Government in the Countryside, detail. Palazzo Pubblico, Siena; right, Adolfo Tommasi, *In the Fields*, detail. Museo Civico Giovanni Fattori, Livorno

Flocks grazing in the Apennines

Hunting in Days of Yore

A land of woods and marshes, Tuscany at one time was a paradise for hunters. Nor was it without more noble quarry, such as stags, bears and wild boar. The Tuscan lords were famous for their feats in hunting, and weapons, trophies and pictures connected with the sport form an important part of the legacy of the Medici. Paintings, tapestries and literary works are full of hunting scenes.

Hunting is also a protagonist of Tuscan literature: one thinks of Fucini, Bonsanti and Sanminiatelli, and of that great witness to a vanished culture that is Eugenio Niccolini's *Giornate di caccia*.

Today, in a changed and devastated environment, there are still some traces of this kingdom of hunting in the Grosseto Maremma, where the wild boar is still native. However, the landscape of the area was radically altered by the vast reclaiming schemes of the first half of the 19th cent., which involved the entire zone between Grosseto and Castiglione della Pescaia (which however left intact the marsh of Castiglione, the one at the mouth of the Ombrone, and the lakes of Burano and Orbetello). The railway connecting this area to Livorno began to function in 1865; but at that time the Maremma was pratically wild, an area dominated by big landowners, but also by bandits and poachers. All these social groups were great hunters. Their prey was not only wild boar, but also fallow deer and roe deer. There was also small game, of course, though this was disdained by the nobility, who still thought of hunting as their "feudal" privilege (and the royal laws on the matter were disregarded).

If hunting for the gentry was

Mosaic depicting a *Wild-Boar Hunt*. Museo Archeologico, Chiusi

Benozzo Gozzoli, *Procession of the Magi*, detail. Palazzo Medici-Riccardi, Florence

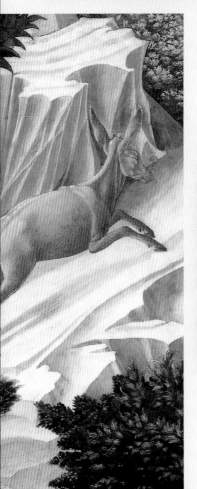

Top, Paolo Uccello, *Battle of San Romano*, detail. Uffizi, Florence

Above, Sano di Pietro, *Falconry*, from the *Codice delle Monache*. Biblioteca Comunale, Siena

Florentine wedding chest with hunting scene. Museo degli Argenti, Florence

a sport and a privilege, for those who did it "illegally" it could be any number of things, from sheer need (and there were poachers who were poor peasants) to an out-and-out profession in which a good income went hand in glove with adventure. Certain 19th century poachers have remained as celebrated as bandits! And it is significant that when the reclaiming schemes started up again at the end of the 19th cent. the lordly hunters and the bandits both found their worlds threatened at the same time. They had been, in fact, the two faces of the same system, of the same delicate ecological and social equilibrium.

left. Readers of Pinocchio will also lament the extinction of the little Tuscan ass with its tender, intelligent eyes (that donkeys are stupid is a calumny spread by schoolboys afraid of the competition). This little animal is no longer even to be found as an ingredient of mortadella, which in any case is an Emilian kind of salame, and no great favourite in Tuscany.

Since we have spoken about hunting and stock-raising, completeness demands that we should briefly mention fishing. And here there is really little to gladden our hearts. Even if fresh fish and crustaceans never seem to be lacking in the summer markets or at parties on the Argentario, the waters of the Tyrrhenian are stinting and subject to constant impoverishment. Gone are the days when there were tunny-fishing nets to be seen on Elba, though a small catch is still made in the Tuscan Archipelago. However, Viareggio, Livorno, the Argentario and Portoferraio are still fishing centres of a certain note, while the occasional lobster is caught at Montecristo and

Giglio. The total production only amounts to a few hundred tons. The fishing-fleet is commissioned in Livorno, but it sails down to Africa or even towards America.

On the other hand, if the woodlands, and hunting and fishing, are not as flourishing as they were, the reasons are well-known, and range from the growth of industry to the overpopulation during the summer months and the question of pollution. Nor are these neutral causes and inevitable happenings, but the results of choices taken deliberately, even if not always properly controlled. In these circumstances the development of industry, and above all manufacturing on the plane of craftsmanship, has in the last few years reached considerable levels in terms of quantity, and by no means always at the expense of quality. In this field the local talent for free enterprise and for producing high-quality goods have gone hand in hand, with the result that products are on the average really good, and sometimes excellent.

The small firm, the break-up of larger units into small-

Fishing boats in Livorno harbor

er ones, and the accompanying subdivision of capital... When people seriously believed in a "one-way" economic development, these features were long considered limitations on the capacity of the business world in Tuscany, which has often been called narrow-minded, egoistic, pusillanimous and out of date. In the long run, however, it has been realized that these characteristics, which from some points of view do certainly hold things back, were in fact not so much a weakness as a strength in an economic world unwilling to abandon the level of individual craftsmanship and move onto an industrial scale; and this not always purely for reasons of economic profitability.

Another long-established feature of Tuscany, which we have mentioned in terms of culture and politics, is that it is "polycentric;" that is, with many centres rather than one. On the level of productivity and labour this leads to a system in which the availability of certain raw materials is in tune with many long-established methods (or even secrets) of manufacture, and pride in one's work, in the best sense of the word. Such areas are sometimes known as "islands" of productivity, and the most conspicuous of them, with roots stretching far back into history, is the textile zone of Prato, where the old "ragshops" have long since been converted into highly modernized, active concerns. In second place come the tanneries and the shoemakers of the "leather district" which stretches between the lower Valdarno and the Valdinievole, along with the "furniture district" more or less in the triangle described by Cascina,

Pontedera and Ponsacco, and its rival in the zone between Prato and Pistoia. Most of this stuff is mass-produced, but there is a proportion of traditional, handmade wares.

Other districts well worthy of mention are those of the glass trade (between Empoli and Montelupo and at Colle di Val d'Elsa), of ceramics (at Sesto Fiorentino and between Montelupo and Signa), and paper-making, including some beautiful mills, some of ancient date, near Barga in the Serchio valley, around Pescia and at Colle di Val d'Elsa, while ready-to-wear clothes are produced in abundance in the Empoli area. Impruneta is the home of famous fired bricks and tiles, the very same that once roofed Brunelleschi's dome on the cathedral of Florence. Stia is a well-known centre for wrought-iron, while Scarperia is famed for its fine cutlery. Goldsmith's work is now concentrated chiefly in and around Arezzo, with mass-production accompanied by the highest standards of craftsmanship. The working of various kinds of stone (alabaster at Volterra, marble around Carrara, *pietra serena* in the Fiesole hills, round Empoli and in the Alto Mugello) is dependent on the quarries existing in these areas. Florence, of course, is a kind of compendium of all these specialities, a shop-window for expert craftsmanship that in many cases reaches the level of art itself. We might mention the workshop for semi-precious stones (Opificio delle Pietre Dure), the leather-working school (Scuola del Cuoio) at Santa Croce, and the goldsmiths' shops which are clustered on and around the Ponte Vecchio. But above all else

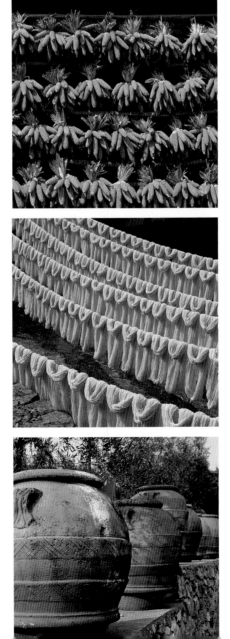

Drying of maize at Monterchi
(Arezzo) and of wool at Reggello
(Florence)

Traditional working of terracotta
at Impruneta

it is in the realm of high fashion that Florence is really and truly on a world level, with its shows and its fashion parades at Palazzo Pitti, as well as its boutiques which are often linked with those of the great names in Rome, Milan, Paris, London and New York.

In comparison to the many and famous enterprises thriving in the world of the arts and crafts, "industry" in Tuscany is in what we might call a minor key. In this case the small scale of the firms themselves and the capital involved may

there are shipyards at Livorno and Viareggio, chemical plants at Rosignano and near Volterra, and cement-works in the province of Florence. This development has had an inevitable impact on the environment, and has brought about constant arguments on one side and the other. There are the old progressives left over from the thirties, for whom industrial development was the sure sign of a higher level of social and technological progress, cost what it may, and there are the ecologists who dream of a region made into an enormous park of natural and artistic beauties. Between these two parties a middle way is now being sought for, in order to preserve and administrate a legacy of incomparable beauty.

Where industry and the environment do still come to blows is in the field of mines and quarries (although now in decline). Tuscany was at one time volcanic, and still has its residue of thermal phenomena, but it is also a land of minerals and metals. Apart from the marble quarries of the Apuan Alps, home of Carrara Marble, we should mention the iron mined in Elba, mercury from Monte Amiata, endogenous steam and borax from Lardarello and lignite from the Upper Valdarno. Up until the sixties Tuscany was responsible for almost the whole of the country's production of mercury and pyrite. The Colline Metallifere are rich not only in pyrite but also in lead, and therefore – or until only a few years ago – silver as well. Massa Marittima has been a centre of the mining industry, and mineralogy is part of its local history and culture.

have slowed up the rate of development. But this might not be such a bad thing after all, considering those unique things that make Tuscany renowned throughout the world, such as the landscape, the specialized agricultural products and the good standard of living. It may be that these would not altogether harmonize with intensive industrialization. All the same, we have a steel industry at Piombino, foundries in Florence and around Livorno, the production of precision instruments in Florence, and of motorcycles in Pontedera, while

What we have said about industry and craftsmanship already gives us the outlines of the main sources of Tuscan exports: handicrafts, olive oil, wine, plants and flowers (with nurseries at Pistoia and large-scale horticulture around Pescia), products of the metallurgic and mechanical industries, textiles, glass products, and finally the famous

An old pyrite mine at
Boccheggiano (Grosseto)

Plant for the exploitation of
geothermic energy at Larderello
(Pisa)

sweetmeats of Siena, such as *panforte* and *ricciarelli.*

All the same, one of the chief industries of Tuscany, and one of the most profitable, is still tourism. If the winter-sports centres in the Apennines are at this time of only secondary importance, of greater interest are the many hot springs, from the celebrated baths at Montecatini to the old-established ones in the provinces of Lucca, Pisa and Siena. The beaches are attractive and reasonably well-equipped all the way from Sarzana to Grosseto, but

fact nearly two-thirds of the tourists are Italians from other regions of the country, or even from Tuscany itself. There is a large network of hotels, but it is well supported, in line with the Tuscan tradition, by small-scale enterprises, such as pensions and farms with accommodation for guests (the latter constantly growing in number) as well as camping-sites and hostels which serve to meet the needs of young people. The general picture would be fairly satisfactory if profiteering were not so rife in the

the majority of the summer crowds choose the Versilia and the coast between Cecina and Piombino, though there are also areas of luxury tourism at Punta Ala, on the Argentario, and on the islands. The artistic legacy of places incomparably endowed with masterpieces (and we are not alluding only to major cities such as Florence, Pisa or Siena) bring tourists by the million from all corners of the earth. Naturally enough, not all tourists in Tuscany are foreigners (from the US, Europe and Asia). In point of

property and building markets, combining with the horrors of pollution to undermine it.

It may at first sight appear odd that this region, so open to visitors from abroad, and therefore so accustomed to comparing itself with other cultures, is also known for the aggressiveness of its inhabitants, a feature that may sometimes have its charm, but also its inconveniences. Faced with a visitor, even if he be a tourist with good money in his pocket, your average Tuscan does not show a lot of enthusiasm.

Nursery at Pistoia

Someone who pays a visit of a few days or even weeks might easily slip by unnoticed; but someone who decides to put down roots for a while sooner or later comes up against a wall built not so much of suspicion and discourtesy as of a mixture of circumspection and indifference.

And it may also seem strange that a region with so many great cultural traditions barely keeps above the national average in terms of education. In Tuscany there are three universities, at Florence, Pisa and Siena (with a branch in Arezzo), as well as a vast number of institutes of higher education, many branches of foreign (largely American) universities, and renowned institutions such as the Collegio di Poggio Imperiale in Florence and the Convitto Nazionale Cicognini in Prato. In spite of this your average Tuscan does not seem to have too much faith in education and culture, and in this regard he is put at an advantage throughout the region by the "family firm," and therefore the possibility of finding work "at home." The result is that he tends to leave school early and take up a money-making job as soon as possible. As far as this is concerned, sociologists and historians of education never fall to point out that until the 15th century the average Tuscan was perfectly capable of filling in his own registers of produce, and indeed this is proved by contemporary documents. It was only later on that illiteracy became so widespread that when Italy was unified it was as high as 70% throughout the region. It would appear that between the 16th and 18th centuries there was a period of stagnation that proved hard to overcome; and this in fact coincides with what we know of cultural tendencies throughout Italy, and indeed throughout Europe.

But the fact is that "culture" is not only a matter of literacy, let alone of faithful attendance at school. The streets of our towns and cities have for centuries been lined with works of art, both religious and civic, that have no match in the world, in terms not only of excellence but also of number. They in themselves were the schools of taste, and character and aesthetics, for the Tuscans. It seems to me

that a child in San Gimignano, who has left school at fifteen but has nonetheless grown up among the mediaeval towers of the town, and its marvellously frescoed church, in a position to meet tourists from all over the world, able to see the exhibitions organized by the Commune and the operas performed in the piazza during the summer, has had as good a schooling as an 18 year-old with a diploma from any town in Lombardy or Calabria. I contend that one

The iron mines of Rio Marina
(Island of Elba)

learns more in a Florentine workshop on the left bank of the Arno than in any art school in Italy, where one scratches the surface of a few textbooks thrust upon one by the Ministry of Education, while Giotto, Botticelli and Leonardo da Vinci are cut down to a paragraph a head.

From all this, without wishing to generalize, emerge the two "exports" most widespread in Tuscany, and the most typical of this land. In these pages written by a true-born Tus-can, the reader will already have discerned the first: this is an absolutely stubborn pride. The other is one of the foundations for this pride, an artistic and cultural legacy unique in the whole world, and this not only because it is incomparable in terms of beauty and abundance, but also (and above all) because it is deep-rooted in the explicit, conscious memory of the people of Tuscany. By which I mean, of course, history. And it is to history that we now have to turn.

Spas and Hot Springs

The Cascate del Mulino at Saturnia
Left, the pool of the ancient baths at Bagno Vignoni

Spas and hot springs have been celebrated in Tuscany since Etruscan and Roman times, and were even famous in the Middle Ages, when hydrotherapy was very popular. The best-known watering-place in Tuscany, at least since the 14th cent., has been Montecatini, where most of the baths offer cures of the digestive system by the use of mineral waters. Also important is Chianciano Terme, with its waters that are good for ailments of the liver. Casciana Terme, near Pontedera, is known for its baths and irrigations. Bagni di Lucca (famous in ancient times as the baths of Corsena, and frequented by the high society of Europe throughout the 19th cent.) offers waters and mud to cure rheumatism, arthritis and hyperuricaemia. The hydrotherapeutic cures at San Giuliano Terme, between Lucca and Pisa, are effective for diseases of the bones. San Casciano dei Bagni, near Cetona, and therefore in the

The Tettuccio Baths at Montecatini Terme

vicinity of Chianciano, has hot-water cures for rheumatism and diseases of the metabolism. Rheumatism and skin diseases are a speciality at Rapolano Terme, between Siena and Val di Chiana. Equi Terme, between Lucca and Aulla, has radioactive waters used since

Roman times with success against chronic diseases of the respiratory system. Near Amiata there are the picturesque Bagno Vignoni (where Lorenzo the Magnificent went in 1490) and Bagno San Filippo. The Terme di Bagnolo near Follonica treat traumatic ailments, arthritis and gout. The same ailments are

treated at the Terme di Caldana, which is not far away and can perhaps be identified with the Baths of Populonia mentioned by ancient writers. The Terme di Saturnia, not far from Sovana, have warm sulphur baths, inhalations and exudative treatments good for troubles in the respiratory system. Pope Pius II visited the baths at Petriolo, not far from the Abbey of San Galgano, which have sulphurous waters effective in the treatment of trouble with the metabolism, arthritis and gout (it was from this last that the Piccolomini pope sought relief).

Mediaeval doctors did not agree on the efficacy of hydrotherapeutic treatment, and nor do doctors today. But from Montecatini to Petriolo a thriving tourist trade has sprung up in the last few decades, and the baths have become equipped to meet the demand. Even if waters and mud only do you a relative amount of good, fresh air and peace are helpful factors in regaining one's health.

Memmo di Filippuccio, *The Bath*, detail. Palazzo del Popolo, San Gimignano

Facing page, Bagni San Filippo

Memory and Identity

The Etruscans

Several tens of thousands of years ago the upper valley of the Arno was a huge lake surrounded by dense forests. Today it abounds in lignite and fossils. The bones discovered bear witness to the fact that the area around Montevarchi and down the Valdichiana was the haunt of elephant, rhinoceros, deer, bear, big cats and monkeys. In the Apuan Alps, Versilia, the Lunigiana and the Garfagnana there are numerous natural caves with traces of fires and artefacts that may date back to the Palaeolithic, Mesolithic or Neolithic ages. This covers a considerable span of time, between 2 million and 3 thousand years before Christ.

It was around the latter date that man began to work in metal here, as well as stone. In the Apuan Alps, dating from about that time, we find numerous metal objects (silver, lead and copper), in conjunction with new funeral rites which were evidently brought in by peoples who had recently arrived in the area. Throughout the Apennines there is much evidence of the Bronze Age and the Villanovian period. However it is between the 2nd and

Top, Etruscan art of the 1st cent. BC, *Urn of the Married Couple.* Museo Guarnacci, Volterra

Reconstruction of the 2nd-cent. BC Inghirami Tomb in Volterra. Museo Archeologico, Florence

the 1st millennium BC, corresponding to the beginning of the Iron Age, that the southern part of what is now Tuscany begins to emerge. This is in fact the area which over the centuries saw the growth of the great culture which was destined to characterize the whole territory and give it its first name.

It is perhaps between the 9th and 8th centuries BC that we may begin to speak of an Etruscan civilization and an Etruscan people, since at that time the territory between the Tyrrhenian Sea and the valleys of the Arno and the Tiber became densely settled by these people. With their funeral rites involving cremation, which we usually associate with Villanovian culture, they have by some scholars been connected with those peoples who gave rise to the culture of "urn burial" in Central Europe and Northern Italy towards the end of the Bronze Age. Various theories have been put forward about the origins of the Etruscans. On the authority of Herodotus (who mentioned Lydia as their original homeland) they have been said to have come from Asia Minor, or according to the above-mentioned theories from the north. Finally, on the basis of hints furnished by Dionysius of Halicarnassus, they have been held to have been "aboriginal:" that is, they were related to peoples inhabiting Italy before the arrival of the Indo-Europeans. However, the historical and archaeological data in our possession make it unlikely that the Etruscan "nation" came into being as the result of some sudden event - such as an invasion by a "new" people - or indeed over a relatively short span of years. On the contrary, it is now commonly held that it came about slowly, with the gradual formation of those ethnical and cultural features which we are accustomed to think of as genuinely Etruscan.

Much has been said about the Etruscan "mystery," mostly concerning the mythical

and religious features of that ancient people, with their strong tendency towards the techniques of divination and deep-seated burial rites. It is to these that we owe the greater part of our knowledge of the mental world and everyday life of the Etruscans. The same is true of the language, the basic structures of which are still hard to understand today, even if we do succeed in reading it letter by letter and grasping the sense (we have, however, come this far by way of a Greek alphabet taught to the Etruscans by emigrants from Euboea during the 8th cent. BC). Judging from analogies with the known language of Lemnos in the 6th cent. BC, it has been suggested that Etruscan (like the language of Lemnos) is a relic of a language spoken throughout the Mediterranean before the arrival of the Indo-Europeans. In any case, from the 3rd to the 1st century BC, the Romans overwhelmed and decimated the Etruscans, who gave up speaking their own language entirely, particularly after 90 BC, the year in which Etruria was granted Roman citizenship.

The great flourishing of Etruscan civilization was therefore between the 8th and the 4th century BC, and it is significant that this coincides with the considerable population growth which took place in the 9th and 8th centuries, and also with the arrival of the first Greek colonists. The latter, settling in Campania, showed a great deal of interest in the metal resources of the island of Elba, and of the whole area between the coast and the Tiber. The exploitation of the mineral resources and intense activity in trade and handicrafts created a flourishing economy and a taste for luxury among the ruling classes in the towns, whose solid prosperity is attested by the wealth of precious and refined

From the top, Etruscan art, *Corsini Fibula* (7th cent. BC); gold bracelet from Vetulonia (6th cent. BC); bucchero (mid-6th cent. BC). Museo Archeologico, Florence

objects with which they were buried. We are told by Greek historians that in the 7th and 6th centuries there was a thorough-going "thalassocracy" of the Tyrrhenian, during which Etruscan civilization – profoundly influenced by Greek culture – extended south of the Tiber as far as Campania and north of the Apennines into the Po Valley, where such centres emerged as Félsina (Bologna) and Spina (at the mouth of the river). That was the period of the so-called "dodecapolis" (the "twelve cities," although in fact they were more than twelve). This was a federation of city-states that were completely independent, but at the same time strongly linked by the awareness of their common ethnic and cultural roots, expressed above all in language and religion. The wealthiest and most important of these were at first the coastal towns such as Populonia, Vetulonia, Roselle, Talamone, Cosa (now Ansedonia), Vulci, Tarquinia, Pyrgi (now Santa Severa) and Caere (now Cerveteri). But the towns of the interior soon gained in importance, with the rise of Fiesole, Volterra, Arezzo, Cortona, Perugia, Chiusi, Volsinii, Falerii and Veii. Trade and communications were assured by a network of roads, running both parallel to the coast (to connect the coastal centres) and at right angles to it to link up the inland towns. Even in those days Tuscany could qualify as a "land of cities," some of which were more ancient than Rome. And even in those days there

was the tendency towards the particular, the local, the specific – a tendency that has remained as a "genuine feature" of the history and art of the region. For every centre, even in those times, had its particular way of making objects, building and decorating tombs and necropolises, or shaping and colouring pottery.

The Roman Reshuffle

It was in the 6th cent. that an Etruscan dynasty, the Tarquins, became kings of Rome, while in the same century the Etruscans, allied to the Carthaginians, were apparently successful in repelling the expansionistic aims of the Greek colonists and keeping a firm grip on the Tyrrhenian. Nevertheless, by the end of that century Etruscan power was shaken by events such as the abortive conquest of Cumae in 525 BC, the fall of the Tarquins in Rome and the rebellion of Latium in 510-505, the growing aggressiveness of the Apennine peoples (Umbrians, Sabines, Samnites), the defeat off Cumae of the Etruscan fleet by that of Syracuse (474 BC) and the sack of Caere in 384, once again by Syracuse. By the early 4th cent., shaken also by a wave of invasion by the Celts (who got as far as Rome), the power of the Etruscans was prostrate. After that the Etruscans were in no position to resist the advance of Rome, which overran the independent cities one by one, or forced them into disadvantageous alliances, while at the same time founding new cen-

Top left, Etruscan art of the 7th cent. BC., gold fibula from Vetulonia. Museo Archeologico, Florence; right, Etruscan art, Canopic jar from Castelluccio near Pienza. Museo Archeologico, Chiusi

Parish church of Socana (Arezzo) with the remains of a 5th-cent. BC Etruscan altar in the foreground

tres and gaining control of the network of communications.

The Roman conquest was not confined to destroying the bases of Etruscan civilization, even where formally and in appearance these were left intact. On the contrary, it brought about a thorough reshuffling of the territory and social structure of Tuscany, favouring the appropriation of the *ager publicus* by the patrician families of the new capital, distributing lands near the old cities to veterans of the Roman army, and finally taking over the road network and rearranging it to make "all roads lead to Rome." In Etruscan times the roads were laid out in such a way as to facilitate communications between the coast and the interior, and the Romans modified all this to provide easy passage to and from the capital. The roads hence came to run prevalently north-south, leading to the decline of the towns which were "out of line." The Via Clodia, the Via Cassia, and above all the Via Aurelia between Rome and Pisa became the chief axes of the new system.

Top, the Roman theater of Volterra and, right, remains of a Roman mosaic. Museo Guarnacci, Volterra

This automatically brought about the economic and cultural decay of many Etruscan centres, a tendency which Augustus attempted to contain by making Etruria part of the *VII Regio* and giving birth to a programme of colonization and social and economic reorganization. These measures included the establishment of huge *villae* farmed by slaves and of manufactories in many of the towns. But the process of decline could not be stopped, and in the 2nd cent. had already taken on several chronic features: the towns began to drop in population, while

From the Longobards to Feudalism

The Longobards organized the region into a duchy with its main centre at Lucca, although it stood in the middle of a flood plain. During the two centuries of their dominion the road network deteriorated still further. The Via Aurelia became almost impassable, being exposed to erosion by the sea and the spread of the marshes; and also marshy was the Via Cassia, which ran from Pistoia and Florence to Rome by way of Chiusi and Bolsena. In the section through the Valdichiana it was also liable to attacks by the Byzantines coming from the Adriatic coast, where the Exarch had his seat. All through the 10th cent. Tuscany was a land of fevers, of ruined monuments, of settlements abandoned or sparsely populated because of the drop in population and the tendency of the inhabitants to live in out-of-the-way places for reasons of safety. The historical and archaeological documents of the time all agree in giving us the picture of a life of hardship, with agriculture at a subsistence level, the plains half abandoned, large stretches of once-cultivated land reduced to grassland, marshes or woods, while the dwellings were wretched huts or – especially in the south of the area – caves.

The marshes that swamped the coast-road and the dangers of the eastern route had even in Longobard times made it necessary to have a new road to Rome through the centre of the region. This indeed came about with the

the southerly coastal areas began gradually to turn into marshes, a process that in every sense changed the *Maritima* into the Maremma. In the early 5th cent. AD the description of the coast of Etruria in the *De Reditu Suo* of Rutilius Claudius Namatianus gives us a picture of decay and pitiful desolation. In the 6th cent. the wars between the Greeks and the Goths and (from 570 on) the arrival of the Longobards and the slaughter and destruction that accompanied their earliest settlements seemed to deliver the *coup-de-grâce* to a region shattered by outbreaks of smallpox and the plague, and sorely tried during the same period by natural disasters such as ruinous floods.

Interior of the church of San Piero a Grado (Pisa) with the remains of the previous building from the 4th-6th cent. AD

Longobard art of the 7th cent., *Plate of Agilulf.* Museo del Bargello, Florence

Longobard art of the 6th cent., gold cross from Santa Giulia in Lucca. Museo Archeologico, Florence

increasing importance of the *Mons Bardonis* road (the Cisa Pass) and consequently of the road leading from there to Rome by way of Lucca, the mid-Valdarno, the Val d'Elsa, Siena, Radicofani, Acquapendente, Bolsena, Viterbo and Sutri.

The Longobard rearrangement of Tuscan territory disrupted and cancelled out the order set up in the region at the end of the Roman Empire. Diocletian had in fact united what came more and more to be known as Tuscia to Umbria, while in 370 Tuscia had been divided into the *suburbicaria* to the south of the Arno and the *annonaria* to the north; as governor of the whole region there was a *Corrector*, with his seat in Florence. But the function of Florence as the chief centre did not survive the Longobard invasion, nor did the city succeed in reclaiming importance after the year 774, when the territory became a "march" of the Carolingian world. In fact Florence lay off the route of the new road which came down from the Cisa Pass and (due to the fact that it was chiefly the artery used by pilgrims travelling from France to Rome) was already known as the Via Francigena. The Tuscan metropolis of the late Middle Ages therefore remained Lucca, which in the course of the 11th cent. was joined by Pisa.

A certain amount of sea-going trade had survived in Pisa even under the Longobards, but throughout the late Middle Ages it was an exception on a coast that was seriously depressed not only because of the encroaching marshes, but also owing to the Saracen and Norman incursions which from the 8th to the 10th century were the scourge of the Tuscan shores no less than those of Corsica and Sardinia. This caused, or hastened, the decline of once-flourishing urban centres, along with the related phenomenon of the transfer of the sees of the bishops towards nearby towns further inland: the see of Luni moved to Sarzana, that of Populonia to Massa Marittima, that of Roselle to Grosseto.

During the 10th cent., however, we begin to discern a few signs of reawakening due to the efforts of the marquises of Tuscany, both at the end of that century with the famous Marquis Ugo, and at the beginning of the next century, when the marquisate passed to the powerful family of the Counts of Canossa, who between feudal titles and alodial estates possessed a real and proper "empire" that stretched from the Tuscan-Emilian Apennines as far as Modena, Reggio, Mantua and Ferrara. Their power, however, began to wane after the death in 1115 of the "great" Countess Mathilda, who with Gregory VII and the emperor Henry IV had been a protagonist of the period known as the Wars of the Investitures. In exchange, 12th-century Tuscany was divided up between great feudal families such as the Malaspina who controlled the Lunigiana, the Alberti with their vast feuds between the Apennines and the mid-Valdarno, the Guidi who dominated the Casentino, and the Aldobrandeschi who were powerful in Siena. Beside these noble dynasties were lesser feudal families who played a minor but often far from negligible role. Many of them settled in the cities, which were even then beginning the process of recovery, thereby creating a town-dwelling aristocracy that was a feature of the first phase of the movement of the Communes, or the free city-states.

Longobard art, peacocks from the shield of San Romano. Museo di Villa Guinigi, Lucca

Illumination from the *Vita Mathildis* depicting Mathilda of Canossa, Henry IV and Hugh of Cluny. Biblioteca Vaticana, Rome, MS. lat. 4922

The Age of the Communes

The characteristic feature of the 11th and 12th centuries in Tuscany was in fact the revival of trade, manufacturing, and the civil and economic life of the cities. While Lucca, in the absence of the powers of the marquisate, went into a slow but dignified decline, Pisa succeeded in linking its rise to power with the struggles (first in alliance but later in competition with Genoa) to free the Tyrrhenian Sea from the menace of the Saracen pirates and gain control of Corsica and Sardinia. In the second half of the 11th cent. a bitter religious and political struggle broke out in Pisa, Lucca and Florence, connected with the reforms of the Church at that time. In a Tuscany until then accustomed to the presence of great monasteries that were also feudal overlords, such as the abbey of San Salvatore on Monte Amiata, these events led to the foundation of new and typically Tuscan religious orders, such as the Vallombrosians and the Camaldolensians, who even built abbeys in the cities, making a considerable contribution to their political lives.

Pisan dominance was sanctioned and confirmed by the Crusades. Even though late in the day, the city took part in the First Crusade, and in 1100, though only for a short time, its archbishop became the Latin Patriarch of Jerusalem; but it also had an important role in the Second and Third Crusades. These exploits gained Pisa a leading place in the Mediterranean mercantile world of the time, and the city founded trading colonies not only on the coasts of Syria and Palestine but also at Byzantium and in Africa. Towards the end of the 12th cent., we begin to discern the emergence of those elements which caused Pisa to lose the leading role in the area. Her constant loyalty to the Hohenstaufen emperors, whose political designs were largely shattered by the resistance of the popes, and the rise of the vigorous communal movement, did nothing to help Pisa. Nor did she show herself capable of coping at one and the same time with the pressure exerted by her two great rivals, Genoa on the sea and Florence, which was pressing from the interior.

At first sight it might appear that the characteristic feature of Tuscany during the 12th and 13th centuries (not very different from what happened in most of central and northern Italy at that time) was the struggle between the Guelphs (sup-

Facing page, the early medieval crypt of the abbey of San Salvatore on Monte Amiata

Top, Ambrogio Lorenzetti, *Effects of Good Government in the City*, detail. Palazzo Pubblico, Siena; right, the Ghibelline Torri Salvucci in San Gimignano

porters of papal power) and the Ghibellines, who backed the power of the Holy Roman Empire in the fight between two "universal" authorities. But this had little to do with great political or ethical principles, and was really the excuse for contesting frontiers, dominating the routes of communication, and seizing new markets, close at hand or otherwise. Its "chessboard" structure, according to which if one city was Ghibelline the others around it became Guelph, and vice versa, is clear proof that these choices were nothing but pretexts. The same thing is reflected in the struggles between the aristocratic families of

gion. This phenomenon was accompanied by the tendency of the larger ones to domineer over the smaller, or at least to make them into allies, needless to say on unequal terms. In other words the communal "city-state" tended by its very nature to grow larger and to transform itself into a territorial state.

This was necessary to establish and maintain free circulation on the roads and to control the markets. Thus, with occasional variants, there came about a difficult equilibrium which, however, implied a constant clash between a Guelph alliance (Florence and Lucca together

Left, Taddeo Gaddi, *Saint Eligius the Goldsmith*, detail. Prado, Madrid

Niccolò di Pietro Gerini, *Scenes from the Life of Saint Matthew*, detail of two bankers. San Francesco, Prato

Bottom, Luca della Robbia, coat of arms of the Crafts of Stone- and Woodcutting. Orsanmichele, Florence

each single town, so that where the Guelphs were on top the families opposing those in power immediately declared themselves Ghibellines, and so on. The reality is not to be found on the political face of things, but on the contrary in a savage struggle for power, which saw cities pitted against feudal overlords, or one town against another, or even family against family in one and the same place.

An objective cause of political instability throughout the 12th cent. was the great number of free Communes that set themselves up in the re-

with cities outside Tuscany, such as Genoa and Perugia) and a Ghibelline league (Pisa, Siena, Pistoia, Arezzo). Also during the 13th cent. the quarrels between the old aristocratic families who formed the governing classes of the old Communes, with their knightly rank and way of life, and houses and towers in the towns and lands outside it, were added to by the struggle (political, but also in part social) of the non-aristocratic citizens who possessed new forms of economic power. These were the bankers, merchants and manufacturers (above all of textiles) who had liquid cash

with which to challenge the power of the old nobility and take a hand in the government. This was the battle between the magnates and the populace, in which "populace" must be understood to mean the classes of businessmen, producers, shopkeepers and so on, all organized into professional associations known as *Arti* (Guilds) or Corporations. Towards the end of the 13th cent. this led in more or less all the cities of Tuscany to the formation of governments dominated by the big commercial organizations. Once they had come to power these organizations became strongly conserva-

possible political role for the masses. These, for their part, aimed to get a say in the government. Beside the *popolo grasso* (the "fat populace" whom we could very roughly compare with the upper middle class), there emerged in the 14th cent. a *popolo magro* or "lean populace" composed of small businessmen and artisans, also provided with their corporations, and even the crowd of employees and subordinates (*popolo minuto*) who were forbidden to enter public affairs and refused the right to set up organizations. In the second half of the 14th cent., when as well as a general drop in popula-

Sano di Pietro,
Charter of the
Merchants' Guild.
State Archives,
Siena

Right, Payment
of the employees
of the Comune.
State Archives,
Siena

Bottom, Andrea
della Robbia,
symbol of the
Wool Guild.
Sanctuary of
La Verna

tive. The bankers and manufacturers (especially in textiles) who were also the protagonists and leaders in the political field tended to marry into the old aristocracy and to inherit its mental attitudes and ways of life, and they invested a conspicuous part of their business profits in buying land.

On the other hand they did not intend to lose a dominance that they had fought so hard to gain. To this end they had to protect themselves against the rise of the lower classes, socially subordinate to them, by attempting to regulate or even prevent any

tion culminating in the Black Death of 1348 there was a grave social and economic depression throughout the whole of Europe, the lower classes made their voice heard in a number of uprisings, such as the famous revolt of the Ciompi (employees of the Wool Guild) in Florence in 1378. These were immediately suppressed by the governments, the reins of which were in the hands of the wealthy merchants.

Tuscan Festivals

Quite a number of towns in Tuscany have their own special way of celebrating Carnival, the most famous of all being Viareggio with its parade of allegorical floats. But Carnival is only one of a number of festivals that are not peculiar to Tuscany.

There are numberless fairs, and feast-days and whatnot. For the most part, perhaps, they are the result of rather dubious "revivals," and fishing up old traditions to make money out of them, in the same way that "local customs" and "country taverns" have

Top, Biccherna tablet representing a tournament in honor of Ferdinando I de' Medici. State Archives, Siena

Right, Giovanni Stradano, *Popular Festival in Piazza Santo Spirito* and, below, *Fireworks for the Feast of Saint John*. Palazzo Vecchio, Florence

sprouted up like mushrooms.

Nevertheless, a lot of good things remain. For example, in the middle of October you simply have to go to Impruneta for the Fair of San Luca, which at one time coincided with the date at which the flocks of sheep, on their way down to winter in the Maremma, were assembled here at the famous shrine of the Virgin Mary. The "Rificolona," in which people parade through the streets of Florence with Chinese lanterns to celebrate the feast marking the birth of the Virgin (September 8th), has deep

Vincenzo Rustici, *The Bullfight in Piazza del Campo*, detail. Historic Seat of the Monte dei Paschi, Siena

Parade for the game of soccer in historical costume in Florence

The Giostra dell'Orso in Pistoia

roots in the consciousness of the people and sound historical origins. Indeed it appears that it is derived from the "fierucolone," or processions of the women from the surrounding countryside coming in to Florence on the eve of the festival in good time to sell their wares next day in the Piazza della Santissima Annunziata. In Pisa the display of lights of San Ranieri is worth seeing, while in Florence it is rather sad to see the great religious and civic festival of San Giovanni celebrated only with fireworks.

However, if you have a chance, there are several other festivals worth the trip. At Querceta near Forte dei Marmi, on the second Sunday after Easter, there is the donkey "palio" (i.e. donkey race), at Pienza there is the cheese fair on the first Sunday in September. But above all there are the "butterate" in the Maremma. These are Tuscan "rodeos" in which cowboys and their mounts compete in agility and ability. It is well known around here that the cowboys of the Maremma were challenged by the world-famous troupe of that over-inflated gasbag Buffalo Bill, and that they beat the Americans hands down.

The Giostra del Saracino in Arezzo

Detail of allegorical float at the Carnival of Viareggio

The Rise of Florence

Left, gold florin

Domenico di Michelino, *Dante and the Worlds of the "Comedy,"* detail. Cathedral, Florence

In any case, in spite of numerous crises and periods of marking time, it was the city of Florence, with its ruling class of bankers and producers of woollen textiles, which imposed its dominion on the whole of Tuscany. In 1252 the Florentines were among the first to mint a gold coin of their own, the florin, which along with the Venetian ducat very soon became the currency *par excellence* of the entire European side of the Mediterranean, and was in effect the main basis for pursuing a "power policy." Pisa, exhausted by its constant struggles with Genoa, and crippled by the end of the Crusades which had put its colonial system into a state of crisis, ceased to be a real rival at the end of the 13th cent. Siena had in the 13th cent. established an important banking system, but it could not keep pace with Florence, which apart from all else enjoyed the support of the two great religious and political powers of the early 14th cent., the papacy and the French monarchy. In spite of this, for much of the 14th cent. it still seemed anyone's bet in Tuscany. For example, Castruccio Castracani, an audacious Ghibelline chief with a good head for politics, succeeded in becoming lord of Pistoia and Lucca, and making them the centres of a territory that posed a great threat to Florence. Later on, at the end of the century, a similar threat appeared to be posed by a non-Tuscan ruler, Giangaleazzo Visconti, Duke of Milan. He had a great number of supporters in Tuscany, who saw him (if nothing else) as the only hope of preventing the dominance of Florence. And in fact as we see from the letters of the city's Humanist chancellor, Coluccio Salutati, a tireless opponent of Visconti, Florence lost no opportunity of presenting herself (and not just to Tuscans, but to the whole of Central Italy) as the most reliable defender of "freedom" against the "tyrants." These "tyrants" were the party leaders or knights of feudal origin who as early as the end of the 13th cent. had seized power in many towns in Lombardy, the Veneto and Emilia, making themselves "lords" of them on the pretext that these towns were unable to sort out their political squabbles and institutional crises.

Illuminations from the *Biadaiolo Codex* depicting the distribution of grain (left) and a greengrocer. Biblioteca Laurenziana, Florence

What is called *signoria* (lordship) is in fact not a Tuscan phenomenon, even if there is no lack of instances of it all through the region (from Arezzo to Lucca, from Cortona to Pisa and Siena). And most of all it is not a Florentine phenomenon, since in Florence the various families fighting each other for power never managed to find a successful leader until the middle of the 15th cent. In the late 14th cent., and well into the 15th, Florence was therefore governed by an oligarchy of wealthy families. To the economic power which they derived from banking, wool manufacturing or other highly remunerative activities, they united a shrewd policy of making good marriages and large investments in land. Estates and castles, out-of-town houses and coats of arms granted them by the pope, or else by one of the European sovereigns who owed them vast amounts of money, very soon enabled them to forget their origins, often very humble, and embrace the aristocratic way of life, becoming part of the late-mediaeval, early-modern process of re-feudalization. Never were there so many tournaments and emblems and heraldic devices as in the Florence of the "people" or of the "bourgeois".

On the other hand, if the solidarity of the oligarchy made up of the great families (who nonetheless fought like tigers among themselves for supreme power) had sheltered Florentine society from institutional changes brought about "from below," there remained the vast problem of transforming the city-state into a territorial state. In late mediaeval Italy this problem became the basis of a whole new political equilibrium, with the erasure of dozens and dozens of small local governments – which in some cases survived perhaps in form if not in substance – in favour of the gradual annexation of small states into larger and more logical units. This is why northern Italy came to be partitioned between the Duchy of Milan and the Republic of Venice. Much the same thing is true of Florence, whose territory in the early 12th cent.

Masolino, *The Healing of the Cripple*, detail. Brancacci Chapel, Florence

did not extend beyond the Valdelsa and the Mugello, and did not even include Fiesole, which was just "at the top of the hill." By conducting a ruthless policy of alternating alliances, of the acquisition of territories and the founding of new centres (the *terrenove* or "new lands," such as San Giovanni Valdarno, Firenzuola, Scarperia), Florence by the end of the 15th cent. had in one way or another subdued almost all of northern and central Tuscany, including the cities of Prato, Pistoia, Arezzo, Cortona, Volterra and even Pisa herself, defeated in 1406 after a long siege. One city to escape from the ambitions of the Florentines was Lucca, for all political manoeuvres and military campaigns aimed at gaining control of the city had failed, and Lucca was still at the head of a republic stretching

from the Valdinievole to the Lunigiana and southern Garfagnana. The other was Siena, mistress of a large if somewhat sparsely populated territory extending from the Chianti hills to Monte Amiata and from the Maremma to Chiusi, including the important town of Grosseto and the port of Talamone, from which the Sienese for a long time vainly attempted to organize their independent maritime policy.

Government by an overlord only began in Florence in 1434, when the group of oligarchical families led by the rich and powerful bankers of the Medici family and with ample support from the more modest strata of society, succeeded in defeating and to a large extent exiling the rival group, led by the Albizzi family. However, the head of the Medici family and firm, Cosimo the Elder, never took on the outward trappings of an overlord. He continued to govern the city, as the phrase goes, "from the back of his shop," which was in fact the splendid palace in Via Larga (now Via Cavour) which he had had built by Michelozzo and from which he controlled the affairs of the family, the family firm and the city. Cosimo always refused official posts and honours, contenting himself with checking on the electoral lists and giving his own apparently modest personal advice to the rulers of the city, as well as to foreign ambassadors. But in reality, though clad in the garb of an affable merchant, his authority was no less felt than that of a Duke of Milan or Marquis of Ferrara, girded as they were with military splendours. After the brief paranthesis of his son Piero, who was an invalid, his work was continued by his grandson Lorenzo, known as "the Magnificent." Lorenzo to a large extent abandoned the principle of outward reserve, and, especially in the last years of his government, openly adopted the stance of a real prince. Lorenzo was celebrated for his political and diplomatic acumen – Francesco Guicciardi-

Jacopo Pontormo, *Portrait of Cosimo the Elder.* Uffizi, Florence

Niccolò Fiorentino, medal with *Portrait of Lorenzo the Magnificent.* Museo del Bargello, Florence

ni described him as the "index of the scale" in the balance of power of 15th-century Italy – and also for his patronage of artists. In fact the years of his government (1469-1492) coincide with the most splendid and creative period of the early Renaissance in Florence. But we should not turn a blind eye to his more negative side: a really harsh policy, both towards his internal enemies and to those parts of Tuscany subject to Florence; the constant subordination of the interests of the republic to those of his own house and banking enterprises; and a political and financial policy that was far from prudent, and brought the state and the Medici bank to the verge of crisis.

And in fact in 1492, when Lorenzo died, black clouds were looming over Florence. The city was stricken by new outbreaks of conflict between the factions, Charles VIII of France swept down into the country, there was the brief but intense and significant dictatorship of Gerolamo Savonarola from 1494 to 1498, and the subject cities (such as Pisa in 1494 and Arezzo in 1502) rebelled against Florentine rule. In the wars between France and Spain, which took place in Italy, Florentine dominance in Tuscany appeared to crumble, while Florence herself seemed unable to decide between the Medici family supported from without (what had been a family of bankers now provided two great Renaissance popes, Leo X and Clement VII) and republican forces stemming from an aristocracy that was by now politically enfeebled.

Anonymous Florentine artist, *Piazza della Signoria with the Martyrdom of Savonarola*, detail. Museo di San Marco, Florence

Left, Raphael, *Portrait of Leo X with Two Cardinals*, detail. Uffizi, Florence

The Medici Villas

At the end of the 16th cent. the Flemish painter Justus Utens made 14 lunettes for the Medici villa of Artimino, each one depicting a house in the region belonging to the granducal family. As a number of these great villas have been subjected to remodelling and alterations that have profoundly changed their character, while others have completely disappeared, these lunettes by Utens (now in the "Firenze Com'era" Museum in Florence) are a valuable source of information.

The villas, with their parklands, were scattered throughout the territory of the State, in such a way that the sovereign could move to any

From the top, Justus Utens, lunettes depicting the villas of Cafaggiolo, Montelupo, Poggio a Caiano and Pratolino (left). Museo di Firenze Com'era, Florence

part of it and yet remain, as it were, at home. Still existing today are: Cafaggiolo in the Mugello, on the road to the Futa pass (and it is something of a "mother house" for the Medici); the villa of Trebbio nearby; Poggio a Caiano near Pistoia, designed in 1485 by Giuliano da Sangallo; Castello, between Florence and Sesto on the Prato road; Seravezza, built by Cosimo I near the marble quarries and silver mines in which he took a personal interest; La Petraia, which was severely remodelled in the 19th cent., when Florence became the capital and the villa became a royal residence; Palazzo Pitti in Florence, with the great complex of the Boboli Gardens and the Fortezza del Belvedere; Lappeggi near Grassina, south of Florence, now much modified and spoilt; La Magia near Quarrata, in the area of Monte Albano; Marignolle; L'Ambrogiana at Montelupo,

The villa La Petraia
Right, the villa of Poggio a Caiano

now a nursing home for the mentally disturbed; Montevettolini on the slopes of Monte Albano; Colle Salvetti; and Artimino. Lost to us is the villa of Pratolino, with its marvellous park (of which a few monuments remain).

The villa of Artimino or "of the hundred chimneys"

The Medici Grand Duchy

The siege of Florence in 1530, conducted by the troops of the emperor Charles V on the request of Clement VII, who was anxious to get his own family back into power in the city, was the last great period of republican and "Savonarolian" Florence, symbolized for us by the efforts made by Michelangelo to prepare the fortifications of the city. In accord with the neo-feudal appearance which the Habsburg empire was giving if not to European politics at least to its outward forms, Florence and its territory, where the disappointed hope of freedom in the early years of the century and the weakness of the city itself had caused a number of fits and starts, had been patiently and laboriously reorganized, and was now raised to the status of duchy and assigned to Cosimo I, who descended from a cadet

branch of the Medici. It was the new duke who in the years 1555-1559 managed to realize the ancient dream of Florence: in a long and bitter military campaign he subdued the entire Republic of Siena. Siena was unable to withstand the combined strength of the duke and the Spanish, who had placed Tuscany under their direct vigilance by creating a garrison state thick with fortresses from the promontory of the Argentario to the south coast of Elba. But the City of the Virgin had no intention of giving way easily to its age-old enemy, and Cosimo personally had to accept the union of the two ducal crowns of Florence and Siena, formally independent of each other.

Tuscan unity became a constitutional reality only later, in 1559, when pope Pius V conferred on the duke the title of Grand Duke of Florence and Siena.

With Cosimo I the structures of the Tuscan state gradually came into line

Top, Giorgio Vasari and Giovanni Stradano, *The Siege of Florence*, detail. Palazzo Vecchio, Florence

Giovanni Antonio de' Rossi, onyx cameo representing *Cosimo I and His Family*. Museo degli Argenti, Florence

they ever succeed in making themselves particularly popular there. For them, however, this was not a disadvantage. Since Florence had for centuries been disliked by the rest of Tuscany, which was justified in identifying it with the forces which in the 14th and 15th centuries had deprived it of its freedom, the Medici understood that the essential basis of their political image would have to be to promote themselves as the princes of the entire region, and not just of the Florentines. Therefore, with their presence and with the public works which were their representatives, they set about underlining, here there and everywhere, their shrewd and provident grand ducal authority. They formed special privileged relationships with several important centres such as Pisa,

with what was the great political fact of the 16th cent.: absolute monarchy. The court became the centre of the grand duchy, while the whole of Tuscany — thanks to a vast programme of princely building, of villas, palaces and fortresses — turned into a kind of extension of the court itself. Cosimo and his successors also saw to the political enfeeblement of the Florentine nobility, whom they loaded with titles while removing not only the least aspiration in politics, but even in the business world which had at one time constituted their strength. From then on the aristocratic world of Tuscany became one of peaceful landowners, who derived safe incomes from the system of share-cropping and the division of the estates into farms, while they viewed the fact of living in contact with the soil as the basic sign of their nobility.

The grand dukes, though they went on living in Florence, and indeed endowed it with a series of great monuments, were not really fond of their capital; nor did

Top right, Giorgio Vasari and collaborators, *Cosimo Visiting the Fortifications of the Island of Elba*. Palazzo Vecchio, Florence

Giorgio Vasari and collaborators, *Cosimo I Studying the Plans for the Conquest of Siena*, detail. Palazzo Vecchio, Florence

Francesco I's Studiolo in the Palazzo Vecchio of Florence

Peter Paul Rubens, *Portrait of Francesco I*, detail. Louvre, Paris

which enjoyed a new flowering during the 16th cent., or the port of Livorno, which thanks to the foundation in 1561 of the Order of the Knights of St. Stephen became the centre of military and maritime activities to defend the coast against the Barbary corsairs, but which at the same time was a "free port." It soon grew to great prosperity, and traditionally provided an exile for the victims of despotic regimes throughout Europe, such as the Jews expelled from Spain or the Calvinists who had to leave France as a result of the revocation of the Edict of Nantes.

After a difficult period coinciding with the reign of Cosimo's son Francesco I (1574-87), during which Tuscany faced a rather severe economic crisis and a widespread outbreak of banditry, the great policies of Cosimo I were continued by his other son, Grand Duke Ferdinando I (1587-1609). His was the real responsibility for the economic launching of the port of Livorno, and he guided Florentine commerce and the textile trade (by now centred on the manufacture of silk) towards a new period of prosperity. Ferdinando can also take credit for having slackened the traditional ties of alliance with Spain, which had become too heavy a political burden, and which Cosimo had already attempted to reduce, and for turning instead to France, thereby taking up one of the threads of the policy of mediaeval Florence.

The 17th cent. brought Tuscany a certain number of problems, as it did to the rest of Europe. War raged more or less everywhere, and it may be that one of the keys to understanding the attachment of the Tuscan people to the grand-ducal family was simply the fact that it managed to keep the region free from the scourge of war. But it could not shelter Tuscany from other troubles, such as the long eco-

nomic crisis that badly hit the textile industry, still conva-lescent after its recovery at the end of the 16th cent., or the plague of 1630 which decimated the population. The free port of Livorno remained flourishing, but its cosmopoli-tan middle class was dominated by the two great econom-ic and maritime powers of the century, the Dutch and the English, so that the Tuscans could derive little benefit from it. Especially with Cosimo III (1670-1723) and Gian Gastone (1723-37), the grand-ducal dynasty seemed to have fallen into a kind of lethargy, not unlike that of the Tuscan aris-tocracy as a whole, converted into a nobility of farmers.

The Lorraine Grand Duchy

The Medici dynasty died out with Gian Gastone, and in the general rearrangement of European in-stitutions following the War of the Polish Succession the grand duchy was assigned to Francis Stephen of Lor-raine, husband of the empress Maria Theresa of Habs-burg. But he lived nearly the whole time in Vienna, gov-erning the region through a council of regents. Things went quite differently when, in 1765, he was succeeded by his son Peter Leopold I, who governed directly and vig-orously until he was recalled to Vienna in 1790 to ascend the throne of the Empire. The strength of purpose of a prince extraordinarily open to reform was echoed by an intellectual environment in which the rationalistic scientif-ic legacy of Galileo was still alive, and in which circulat-ed the physiocratic theories which had their chief motive force in the Accademia dei Georgofili. An indication of this interest in innovation is the fact that the French *Ency-clopédie,* that out-and-out manifesto of the Enlightenment in Europe, was published twice in Tuscany, in 1758 in Lucca and in 1770 in Livorno. Leopold carried out a pol-icy of limiting or suppressing the feudal privileges hither-to held by the aristocracy and many ecclesiastical institu-tions, put the state finances on a new footing, and laboured to revive agriculture, the meagre yields from which were a problem that increased with the intense pop-ulation growth which started in the mid-18th cent. In this context vast reclamation schemes were undertaken in Valdichiana, the Pisan plain, the Sienese Maremma and the Valdinievole, while laws were passed to allow the free circulation of grain. Plans were drawn up to sell or long-lease the grand-ducal possessions and those of the privileged institutions. The aim of these last two measures was to enlarge and reinforce the class of small landowners and to broaden the base of the ur-ban and rural middle class-

Facing page, bottom, Matteo Rosselli, *Ferdinando I Resumes Work on the Port of Livorno.* Casino Mediceo, Florence

Top, Johann Michael Millitz, *Portrait of Peter Leopold.* Uffizi, Florence; above, Nicola Monti, *Ferdinand III of Lorraine.* Museo Civico, Pistoia

es. A new Penal Code largely inspired by the ideas of reform then circulating in Europe was issued in 1768. Nor did ecclesiastical life go unchanged, both with the suppression of the courts of the Inquisition and various fiscal privileges of the clergy, and by encouraging a kind of religious reform put forward by the Jansenists in Tuscany.

The departure of the grand duke to ascend the throne of the Holy Roman Empire in 1790 produced a considerable movement of discontent. Increasingly connected to the alarming news coming from France, in 1799 (after the French invasion of Italy) this movement led to the formation of the traditionalist faction known as "Viva Maria." Brought into the Napoleonic system in 1801, the grand duchy first became the kingdom of Etruria under the dynasty of the Bourbons of Parma, and then – from 1807 on – a department of the French Empire. Under

Napoleon the projects started during the period of Leopoldo came to fruition, though accompanied by strong new administrative centralization and a series of severe, and in many cases brutal, plunderings and forced annulments of old institutions and ancient traditions.

When the Bonapartist adventure came to an end, the Restoration brought Grand Duke Ferdinand III back to the throne, while the Garrison States and the Principality of Piombino were annexed to the grand duchy. The year 1847 saw the annexation also of the duchy of Lucca, so that the first half of the 19th cent. substantially saw the completion of regional unity. Though remaining outside the great social and economic changes that during the same period altered the face of Lombardy and Piedmont, Tuscany travelled slowly and cautiously along the road of progress, retaining most of the reforms brought in under Pe-

ter Leopold and Napoleon and remaining faithful to a tradition of moderation and tolerance that permitted the development of important cultural initiatives animated by liberal tendencies, such as the scientific and literary "Gabinetto" founded by Giovan Pietro Vieusseux and the *Antologia Vieusseux*, a magazine which between 1821 and 1833 prepared the educated Tuscan public for the idea that the grand-ducal regime should gradually change into a constitutional monarchy. This had, in any case, been a project of Peter Leopold's.

In 1847-48 it was moderate public opinion that led the struggle that ended in the issuing of the Statute in February 1848 and the brief military campaign against Austria in alliance with the Piedmontese. Grand Duke Leopold II, though he was beginning to worry about the final outcome of the movement which had thus been started, remained loyal to the agreements he had made with the most determined group of moderates led by Baron Bettino Ricasoli. But in October 1848 events overwhelmed even Tuscany, where as a result of violent protests, especially in Livorno and Florence, power was taken over by a revolutionary triumvirate composed of Montanelli, Guerrazzi and Mazzoni, whose immediate aim was to call an Italian constituent assembly and to join up with the Roman republic. In the meanwhile, in February 1849, the grand duke had abandoned Florence for Gaeta.

Leopold returned to Florence on July 28th of that year, when the situation caused by the revolutionary years of 1848-49 had already crumbled. In the grand duchy there were neither vendettas nor repressions, but the sovereign repealed the Statute and once again became an absolute monarch, preferring to govern with the aid of military support from Austria. But in spite of all this the last decade of the grand-ducal regime was inspired by the customary sense of moderation. In the meanwhile, moderate-thinking people in Tuscany were swinging over to Cavour's ideas of the unity of Italy, while there was also the fear that the end of the Habsburg-Lorraine regime, written on the wall by this time, would bring with it all kinds of social upheaval. The insurrection of April 1859 and the plebiscite concerning the annexation of Tuscany to Piedmont, both of them incited by the middle classes and aristocracy won over to the cause of a united monarchy of Italy, brought this annexation into being. Six years later, in 1865, the need arose to move the capital of the kingdom of Italy away from Turin, which was geographically too marginal with regard to the rest of the country, as well as being too obviously linked to the dynastic continuity of a single family, the Savoy, who had to work hard to show that they did not consider Italy as a whole as being annexed to Piedmont! At the same time there was a wish to shift the capital nearer to what on many sides was hoped to be the future capital, which is to say Rome. Along with the fact that it was considered the historical and cultural "capital" of the country, this led to the decision to make Florence the political capital of the new State. And so it remained until 1870, and it was during this period or shortly after that the city was in part demolished and modernized in ways that to a certain degree deformed its traditional design, but which were at that time thought necessary to give it the outward appearance of a great modern city.

Tuscany as Part of the Italian World

Following unification the country underwent a gradual process of transformation. The wool industry of Prato, the shipyards of Livorno, the mines of Elba, the steelworks of Piombino and the numerous ironworks of Florence and Pistoia, were all giving it a more modern and dynamic appearance. Already begun under the grand duchy, the railway network was being extended, while the traditional resources of the region – the land and its special products, wine and oil – still anchored to the share-cropping system, inevitably generated social and mental conservatism. The ruling classes continued to be moderate, with a more "clerical" tendency in the Lucchesia and a more free-thinking one in Florence and Livorno, where there was no lack of democratic and republican feeling. The growing labour movement was at first influenced by the ideas of Bakunin,

but then became socialist not only in Florence, Livorno and Piombino, but also in smaller centres such as Empoli and Colle di Val d'Elsa, while among the marble quarrymen of the Carrara area there grew up a tendency to anarchy which has become a tradition.

The local governments at that time were for the most part democratic-liberal, often making use of implicit support from the Catholics, though here and there were discernible signs of the growth of the socialist movement, the strength of which would be seen later on with the introduction of universal suffrage, while the deep-rooted Catholicism of the people found expression through the organization of the so-called "white" unions of workers.

The early 20th cent., especially in Florence, was marked by furious warfare between intellectuals and newspapers with various views, some of which soon became well-known or notorious throughout the nation. Examples are Papini and Prezzolini's *La Voce*, Corradini's *Il Regno* and Salvemini's *L'Unità*. Battles were continuous and violent, with their epicentre in the "salon" frequented by militant writers and artists, the "Caffè delle Giubbe Rosse" in the Piazza della Repubblica in Florence. And then, Florence can lay claim to being the birthplace of the Futurist movement in painting, while on another plane it was often the scene of furious diatribes (which frequently came to blows) between "interventionists" and "neutralists" at the outbreak of the First World War.

As in the rest of Italy, the immediate post-war years threw Tuscany into a critical period, worsened by the fact that the war itself had temporarily concealed such problems as unemployment, and with the "wartime economy" had given rise to a whole series of industries which were bound either to be abolished or be drastically cut down with the coming of peace. Discontent was soon transformed into strikes, the occupation of factories and protests in the streets, backed now by the "white" and now by the "red" unions. And in fact it was in opposition to these two factions that in

Ottone Rosai, *Via Toscanella*.
Private collection, Florence

1920-22 Fascism emerged, taking on the two faces (destined to remain quite distinct from one another, and sometimes on opposite sides) of reaction from the agrarian community on the one hand, and on the other the brutal, nihilistic behaviour of the Fascist "squads," with their more or less republican aims and their irreverence towards the clergy. Fascism was caught between its objective stance of being against the workers and its deep-rooted prejudice against the middle classes.

Between 1922 and 1925 the more brutally subversive side of Fascism died down, as the movement had become legitimized by an established regime that was obliged to repress its most arbitrary and violent features. But the political debate was not altogether silenced. The Livorno Congress of 1921 saw the foundation of the Italian Communist Party, and no sooner had the government made Mussolini the "legitimate" dictator of the country than the first anti-Fascist newspaper was founded, and in no other city than Florence. This was *Non Mollare*, edited by Carlo Rosselli, Gaetano Salvemini, Ernesto Rossi and Piero Calamandrei.

As far as the Fascist regime was concerned, it found Florence a hard place to deal with, even among its own most fervent supporters. Within the Fascist party in Florence there were many with republican and libertarian views, and we need only mention one, a person of the stature of Ardengo Soffici. If Fascism was to get a grip on Tuscany it had not only to show its face of repression, but also the other one: the face that was in its way the heir of Futurism, an area in which there was room for suggestions for future progress or for attitudes that were at least less forcefully "under control." This gave rise to the sort of social and intellectual tension expressed in papers such as "Il Bargello" and which (partly in response to the crisis of 1929, which particularly hit the industrial and mining sectors) caused the characteristic tendency to launch into vast public works which absorbed manpower and gave an impression of progress and activity. Some results of this were the Firenze-Mare motorway, the direct railway-line from Florence to Bologna, and a number of buildings which for a long time remained exemplary of their kind, such as the Santa Maria Novella railway station in Florence. The Tuscan "capital" was also the scene of continuous artistic and cultural experimentation on the part of the regime, with a wealth of ideas some of which were fairly non-conformist, especially when the Florentine Alessandro Pavolini became Minister of "Popular Culture."

The Second World War, and particularly the terrible years of 1944-45, hit Tuscany extremely hard, partly be-

Emilio Pettoruti, *"La Voce."* Private collection, Paris

Top, Ardengo Soffici, *Composition with "Lacerba."* Private collection, Florence

cause the territory was split in two by the so-called "Gothic Line," the heavily fortified line from Pisa to Rimini which the Germans were determined to hold. During the summer of 1944 the Allied advance was very slow, while the population was subjected to considerable hardship, and there was much damage from bombing and artillery fire. At the same time there were some ugly episodes of repression and on certain occasions downright barbarity, such as deportations, mass shootings and indiscriminate massacre such as that of the Fucecchio swamps or at Sant'Anna di Stazzema. However, even in such sad and dramatic times the character of the Tuscans (factious perhaps, but also courageous) had a chance to reveal itself. The Resistance was not only and not principally a matter of groups of partisans, but a kind of spontaneous movement on the part of the people, shown by hiding fugitives and wanted persons, helping the homeless and refugees, and putting up resistance, albeit passive, to

the harsh measures imposed by the forces of occupation.

As we have seen, the post-war reconstruction once more placed Tuscany in the vanguard of Italy and Europe as a land of culture and economic activities directed not merely at development in terms of quantity, but also at safeguarding traditions and quality. Even agriculture, which in the immediate post-war years was perhaps rather too neglected in the name of the aprioristic need for "progress" in terms of industrialization, has for some time now been regaining its normal role in the region. This, however, has been achieved with the aid of the most advanced techniques and the determination to improve the level of the produce, so as to find a place for Tuscan wines and olive oil, for example, in a world market that is becoming more and more sophisticated and demanding.

Giovanni Michelucci, the church of San Giovanni Battista (Autostrada del Sole), and the station of Santa Maria Novella in Florence

Hypergothic and Hyperexotic

Among so many things, one comes to Tuscany to find things mediaeval. And indeed one finds them often, in cities, in villages and out in the country, set among hills and cypresses. But take care! Those battlements, those lovely towers, those embrasures and double-light windows, may conceal a fake. Usually, the more mediaeval a thing looks the less likely it is to be so.

The Romantic age and the later Neo-Gothic period, along with the eclectic and decadent taste of the turn of the century, filled Tuscany with fakes, follies and unfaithful restorations. This does not of course mean that many of these buildings are not very beautiful, and have much artistic merit of their own, and are works of art or at least monuments of interest, bearing precious witness to the taste of a certain epoch. It is just that they have nothing to do with the Middle Ages, or even with a correct philological and archeological approach to them.

In Via Calimala in Florence you find the "Palagio dell'Arte della Lana" (Palace of the Wool Guild), the nucleus of which dates from the very early 15th cent. But in 1905 Enrico Lusini "restored" it in a manner that is just too "mediaeval" for words. On the outskirts of Florence, on the road up to Fiesole from Ponte a Mensola, is the ancient castle of Vincigliata, a Visdomini property already in existence in the 11th cent. But it was remodelled in neo-mediaeval style by Giuseppe Fancelli in 1855-65. Brolio, Strozzavolpe near Poggibonsi, and even the town centre of San Gimignano have had a good few coats of 19th-century mediaeval paint.

Nor did the Neo-Gothic satisfy a certain number of eccentric spirits, and these preferred to go in for the exotic. The Villa di Sammezzano, near Pontassieve in the Valdarno, is a kind of

The Palagio dell'Arte della Lana

phoney Alhambra, while on the Porrettana near Riola (between 1850 and 1896) Cesare Mattei had a fairytale castle built for him. A jumble of styles, with plenty of Moorish and Russian echoes, it is called La Rocchetta, and may be viewed as a sort of Tusco-Emilian Neuschwanstein. And indeed among its guests were Ludwig II of Bavaria and Elizabeth of Habsburg, wife of Franz Joseph.

Left, the castle of Brolio in the Sienese part of Chianti; below, the castle of Vincigliata

INVITATION TO
THE JOURNEY

Where Can We Start From?

Let us take at random any Italian or foreign tourist who wishes to visit Tuscany, an undertaking which if confronted with passable seriousness will require at least a fortnight, whether he does it by train and bus, in his Toyota or thumbing lifts. The first problem he faces is: how to enter the region? What side should one besiege Tuscany from?

The idea of starting from Florence, given the city's central position in the region, and branching out from there on excursions of one or more days, makes sense if our tourist flies to the airport in Florence or the one in Pisa, which is connected to the provincial capital by a shuttle rail service that takes around an hour.

But otherwise?

There we have the question: "where does Tuscany begin?" The Etruscans first saw the coastline, coming from the sea – on the assumption that they did in fact arrive that way. But today one is rather unlikely to come in from the sea. Is there any "special" route to assure us of an enjoyable and profitable journey?

Before answering, and before we set off, it would be as well to set down a few facts. The road network of the region is considerable, with nearly 20,000 Km of roads, apart from more than 300 km of motorways. The latter comprise the A1 (Autostrada del Sole), the A12 (Tirrenica or Autostrada dei Fiori) the A11 (the Firenze-Mare opened in 1933, one of the earliest of its kind in Europe) and the A15 (della Cisa) which runs along the valley of the Magra, connecting the A12 with the A1. A series of *superstrade* or expressways radiate from these. Well known, for example, is the Florence-Siena-Grosseto link, joining the Autostrada del Sole to south-western Tuscany,

while in the Valdichiana there is another motorway leading to Umbria and the Adriatic. The Strada Statale 2, the glorious Via Cassia, is little used today, and mostly by local traffic, while long-distance drivers prefer the A1. This is a pity, for it is a beautiful road passing through enchanting landscapes and towns abounding in art and history. Another road of great charm is the Statale 1, the ancient Roman consular road known as the Via Aurelia which runs along the coast to the south of Pisa, a long stretch of which has for several years been flanked by the faster expressway leading to Grosseto.

We should mention that Tuscany has an extensive and efficient network of bus services, which tourists seldom know about or use as much as they might.

After a long delay – in line with a general tendency, related to the rise in public and private road traffic – the development of the railways has continued with the construction of high-speed lines.

Anyone who has travelled in Italy, be he Tuscan or otherwise, is familiar with the two main lines: the Turin-Rome line along the coast and the Milan-Rome inland route. But a tourist with a liking for revivals and enough time, patience and imagination, might think of taking some lesser line, such as the "trenino" from Borgo San Lorenzo to Faenza, or the Pisa-Cecina-Volterra line, or yet again the one (under private management) from Arezzo to Pratovecchio and Stia. He would find himself in contact with a different Tuscany, with glimpses of a landscape seldom seen and hardly even guessed at, old skills and technologies still in use, and a sense of time and human relations quite different from what one is used to in the big cities or along the main roads. But maybe this advice is

pp. 80-1, the "Italian-style" garden of Villa Gamberaia in the environs of Florence

best offered to a special kind of traveller: one who travels less to discover places than to discover himself.

As for the airports, it suffices to say that the main ones, and the only ones open to international civil aviation, are those of Pisa and Florence.

The situation with regard to ports is good. In addition to the great port of Livorno there is that of Piombino, rather smaller but nonetheless important for the local steel industry and communications with the island of Elba. Carrara and Viareggio both have fair-sized ports, while Vada, Baratti, Castiglione della Pescaia, Talamone, Porto Ercole and Porto Santo Stefano are little harbours for fishing and tourism. Portoferraio, important before the war because of its many industrial plants (now destroyed) has regained some measure of vitality thanks chiefly to tourism.

This is not a tourist guide, nor can it in any way replace guides, maps and so on. All the same, as its intention is to be a *vade-mecum* for the tourist who has no intention of going mad or joining the crowd, it too will offer a choice of routes. And for convenience and more logical presentation we will proceed as far as possible in the directions that seem most natural to the modern Western mind, which is to say from north to south and from west to east. Bearing in mind, above all, that the good traveller is a sage. He does not allow himself to be carried away by the desire to see everything; he does not tear his hair if he misses some objective that has three asterisks in his guidebook. When he feels the need he does not deny himself the pleasure of a swift gallop, a trip taken all in one breath, without ever leaving the window of a train or the wheel of a car. Such journeys do not enable him to pause over details, but give him the feeling and as it were the "aroma" of a region. Nor, on the other hand, will he deny himself the luxury of deviating from his route, of making unforeseen incursions, of "wasting" an afternoon sipping a glass of wine, or watching the sun go down over the vineyards of Chianti or, in the Maremma, over the sea. Anyone unwilling to do at least one of these things would do better not to come travelling in Tuscany. In fact, he would do better not to travel at all.

Florence

Out of the many possible ways to embark on this "journey," from the gradual descent into the city from the more picturesque of the surrounding hills (Fiesole, Settignano, Pian de' Giullari) to the classical but always stirring first glimpse from Piazzale Michelangelo, where the city is laid out below, we prefer to take a chronological approach, the one best suited to presenting a picture of Florence that is directly connected with its centuries of history. We will have to start out from the city's religious hub, the large space

in which stand the cathedral and the baptistery. The latter, traditionally regarded as one of the oldest buildings in the city, was constructed on the ruins of a large Roman building, part of whose mosaic floor has been brought to light. But its actual date, placed at various times between the 5th and 9th cent., is still an open question. The outer facing of white and green marble, with a geometric decoration of Oriental derivation, dates from the 11th to 13th cent. and, together with the 14th- to 15th-cent. doors (including the famous "Porta del Paradiso," 1425-52), is a symbol of great visual impact. Inside it is characterized by the great cycle of mosaics in the apse and the octagonal dome on which artists from Venice and Tuscany worked, by its inlaid marble floor and by the *Tomb of the Antipope John XXIII*, a fully Renaissance work by Michelozzo and Donatello.

In front of the baptistery

School of Verrocchio, *Madonna and Child with Saints*, detail with Florence. San Martino, Grassina

The baptistery of San Giovanni and, right, detail of the mosaic decoration of the apse with the *Last Judgment*

was embellished with 15th-cent. masterpieces by some of the greatest artists in Florence (Paolo Uccello, Andrea del Castagno, Luca della Robbia, Donatello). Later the dome was decorated with frescoes by Giorgio Vasari and Federico Zuccari representing the *Last Judgment*.

Alongside, completing the exceptional architectural complex, rises Giotto's campanile (1334-59), a monument to the city of burghers whose values are celebrated in the sculptural decoration centering on

The religious center with the baptistery, cathedral and campanile; bottom, the interior of the cathedral

stands the immense cathedral of Santa Maria del Fiore, a building constructed over the course of many centuries, to which the present Neo-Gothic façade was added only in the second half of the 19th cent. The previous cathedral of Santa Reparata had become

insufficient to meet the needs of a rapidly growing city. Its reconstruction was entrusted to the architect Arnolfo di Cambio (1294), and after his death the work continued with difficulties and frequent changes of hand up until the second decade of the 15th cent, when Filippo Brunelleschi took charge of the work, tackling and solving the technical problems connected

with the creation of a structure of such exceptional size in masterly fashion. By 1436 the dome (apart from the lantern) was already finished, a true manifesto of the Renaissance that was to leave a permanent mark on the city.

Its interior, with a nave and two aisles of great size, was built in a Gothic style tempered by touches of the classical and

Andrea del Castagno, *Monument to Niccolò da Tolentino*; bottom, Paolo Uccello, *Monument to John Hawkwood*, cathedral

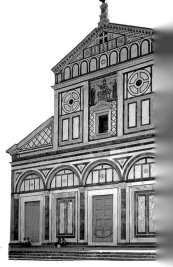

humanity's progressive conquest of civilization.

Along with the baptistery, the earliest places of worship to be built in the city with the arrival and spread of Christianity were the basilica of San Lorenzo (393), which was for a long time the seat of the bishop (but the building we see today is a Renaissance reconstruction), Santa Felicita, completely reconstructed in the 18th cent.,

and San Miniato al Monte. This last, built in the form of an oratory on the site chosen by the Christian martyr Miniatus for his hermitage, was restructured in the Romanesque style from the 11th cent. onward. With its beautiful façade of marble inlays and geometric designs of symbolic significance, and its harmonious interior in which Romanesque sculpture coexists

with Gothic frescoes and Renaissance works, it is perhaps the most fascinating church in Florence.

Many of the other religious buildings of the time have been lost in the incessant process of urban renewal, or adapted and renovated to suit current tastes. This has been the fate of the church of the Santi Apostoli, although an ambitious restoration carried out in the 20th cent. attempted to bring it back to its original Romanesque character, as well as of the former church of Santo Stefano al Ponte and the Badia Fiorentina, the first city's first

San Miniato al Monte with its Romanesque pulpit (bottom) and, top left, a detail of the decoration of the marble enclosure

monastic institution founded at the end of the 10th cent.

The same thing has happened to a lot of the civil buildings, including the ancient and distinctive Torre della

Pagliazza, formerly thought to be Byzantine, and several tower-houses that have managed to survive the ravages of men and time, bearing witness to an age of social and political insecurity in which people's homes required an almost military defense. These requirements also seem to have shaped the massive Palazzo del Capitano del Popolo, now the Palazzo del Bargello, an early example of Florentine public building constructed according to Vasari by Lapo Tedesco in the middle of the 13th cent., but more probably by the Dominicans Fra Sisto and Fra

The Tempietto del Santo Sepolcro in the Rucellai Chapel and, bottom left, detail of the façade of Santa Maria Novella, both by Leon Battista Alberti

The interior of Santo Spirito and, right, the Pazzi Chapel in Santa Croce, both by Filippo Brunelleschi

Ristoro. Used as the seat of the podestà, it went on to become the place for the administration of justice, and, at the time of Medici rule, the headquarters of the chief of police, known as the *bargello*.

The Palazzo dei Priori, or Palazzo Vecchio, dates from a few decades later and is the product of a period of somewhat less troubled politics. Begun in 1299, it was built as a seat for the government of the Priors, a manifestation of the new social classes organized into guilds. Its design is traditionally ascribed to Arnolfo di Cambio, who built a sort of large square fortress out of rusticated masonry with two-light windows, a

projecting balcony and a tall tower that is off center because it was constructed on the foundations of a preexisting Ghibelline one. For centuries the palace was the center of civil power and political life in Florence, but was never particularly popular with the Medici. Though it was Cosimo I himself who, along with his favorite architect Giorgio Vasari, undertook its radical renovation, he lived there for only a few years, preferring Palazzo Pitti. It made a comeback with the proclamation of Florence as the capital of Italy (1865-71), becoming the seat of the national parliament. Today it is occupied by the mayor and houses many offices of the commune.

At the time of the construction of the Palazzo dei Priori, Florence was already changing its character, from a gloomy city that had grown vertically to one that was progressively

spreading out, taking over new spaces, opening up ever broader and straighter streets and building more comfortable houses. Above all, however, it had already welcomed the principal mendicant orders, which started to erect their own places of worship at the end of the 13th cent. Over the course of a few decades the great basilicas of Santa Maria Novella and Santa Croce were created: masterpieces of Italian Gothic and treasure troves of some of the finest art in Florence, housing paintings and sculptures by artists of the stature of Giotto, Taddeo and Agnolo Gaddi, Andrea Orcagna and Nardo di Cione, Brunelleschi, Masaccio,

Facing page, Masaccio, *The Tribute Money*, detail. Brancacci Chapel

Donatello, Ghirlandaio and Filippino Lippi.

More or less contemporary was the construction, or in some cases the renovation, of other important religious buildings such as Santa Trinita, from the 11th cent. but restructured on the inside in the Gothic style; Santa Maria Maggiore; Ognissanti with its adjoining monastery (although modifications made in the 17th and 18th centuries have altered its appearance); Sant'Ambrogio; San Marco, founded in 1299 by Sylvestrine monks but restructured several times; and Orsanmichele. This last is a singular structure – one of the most interesting examples of 14th-cent. architecture –

Top left, the Palazzo Vecchio; top right, the interior of the Salone dei Cinquecento

Left, Donatello, *Judith and Holofernes*. Palazzo Vecchio; bottom, Palazzo Pitti

that was originally intended to house the grain market (1290), was rebuilt after a fire and used as a warehouse as well and finally was transformed into a place of worship for the guilds. Inside stands the sumptuous tabernacle created by Andrea Orcagna (1359) for a miraculous image of Mary, while it is decorated on the outside with the niches of the various guilds. These hold statues of their patron saints that present a significant cross-section of Florentine sculpture from the 15th to the 17th cent.

In the adjoining Piazza della Signoria it is possible to admire another important work of 14th-cent. architecture, the Loggia dei Lanzi, created in the second half of the century to house the priors during official ceremonies. Not far off, Palazzo Davanzati, in spite of a number of restorations carried out last century that have somewhat altered its appearance, is a typical example of a 14th-cent. noble residence (it now houses the Museo della Casa Fiorentina, or Museum of the Florentine House).

Under the impetus of brilliant artists, 15th-cent. Florence was enriched and renewed but without fundamentally altering its appearance. It was Brunelleschi with his research into perspective and his precocious ideas about city planning who dominated the art scene in the first half of the century. Not only did he build the great dome of Santa Maria del Fiore and the Ospedale degli Innocenti, but he also reconstructed the basilicas of San Lorenzo – designing the splendid Old Sacristy – and Santo Spirito, built the Pazzi

Chapel in the monastic complex of Santa Croce and designed the rotunda of Santa Maria degli Angeli, as well as the central block of Palazzo Pitti.

Generally speaking, it was an extraordinary time in the artistic life of Florence, with painters like Masolino and Masaccio at work in Santa Maria del Carmine, Paolo Uccello in the Green Cloister of Santa Maria Novella, Fra Angelico in the convent of San Marco and Domenico Ghirlandaio in the Main Chapel in Santa Maria Novella and the Sassetti Chapel in Santa Trinita, along with sculptors like Lorenzo Ghiberti, Donatello and Luca della Robbia.

Undoubtedly a primary role was played by the Medici family, which in the meantime had established a seigniorial government headed by Cosimo the Elder (1434). Cosimo, with the aid of his favorite architect, Michelozzo, promoted a number of important architectural interventions, ranging from the construction of the Dominican convent of San Marco with its rich library and the radical alterations to the ancient basilica of the Santissima Annunziata, to the building of his own residence, the severe palace on Via Larga (now Via Cavour) that was to provide a model for much of the civil construction of the 15th cent. This was the case, for instance, with the large palace that Filippo Strozzi had built by Benedetto da Maiano on his return from exile (1489), while Palazzo Rucellai, with its

Benvenuto Cellini, *Perseus*. Loggia dei Lanzi

pp. 92-93, Leonardo da Vinci, *Annunciation*, detail. Uffizi

above all a cultured man. A poet and writer himself, he chose to surround himself with men of keen intelligence, gathered in the celebrated Accademia Platonica situated at the Medici villa at Careggi. This was his greatest legacy to Florence, before the period of political upheaval to which the city was subjected for several decades after his death (1492).

At the beginning of the century the most significant artists in Florence were without doubt Leonardo and Michelangelo. Each was commissioned by the gonfalonier Pier Soderini to fresco a battle scene (never finished) in the Salone dei Cinquecento in Palazzo Vecchio: Cellini would later describe their preparatory drawings as the "world's school." But the former soon left the city (1506), never to return, while the latter – though he left works of the greatest importance in Florence – had

Raphael, *Madonna della Seggiola*, Galleria Palatina

Top left, Giotto, *Ognissanti Maestà*, Uffizi

Bottom left, Sandro Botticelli, *Birth of Venus*. Uffizi

Bottom right, Michelangelo, *David*. Galleria dell'Accademia

Facing page, Michelangelo, *Pitti Tondo*, detail. Museo del Bargello

rigorous superimposition of orders on the façade, erected (1455-70) by Bernardo Rossellino to a design by Leon Battista Alberti, was directly inspired by treatises on ancient architecture.

The golden age ushered in by Cosimo the Elder was

continued, after the interlude of rule by his son Piero, by his grandson Lorenzo, the "magnificent" lord who, unlike his grandfather, liked to present himself in the guise of a prince. While not a particularly able businessman, he had great political foresight and was

already begun to pay frequent visits to Rome and would go on to live for long periods in the city of the popes. Among his greatest creations, in addition to the works on show in the museums, were the Biblioteca Laurenziana and the New Sacristy of San Lorenzo.

The definitive reestablishment of Medici rule (even if by a cadet branch of the family) in the figure of Cosimo I (1537), ushered in a long period of political stability centered on the strong personality of the duke, the true architect of regional unification. A good organizer, he set about the creation of a strong state, partly through an intense program of military constructions in border areas. In the city he sought to increase his own prestige through marriage to the daughter of the viceroy of Naples, Eleonora de Toledo, and the transfer of the court to the former Palazzo dei Priori, then subjected to incessant works of restoration and enlargement to which the most important artists of the day contributed. While lacking the refined Humanistic culture of Lorenzo, he continued the family tradition of patronage. He embellished Florence with fountains, statues, columns and arcades, often in connection with the lavish ceremonies he staged to celebrate the arrival of high-ranking personages.

The building that now houses the Galleria degli Uffizi was also intended to produce a scenic effect: a curious structure in the shape of a U, it was built between Piazza della Signoria and the river to house the principal magistracies (the *uffizi*, or "offices") of the duchy of Tuscany. Designed by Giorgio Vasari (1560) and concluded twenty years later by Bernardo Buontalenti, it was then extended with a corridor that connected it to Palazzo Pitti, passing over the ancient Ponte Vecchio. This was a bold idea on Cosimo's part, an attempt to establish a "secret" link between the heart of political life, represented by the Palazzo Vecchio, and the new family residence of Palazzo Pitti.

In fact Eleonora's dislike for the enclosed spaces of the building on Piazza della Signoria and her delicate health had for some time been urging a move to the more salubrious suburban palace that had been built in the middle of the 15th cent. for the banker Luca Pitti. Little more than a parallelepiped of stone with three portals and a double row of seven windows, the building was subjected to the modifications needed to turn it into an official residence which would also provide the comforts of a country house. Enlarged and given a fine courtyard opening onto the scenic Boboli Gardens by Bartolomeo Ammannati, it has in fact been

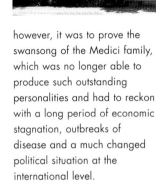

continually renovated and added to, all the way up to the 19th cent. Today it is one of the city's most important monumental complexes, a sort of "citadel" of museums housing the ducal collection of paintings (Galleria Palatina) along with collections of silverware, semiprecious stones, gems, ivories and porcelain that used to belong to the ruling dynasties.

There is no doubt that under Cosimo, and then his sons Francesco and Ferdinando, there was a shift in the traditional centers of power within the city. While under Cosimo the Elder and Lorenzo the Magnificent the urban area "of choice" was comprised between the basilicas of San Lorenzo and the Annunziata, including San Marco, the hub of political life was now located between Piazza della Signoria and Palazzo Pitti. But this did not prevent the Medici grand dukes

from leaving symbols of their authority all over the place.

The basilica of San Lorenzo continued to receive the family's attentions. It was the setting for the solemn funeral of Francesco, the grand duke with a complex and mysterious personality whose name is indissolubly linked with the Studiolo in Palazzo Vecchio, and it was here that Ferdinando created the family pantheon, the sumptuous Chapel of the Princes lined in its entirety with semiprecious stones on which work was to continue for centuries.

Ferdinando was also responsible for the construction of the Belvedere Fort at the top of the Boboli Gardens, probably to a design by Buontalenti, and the splendid Villa di Artimino, known as the "Ferdinanda," outside the city walls. His rule was characterized by a number of important initiatives in the cultural field. In some ways,

however, it was to prove the swansong of the Medici family, which was no longer able to produce such outstanding personalities and had to reckon with a long period of economic stagnation, outbreaks of disease and a much changed political situation at the international level.

Major new works of art were still being created to embellish Florence, but they were smaller in quantity and more sporadic. Often they were limited to the continuation of projects that had already been started or the decoration of existing structures.

Yet the grand dukes of this period did not renounce the patronage for which the dynasty is so renowned,

The elegant 19th-cent. structure of the tepidarium in the Giardino dell'Orticoltura

Two rare examples of art nouveau architecture in Florence: small villa on Via Scipione Ammirato (top) and a detail of the house-gallery in Borgo Ognissanti

Ponte Santa Trinita

showing an interest in painting, music and the world of science, which benefited in those years from the presence of Galileo Galilei and his pupil Evangelista Torricelli, received at court with great enthusiasm.

The succeeding dynasty of Lorraine, on the other hand, was obliged to concentrate on turning around the dreadful economic state into which the duchy had sunk. The most enlightened figure was that of Peter Leopold, who in the space of just over twenty-five years (1765-92) managed to make fundamental changes in the economy and the law, to revitalize the lifeless atmosphere that had held sway in the city since the final period of the Medici dynasty with cultural initiatives and to leave several concrete marks in the field of city planning.

More incisive interventions in the urban fabric were to come in the 19th cent., with the opening of ever wider and straighter streets, the construction of new bridges, the realization of the Neo-Gothic façades of Santa Croce and Santa Maria del Fiore and, above all, the projects drawn up by the architect Giuseppe Poggi for the transformation of the city into the capital of the new kingdom of Italy. Florence was subjected to a radical reorganization that over the space of a few decades would alter its appearance drastically, bringing it closer to the contemporary cities of Europe, but at the same time inflicting on it wounds that would never be healed: two will serve as examples for all: the demolition of the ancient city walls and their replacement by a ring of roads on the model of the Parisian boulevards, and the destruction of the old marketplace along with the Jewish ghetto in the area now occupied by the grand Piazza della Repubblica and its adjacent streets.

A past as important as Florence's, and one which we have come to understand much more over the last few decades, is not represented by its architecture alone. It is also documented by an extraordinary range of museums. Here there is no room for either an exhaustive account or even a cursory list of the city's institutions. So we will do no more than make a few suggestions on the basis of personal preference, or of overriding importance.

The Galleria degli Uffizi, undoubtedly the best-known museum in the city, offers an unparalleled cross-section of Tuscan painting (as well as works from other schools in Italy and Europe) up until the 16th cent., including the singular collection of self-portraits on show in the Corridoio Vasariano, while the nearby Museo del Bargello boasts the most important collection of medieval and Renaissance sculpture in Italy, along with precious collections of the minor arts.

The numerous tourists drawn to the Galleria dell'Accademia by the magnet of Michelangelo's *David* should not overlook the fact that the gallery's many rooms also house a rich panorama of 14th-cent. Tuscan painting. The nearby museums of the Cappelle Medicee, San Marco (where Fra Angelico left the most substantial corpus of his paintings) and the Opificio delle Pietre Dure are all linked to memories of the Medici. In fact the last institution, the "Hard Stone Works," was created by them (1588) and its museum houses works in *commesso*, or Florentine mosaic, made out of semiprecious stones, marble and painting on stone.

The Medici family's fondness for collecting was not confined to painting and sculpture, but also embraced relics of antiquity. This is reflected in the Museo Archeologico, situated in the 17th-cent. Palazzo della Crocetta, which contains the collection of antique bronzes, coins and gems initially formed by Cosimo the Elder and Lorenzo the Magnificent and later enriched by Cosimo I, with

important examples of Etruscan art, and the Lorraine. The Etruscan collection is flanked by an important Egyptian section.

For those who are interested in the endless history of the construction of the cathedral there is the recently reorganized Museo dell'Opera, where it is possible to see the originals of the statues once on the façade, the panels made by Andrea Pisano and Luca della Robbia for the campanile and the gilded panels of the Porta del Paradiso.

The scientific tradition of the city is reflected in the Museo di Storia della Scienza in Palazzo Castellani. Founded last century (1930), it houses scientific instruments from the Medici and Lorraine collections and the original instruments used by Galileo and the Accademia del Cimento.

Among the numerous institutions located in the Oltrarno area, in addition to the Museo Bardini (an eclectic

and refined collection that used to belong to the antiquarian Stefano Bardini and is currently undergoing reorganization,) and the curious Museo della Specola with its collection of anatomical waxes, attention has to be focused on the museums in Palazzo Pitti. As has already been pointed out, this is a complex of large dimensions housing collections

The Ponte Vecchio with the Corridoio Vasariano

of very different character, from the Museo degli Argenti to the Galleria Palatina, from the Appartamenti Monumentali to the Galleria d'Arte Moderna and from the Boboli Gardens themselves to the collections of costumes and porcelain in the Galleria del Costume and the Museo delle Porcellane.

Fiesole

et on the saddle formed by
two hills that overlook
Florence from the north,
the small city of Fiesole has long
been a magnet for tourists from
all over the world, drawn by its
monuments and the enchanting
scenery in which it is immersed,
dotted with old villas belonging

to Florentine noble families.

A few stretches of cyclopean
walls are all that remains today
of the two-kilometer-long ring
that once protected the city
founded by the Etruscans
around the 6th cent. BC. In 80
BC Fiesole became a Roman
colony and at the beginning of
the imperial era the city was
provided with a theater and
baths. Excavations carried out
in the 19th cent. brought to
light the large theater, capable
of seating 3000 people, as
well as the remains of the baths
and an Etruscan temple. The
ruins are now part of a well-
conserved archeological park
that also houses a museum.

In the 5th and 6th cent. the
territory of Fiesole was

subjected to raids by the Goths
and conquered by the
Byzantines. With the arrival of
the Franks it became an
episcopal see and its bishops
acquired growing power, in
competition with nearby Florence.

**Above, the Roman theater; left,
the church of San Francesco**

The conflicts that arose as a result
culminated in the destruction of
the fortress in 1125 and the
subjugation of the city in the
13th cent. From then on events
in Fiesole were to all intents
and purposes part of Florentine
history.

The principal monuments are
gathered around Piazza Mino da
Fiesole, in the place where the
forum was located in Roman
times. Work on the cathedral
dedicated to St. Romulus,
martyred bishop and patron of
the city, commenced in 1028
and lasted until the 13th cent.
During a radical restoration in
the 19th cent. the façade was
completely rebuilt and the interior
returned to its original basilican

**The Palazzo Pretorio
Facing page, detail of the façade
of the Badia Fiesolana at
San Domenico**

form. It contains many works of great value that bear witness to Fiesole's prestige as an episcopal see, even after the loss of its temporal power. In addition to the frescoes of the presbytery and the chapels, including a *Saint Sebastian* attributed to Pietro Perugino, the large triptych on the high altar, which is a 15th-cent. work by Bicci di Lorenzo, the crypt dating from the 11th cent. and the decoration of the Salutati Chapel, with sculptures by Mino da Fiesole and frescoes by Cosimo Rosselli, are all worthy of attention.

In front of the cathedral stand the Palazzo Vescovile, built in the 11th cent. but extensively altered, and the 17th-cent. Palazzo del Seminario. On the upper side of the square is the Palazzo Pretorio from the 14th and 15th cent., decorated with the coats of arms of the podestà of Fiesole and, alongside, the ancient oratory of Santa Maria Primerana.

Not far away is the Museo Bandini, with an interesting collection of paintings and sculptures of the Florentine school dating from the 14th to the 16th cent. and many Della

Top, vessel for bathwater (loutrophoros) with representation of the deceased, detail; below, Attic black-figure kylix, detail. Museo Archeologico

Robbian terracottas.

A steep slope with a panoramic view of Florence leads to the basilica of Sant'Alessandro, constructed in the 6th cent. in the area where an Etruscan temple once stood and renovated in the 11th. Today it is used to stage temporary exhibitions. Continuing the ascent, we come to the top of the hill where the site of the Etruscan acropolis is now occupied by the church and monastery of San Francesco. Notwithstanding successive interventions, the church preserves much of its 14th-cent. appearance and fine decorations, including an *Annunciation* by Raffaellino del Garbo, a *Holy Conception* by Piero di Cosimo and the woodcarvings of the 15th-cent. choir.

In the locality of San Domenico, about three kilometers away on the road that leads down to Florence, we find the Badia Fiesolana, the former cathedral of Fiesole erected on the site of St. Romulus's martyrdom. First reconstructed after 1028 and given the fine marble façade we see today, the church was enlarged and its interior restructured in the Brunelleschian manner at the behest of Cosimo the Elder. The adjoining monastery, once assigned to the Camaldolensians, is now the seat of the Institute of the European University.

Tuscan Cooking

Fabio Picchi is the patron of the "Il Cibreo" restaurant in Florence, where they make traditional Tuscan dishes based on historical research but are not entirely against innovation and even certain cautious but sprightly inventions. But he is absolutely categorical on a number of points. Above all, he serves no pasta whatsoever. In his restaurant the first courses are all soup, both thick and thin, or "pappa" (almost a porridge of bread and vegetables, a fine old Tuscan peasant dish). And indeed he is right. Pasta and risotto were latecomers to Tuscan cooking, and have always remained somewhat clumsily on the sidelines, even if they are now part of a national gastronomic fad that includes such shameful stuff as pasta with caviare or salmon.

Tuscan cooking relies on a handful of down-to-earth things, a lot of myths, and all too many commonplaces. It is a gross error to judge by the scant imagination of the Florentines, who apart from spiced roast pork (*arista*), *fagioli al fiasco* (beans cooked in a wine-flask) and *castagnaccio* (chestnut-flour cake, which in any case comes from the mountains), have invented nothing at all. The *bistecca alla fiorentina* is more English than Florentine, and requires the meat of the cattle of Val di Chiana. Truly Florentine is *zuppa inglese* (trifle), a ghastly sweet mess evidently made for discontented spinsters. Unless we wish to take shelter behind the delights available in the slums of San Lorenzo, Sant'Ambrogio and the Porcellino, simple boiled tripe and other offal are fighting a

rearguard action, while (alas!) the wonderful fried-food vendors of days gone by - now fallen to the level of running a *tavola calda* or prostituting themselves selling sandwiches, have almost entirely forgotten their fried gnocchi made of maize flour, and totally abandoned the *roventini* (pancakes made of pig's blood, eaten folded in half inside a round roll) and the *pattona*, a kind of polenta made of chestnut flour, sliced with a cheese-wire and eaten boiling hot.

But Tuscan cooking, where for meat and fish the spit and the grill are king, can boast an infinite variety of local dishes. *Cacciucco* (fish soup) is now found all up and down the coast, but was originally from Livorno and is a speciality typical of that "free port," with all its bits and pieces of fish made into a piquant stew served on a base of brown bread.

Among the main dishes, the

Giovanna Garzoni, *The Man from Artimino* and, left, *Tray with Artichokes*. Galleria Palatina, Florence

rather monotonous series of roast meats is now very much *à la mode* because it is considered more healthy, more "natural" and less high in cholesterol. But what are we to say of the many, all too many restaurants which push their lack of imagination so far as to offer a more or less varied dish called *arrosto misto*? This is a dish of extremely modest origins put together in the kitchens of aristocratic homes from the scraps of roast meats left over by the masters, who had themselves nibbled away at them with discretion, one at a time, and in a designated order.

Certainly it is a poor man's table, and often frugal. Sometimes it seems designed for people in a hurry. But poverty and haste are not always allies. On the contrary, there are poor people's foods over which the most extraordinary care is taken. One need only think of the Sienese *acquacotta*, a modest soup based on bread, broth, herbs and fresh eggs. It seems like a mere nothing. Or there is the great and glorious *carabaccia* the onion soup which is the ancestor of the French *soup à l'oignon* (or at least appears to be so). Red onions sliced fine, of course, and an earthenware pot... a little chopped carrot and celery... half a glass of good olive oil, plus salt and pepper. Cook on a slow fire, stir gently but often, then add the broth. Then pour onto slices of toast

and add pecorino. That's all there is to it. It is a poor man's cookery, invented by people who had to earn their bread, knew how much things cost and how much sweat it took to make them grow, and who therefore loved and cherished them.

We should also mention the long series of stews and dishes of various kinds of offal that are the pride of the Pistoia area. But from Siena down into the Maremma the main attraction is either fresh meat or highly aromatized salami or the truly noble sweet-and-sour wild-boar, with raisins, pinenuts, a touch of vinegar, and a carefully calculated ration of dark, bitter chocolate.

What about cakes and sweetmeats? In the vanguard come the *panforte* and *ricciarelli* of Siena, both of them inspired inventions. But another of the joys of living, when you can find them, are the *necci* of the Garfagnana. They are thin sheets

of pastry made with chestnut-flour and stuffed with the most delicately-flavoured ricotta. It is hard to find them really well made, but when you do, my friend, I tell you it is a treat.

The Lunigiana and Versilia

Rather than taking the A15 motorway, which passes under the Cisa in a tunnel, the tourist would be well advised to come from Emilia by S.S. (Strada Statale) 62, perhaps after stopping off in Berceto, where he can taste the best mushrooms in the district. In this way he will cross the ancient pass, sacred to pilgrims on their way from France to Rome, and will traverse the Lunigiana, which is the valley of the Magra (the last reaches of which are, however, in Liguria, between La Spezia and Sarzana). The first important centre to the south of the Cisa Pass is Pontremoli, mentioned for the first time in AD 990 as a staging-post on the Via Francigena, and also traditionally important as a centre for the travelling booksellers of central Italy. For this latter reason the "Bancarella" Prize is awarded here annually (bancarella = bookstall). At the meeting of the Magra and its tributary the Verde, the old town has retained its slate roofs and its tiny fields along the river banks which are features of the Lunigiana. Continuing south, we pass beneath the village of Filattiera, where we can visit a (restored) Malaspina castle on the left of the river, but almost opposite, on the right, we advise a short deviation to visit Mulazzo, a Malaspina castle where Dante found hospitality in 1306. Other castles built by the Malaspina family can be seen as we go down river, at Villafranca, Lusuolo and Monti, near

where the Taverone flows into the Magra. If we turn up the Taverone we will find still more castles (Pontebosio, Licciana Nardi, Bastia); or else we can go on to Aulla, and make a deviation from there to visit the fortresses of Fosdinovo and Podenzana.

At Aulla the tourist has two possible routes. If he takes S.S. 445 he will enter the upper valley of the Serchio, which is to say the Garfagnana, visiting Castelnuovo, Barga and Bagni di Lucca. Thence he will follow the valley to the east of the Apuan Alps and reach Lucca by way of S.S. 12. The second route, along S.S. 62, will lead him to Sarzana, where he can join the Via Aurelia as far as Massa, and reach Lucca and Pisa from there. In either case his journey is overshadowed by the massif of the Apuan Alps.

The remains of Luni, on the border between the present regions of Liguria and Tuscany, are now sandwiched between the A12 motorway and the Via Aurelia. A Roman colony near the mouth of the Magra and important for its trade in Apuan marble, it began to decline in the 4th cent., largely on account of malaria, and in the late Middle Ages was several times sacked by the Saracens and the Normans. In 1204 the bishop's curia was once and for all transferred to Sarzana. Apart from an interesting archaeological museum, worth looking at today remain the

The fortress
of Fosdinovo

ruins of the amphitheatre and the cathedral. Between Sarzana and Luni, with short deviations, we get to Castelnuovo Magra, with splendid views over the Gulf of La Spezia and the fortress of Fosdinovo.

Carrara is the "capital" of the marble industry. Quarrying has been going on here for two thousand years. Things to visit here are the cathedral, the façade of which is Romanesque and faced with stripes of grey and white marble in the Pisan style, though the building as a whole only dates from the 14th cent.; the 16th-century Accademia delle Belle Arti, once the palace of the Cybo Malaspina family, rulers of the city; and the Baroque church of the Madonna delle Grazie. From Carrara one can make a number of excursions to the marble quarries and to panoramic viewpoints in the Apuan Alps. The present layout of Carrara is modern, with some interesting echoes of neoclassicism. Massa, on the other hand, is distinguished by a mediaeval nucleus (on which in the 15th and 16th centuries the Malaspina erected their Renaissance residence) dominated by the recently restored fortress and a 16th-century layout centred around Piazza degli Aranci, over which towers the Palazzo Cybo Malaspina (now the Prefecture).

It is from Massa, or rather from Seravezza just to the south-east, that the most beautiful excursions may be taken into the Apuan Alps, amid chestnut woods and really high peaks such as the Sumbra (1764 metres) and Pania della Croce (1858 metres), which owing to the Apuan marble appear to be snow-covered even when they are not. A road with wonderful views crosses the Apuan massif, leading on the far side to Castelnuovo Garfagnana, where one should pay due homage to the fortress where the great poet Ludovico Ariosto lived when he was a delegate of the d'Este government. From here one can bravely start on the climb up S.S. 324 that crosses the Apennines at the breathtaking pass of Foce delle Radici (and on the way down can choose between the opulent Sassuolo, the smiling Frignano or the picturesque mountains around Porretta), or else one can take the road towards Castiglione di Garfagnana, which also leads one to the Passo delle Radici, but by way of San Pellegrino in Alpe where there is an ancient hospice and a famous sanctuary dating back to the 7th cent. The hospice is now

Aerial view of the Luni amphitheater

Stelae from the Lunigiana.
Museo Civico Ubaldo Formentini,
La Spezia

an interesting ethnological museum, containing a wealth of traditional tools of the Garfagnana, a collection well known to students of artisan culture.

If our tourist has a certain sense of nostalgia, and is not put off by kitsch, then an itinerary we can recommend – though not during the summer – is to take the coast road from the mouth of the Magra to that of the Serchio, or the Arno, or even as far as Livorno, where the coast changes entirely in character, becoming high and rocky. The whole stretch can be done on the motorway, or better still on the Via Aurelia – and a truly amazing ride it is. For much of the way there are pinewoods on the left-hand side, with the soaring Apuan Alps in the background, while on the right, from Marinella di Sarzana near Luni all the way to Viareggio, one is separated from the sea by an uninterrupted series of towns whose names until a few decades ago called up irresistible echoes in literary life and elegant society: Forte del Marmi, Marina di Pietrasanta, Lido di Camaiore and Viareggio itself. Until this point one can take the coast road (S.S. 328), keeping the seaside resorts on the left, and the beach with its bathing establishments on the right. The place-names we come across and the people they bring to mind recall the cultural and social splendours of the early years of the century, with the cafés frequented by fashionable intellectuals. Viareggio, when it is not swamped with thousands of summer bathers or the crowds who come to see the Carnival, is worth a trip in itself. The Viareggio I love best is the Viareggio of late autumn or perhaps even early spring, very likely windswept and lashed with rain, or warmed just faintly by a timid sun. It is then that the art nouveau architecture and the semi-deserted Edwardian hotels exude all their charm, and it is then that Shelley, D'Annunzio, Puccini and Viani seem to be still there, haunting the Lido of "their" Versilia.

After Viareggio we lose sight of the sea until we get to Marina di Pisa, for we have reached the long series of

dense forests that give directly onto the sea, with stretches of Mediterranean scrub mingling with the ancient spell of the pinewoods. We have the maquis of Migliarino, the once-royal (now presidential) estate at San Rossore, Barbaricina with its splendid horses, and then, between Pisa and Livorno, the estates of Tombolo and Coltano, with their sad memories of the war and the years just after it, but preserving some natural scenery that is still wild and intact.

This is also one of the areas which most forcibly reminds us of the times when the low coastlines along the Tyrrhenian Sea were invaded by marshes. The straight roads between the tall pines, and the youth of the trees themselves, speak of recent planning and rationalization. The stretch between the Serchio and the Arno is alluvial soil and relatively recent, for at one time the mouths of the two rivers were far closer together, and Pisa was a city on the sea.

But between Viareggio and Pisa, before proceeding beside the maquis of Migliarino, music-lovers will want to pay homage to Giacomo Puccini. From Torre del Lago a tree-lined avenue leads to the western shore of the Lago di Massaciuccoli, the last remnant of the lagoon formed in prehistoric times by the common delta of the Serchio and the Arno. Eels, tench and pike still live in its shallow waters, while one can still wait in the canebrakes for the flight of waterbirds. Overlooking the lake is Villa Puccini, containing many souvenirs of the composer, and there every year in the summer they hold the Puccini Festival, one of the operatic events dearest to the hearts of Tuscans.

Top, the Castello Malaspina
Right, Palazzo Cybo Malaspina
and its courtyard

Massa

The earliest record of a settlement in the area of Massa is provided by the *Peutinger Table*, the famous copy of a map of the ancient world dating from the 3rd-4th cent. AD, which documents the presence of a *taberna* on the Via Emilia Scauri at the point where it crossed the Frigido River. Other references over the course of the Middle Ages speak of small rural settlements in the valleys running down from the Apuan ridge. However, it was not until the 12th cent. that the fortified burg of Bagnara, the first nucleus of Massa, was formed around a parish church dedicated to St. Peter.

A fief of the Ligurian family of the Obertenghi, long disputed between the cities of Pisa, Lucca, Florence and Genoa, the burg passed into the hands of the Malaspina in the 15th cent., who soon turned it into the capital of a small state with the modern characteristics of a Renaissance signoria. During the 16th cent., under Alberico I Cybo Malaspina, the urban fabric was extended and, like that of nearby Carrara, was embellished with large squares and imposing palaces decorated with graffiti. In the 18th cent., following the marriage of Maria Teresa Cybo Malaspina to Ercole Rinaldo d'Este, the marquisate was annexed to the duchy of Modena. Further urban development and reorganization were promoted in the early 19th cent. by Elisa Bonaparte Baciocchi, Napoleon's sister. Among other things, she was responsible for the layout of the Piazza degli Aranci, the heart of social life in modern Massa.

Piazza degli Aranci is dominated by the Palazzo Cybo Malaspina, constructed by Alberico I in the 16th cent. on the site of a previous building and provided with a lavish 18th-cent. courtyard and a frescoed chapel.

Not far off, at the top of an elegant flight of steps, rises the 20th-cent. marble façade of the cathedral. Erected in the 15th cent. on the site of the parish church of San Pietro in Bagnara, the building we see today is the fruit of reconstructions. It houses

valuable works, among them a wooden crucifix of the 13th cent. and a fragment of a fresco by Pintoricchio. An underground chapel holds the tombs of the Cybo Malaspina family, dukes of Massa.

On the top of the Rocca, overlooking the city and the sea, stands the Castello Malaspina ringed with walls and made up of a medieval burg and the sumptuous Renaissance palace built by the Malaspina in the 15th and 16th cent. as the seat of their duchy. The nearby church of San Rocco houses a wooden crucifix considered by many to be an early work by Michelangelo.

Carrara

Set in the narrow strip of plain that separates the Apuan Alps from the sea, Carrara owes its fame to the marble extracted from its quarries, considered the finest since ancient times for its snow-white color and for the purity of its grain, which made it easy to work. As early as the 2nd cent. AD, in fact, Roman ships sailed from the nearby port of Luni with cargos of large blocks of marble that would be used to face the most important buildings of the Mediterranean basin.

Abandoned in the early Middle Ages, extraction was resumed in the 12th cent., and with it the area's population began to grow. The first nucleus of what was to become Carrara emerged around a parish church built in the 11th cent. and later to be replaced by the cathedral of Sant'Andrea. The medieval burg developed rapidly along the axis of Via Santa Maria, was surrounded with a ring of walls and began to attract the attention of the neighboring powers of Pisa, Lucca and Genoa, as well as the ruling Della Scala and Visconti families of Milan, who succeeded in conquering it at various times.

Falling into the hands of the powerful Malaspina family, lords of Massa, in the 15th cent., Carrara was subjected to a first major urban reorganization, launched in 1557 by Alberico I Cybo Malaspina, who provided it with ample squares and a

The cathedral with detail of the rose window on facing page

Piazza Alberica and a detail of
the 16th-cent. Palazzo Sarteschi

larger circle of walls. Further interventions were made in the 17th and 18th cent., giving the medieval burg the dimensions and dignity of a city.

Although flanked by other industrial and tourist activities that have emerged over the last century, encouraging its expansion toward the sea, the production of marble is still the city's principal resource. Over the course of time a strong sense of identity and pride has grown up around the material and the heavy labor of its quarrying and working. Built on the site of the ancient parish church of Sant'Andrea, the cathedral is the city's principal monument. The fine facing of gray and white marble is the culmination of a process of construction that lasted for three centuries, with Pisan, Luccan and Genoese craftsmen and influences alternating in the work between the 12th and the 14th cent. The lower part of the façade and the portal are in the Romanesque style, while the upper part is typically Gothic, with an elegant rose window and an arcade. The basilican interior still retains traces of its old fresco decoration, along with several other fine works that include a white marble group representing the *Annunciation* by Andrea di Francesco Guardi, a 15th-cent. relief with the *Madonna and Saints* and a *Painted Cross* from the late 14th cent.

The historic core of the city, characterized by palaces and churches of the 17th and 18th cent., is comprised between the cathedral, the beautiful Piazza Alberica and Piazza Matteotti. At the center of this triangle stands the imposing edifice of the Accademia di Belle Arti, built in the 16th cent. on the ruins of an ancient Malaspina castle and enlarged over the following centuries. It houses an archeological collection, with important finds from the Roman era, and a gallery of plaster casts of works by Antonio Canova and other celebrated sculptors.

The Museo Civico del Marmo, situated outside the historic center, displays objects and tools documenting the activity of quarrying and working marble from antiquity to the present day.

From the rear of the cathedral steep, winding roads run up to the villages of the quarrymen. These include Colonnata, celebrated in Italy for its lard, whose delicate flavor is attributed to its long seasoning in tubs made from the marble of the mountain.

Viareggio

Hemmed in by the sea and the white marble mountains of the Apuan Alps, the Versilia today is a fertile and densely populated coastal plain, lined with seaside resorts that have by now joined up to form a sort of uninterrupted conurbation.

Conditions were very different just a few centuries ago, when the continuing existence of coastal marshlands – whose memory is preserved today solely by the lake of Massaciuccoli – discouraged significant forms of settlement. The systematic work of reclamation commenced in the 18th cent. and then continued incessantly up until the beginning of the last century has opened up an environment of great natural beauty for human habitation, and at the same time made possible the tumultuous economic development that is all too evident.

The main center of the Versilia district is Viareggio, an ancient coastal fort given in fief by Frederick II to a citizen of Lucca in order to defend the Via Regia (*castrum de via regia*) that ran along the coast, disputed for some time between Pisa and Lucca. The entire area, and in particular the piedmont belt, was moreover an object of the territorial designs of several contenders and underwent frequent changes in its political masters, with the exception of Viareggio, which remained constantly within the orbit of Lucca. During the 15th cent., in fact, it was the city's only outlet to the sea and for this reason acquired more and more

A view of the Gran Caffè Margherita and, bottom, the Grand Hotel & Royal

importance. Evidence for this is provided by the first reclamation works carried out in its hinterland, by the construction the following century of a new and large tower that still stands, known as the "Torre di Matilde," and by the construction of the Burlamacca Canal to drain water from the surrounding area.

In 1820 the small center of Viareggio, where the port was beginning to expand rapidly, was elevated to the rank of city by Marie-Louise of Bourbon, then duchess of Lucca, who also commissioned an urban development plan from the architect Lorenzo Nottolini and had the monumental Viale dei Tigli constructed to link the center with her villa situated in the Pineta di Levante. The result was an urban layout characterized by a regular grid

Above, the Galleria del Libro and the Bagno Balena; bottom, detail of the former Bertolli Villa

that is still visible, in spite of the successive layers of building.

The 19th cent. also saw the creation of the first bathing establishments that in the following century made Viareggio the capital of Versilia and one of the most important tourist resorts in Italy. Certainly, it no longer has the atmosphere of an elegant town that it had at the beginning of the 20th cent., designed to meet the recreation needs of an emerging middle class which gratified its own

sense of aesthetics by attending artistic and cultural events in a setting of refined art nouveau architecture. Yet Viareggio still demonstrates considerable cultural vivacity, with exhibitions, literary prizes and the important season of musical performances at nearby Torre del Lago. And then there is the celebrated carnival with its gigantic masked floats to which a special "citadel" has recently been dedicated.

With the wooden structures of the bathing establishments and the stores on the promenade destroyed in a fire (1917), all that remains to testify to the atmosphere of the past is the graceful Padiglione Martini. Along the promenade, however, there are some other significant works of architecture from the early decades of the 20th cent., including the Gran Caffè Margherita, built by Alfredo Belluomini and decorated by Galileo Chini, with its characteristic Oriental-style domes; the Supercinema,

again designed by Belluomini and with ceramic decorations by Chini; the Duilio 48 department store, typical of the art nouveau style of those years; and the art deco Bagno Balena. Among the great hotels that are now part of the town's history, we cannot fail to mention the Principe di Piemonte with its own bathing establishment, the Hotel Excelsior and the Grand Hotel & Royal. More in general, many of the large and small villas of the last century preserve traces of the eclectic and extravagant decorative style for which the town was famous and which can still be uncovered by the more attentive visitor.

The Duilio 48 department store

In the pinewood known as the Pineta di Levante stands the Villa Borbone, a hunting lodge built for Marie-Louise by the architect Lorenzo Nottolini. Set in a large park, it houses the family's elegant mortuary chapel, built in a Neo-Gothic style by the Purist architect Giuseppe Partini.

Pietrasanta

At the foot of the Apuan Alps, in a natural setting that has been spared the rapid changes of the coastal plain, stands the small city of Pietrasanta.

In contrast to the peaceful industriousness of the present, centering on quarrying activities in the nearby mountains and an important craft tradition of marble working, the city has had a troubled history. For centuries it was the object of the military and political ambitions of many rival powers, continually changing hands between Lucca, Pisa, Genoa and Florence. A definitive solution came only with its entrance (1513) into the new Medicean state, where it was made the seat of a captaincy.

It was founded in 1255 by the podestà of Lucca, Guiscardo Pietrasanta, as part of a policy that aimed at defending the city's borderlands through the creation of new colonies, or *terrae novae* as they were called, to garrison major lines of communication, in this case the ancient Via Aurelia. Pietrasanta, like nearby Camaiore, preserves the character of a colony in its orthogonal urban layout, with long blocks and parallel streets inside a rectangular perimeter on which the walls were built later (early 14th cent.). The walls also extend along the side of the hill to link up with

Top, the interior of the baptistery with the two precious baptismal fonts; above, the marble stalls of the choir

The cathedral of San Martino and, on facing page, the marble pulpit the ancient Rocca di Sala, founded by the Longobards and then reinforced and enlarged by Castruccio Castracani degli Antelminelli, the lord of Lucca who, in homage to his bride, born in the burg, made Pietrasanta his residence.

The central square, in line with the fortress above, is an elongated rectangle splitting the city in two and representing its civil and religious fulcrum. The main public buildings face onto it: the cathedral of San Martino with its fine marble façade, the Palazzo Pretorio, the Torre delle Ore, the church of Sant'Agostino and the remains of the Rocca Arrighina, one of the bulwarks of the system of defense created by Castruccio.

San Martino is the most monumental of the religious buildings in the area. We do not know the date of its foundation with certainty. It is generally considered a 14th-cent. construction because part of it was already in existence by 1330, as we are informed by an inscription on its flank, but it is certain that the work lasted into the following century given that papal indulgences were still being granted to anyone who contributed to its completion at the end of the 14th cent. And as always happened in the past with buildings of large dimensions, interventions of restoration and restructuring were carried out in every era. The interior has several interesting features, although all that remains of its oldest decorations are a wooden *Crucifix* and a much venerated image of the *Madonna del Sole* (shown to the faithful on only three days a year), invoked to ward off the dangers of bad weather.

Numerous marble ornaments of particular value were made specially for the cathedral in the 16th cent.: the pulpit, the baptismal font, the holy-water stoup, the choir, a tabernacle and the enclosure of the presbytery, as well as the high altar and the altar of the chapel of the Santissimo Sacramento. Although some have been dispersed or transferred

elsewhere, these works testify to the ancient activity of marble working in a place where large numbers of craftsmen and quarrymen worked alongside important local dynasties of sculptors and decorators (the Riccomanni, Stagi and Civitali), constituting the backbone of the city's economy. In fact it was to the quarries of Monte Altissimo and Ceragiola, opened at the

beginning of the 16th cent. not far from Pietrasanta, that Michelangelo used to go to choose the marble for his sculptures.

The Gothic church of Sant'Agostino also faces onto the Piazza del Duomo. Housing numerous cycles of frescoes dating from the 14th-15th cent., it is now used to stage cultural events and exhibitions. The small church of the Misericordia, adorned with two important wooden sculptures by Antonio Pardini and Jacopo della Quercia, is known above all for two frescoes depicting the *Gates of Hell* and the *Gates of Paradise*, a gift of the Colombian Fernando Botero, one of many artists who have chosen to make their home in Pietrasanta.

Fernando Botero, *Gates of Heaven and Hell.* **Church of the Misericordia**

Pisa

Phocaean or Ligurian city, later Etruscan, Greek and Roman: not even the most recent archeological researches have been able to settle the controversial question of Pisa's origins. Its history tends to dissolve into mythology: there are even fabulous legends of a Pisan participation in the siege of Troy or of Pisan aid to Aeneas in the war against Turnus. Pisa's more or less official entry into history came in the 2nd cent. BC when, allied with Rome, it took part in the 2nd Punic War. This laid the foundations of its subsequent naval and military power, which would see it exercising a leading role as the "guardian" of the Tyrrhenian coast against frequent Saracen and Norman incursions.

A city with natural ties to water, to which it owed its origin and then its decline, Pisa grew up at the confluence of the river Arno with a branch of the Serchio in an environment very different from that of the present day. The coastline was further inland than it is now (a fact confirmed by the recent discovery of four ships at San Rossore) and much of the area was marshland, constantly subject to flooding by the Arno. Even Pisa's harbor, which played such a part in the history of the glorious maritime republic, was eventually silted up by the river and then abandoned in favor of the emerging port of Livorno. The extensive works of reclamation and regulation of the flow of water, which involved the displacement of the mouth of the Arno, brought about irreversible modifications in the surrounding landscape.

A busy commercial center throughout the Roman era and an important halting place on the route between Rome and Gaul after the opening of the Via Aurelia, Pisa seems to have long maintained a position of control over a vast region, although the arrival of the Longobards and subsequent Carolingian domination curbed its territorial ambitions. Its role as a bastion against the endemic pirate raids went hand in hand with a growing emphasis on trade that led it to establish contacts and bases as far away as the coast of Africa, and made it the most flourishing center in Etruria by the end of the 10th cent. The drawing up of the first maritime code (1075), the participation in the Crusades, the acquisition of papal privileges that sanctioned the Pisan Church's jurisdiction over Sardinia and, finally, the drafting of the city's own statutes (1162) marked the stages in a constant rise.

By contrast, the heavy defeat in the battle of Meloria at the hands of the Genoese fleet (1284) is traditionally taken to mark the beginning of Pisa's decline, but it would be more accurate to regard it as the culmination of a series of factors that had already weakened the city over the course of the 13th cent. These included its support for the Ghibelline faction and resulting conflict with Florence and Lucca, the internecine strife that undermined its stability, the enmity with Genoa and the rise of Venice as a power in the Mediterranean. The succession of a series of different noble families to power over the course of the 14th cent. was brought to a dismal conclusion in 1399, when Gherardo d'Appiano sold the city to the Visconti, who in turn ceded it to the Florentines (1406) in exchange for other territorial concessions. At the end of a long and bloody resistance Pisa was forced to capitulate and resign itself to rule by Florence.

In point of fact Medici rule resulted in a series of important

initiatives that were aimed at revitalizing the city's stagnant economy, such as the opening of the Canale dei Navicelli to permit rapid access to the port of Livorno, the start of substantial works of reclamation

Top left, painting from the early 14th cent. representing *Saint Nicholas Saving Pisa from the Plague*, detail with the city. San Nicola

Piazza dei Cavalieri and, top right, the monumental complex of Piazza dei Miracoli

in an effort to reduce the danger of flooding and the launch of a policy of promoting public works. But the city was no longer capable of regaining the prestige of past centuries and its role within the grand-ducal state was primarily an administrative and cultural one, underlined by the reopening of the ancient university, which was to make it a scientific center of the first rank.

Today the most tangible testimony of Pisa's former grandeur is the harmonious complex of buildings in white marble that are set in the Campo dei Miracoli, or "Square of Miracles." The present layout of the space, bounded on two sides by the medieval walls (1154), dates from the second half of the 19th cent.

The cathedral of Santa Maria Assunta was the first of the buildings to be erected in the square and provided a model for the baptistery and the tower. Its construction was made possible by the rich booty brought back from a successful raid on Palermo (1063), and the church built under the supervision of Buscheto was inaugurated when still incomplete in 1118. Over the following decades the work continued under the architect Rainaldo, who extended the nave and aisles and started on the façade, which was finished in the second half of the century. The result is one of the most fascinating creations in the whole of Western civilization, where different languages meet and are fused: on the one hand the monumentality of classical Roman art, evident in the

pp. 116-17, the baptistery and the flank of the cathedral

The interior of the baptistery; bottom left, Nicola Pisano's pulpit; right, view of the transept of the cathedral

solemn basilican plan and the decoration, and on the other the refined style of the Orient reflected in the pointed profile of the dome, the use of two colors in the marble cladding, the repeated adoption of the lancet arch and the massive presence of columns. The entire monument suggests a profound understanding of Oriental art, deriving from centuries of contact with the Islamic world of the Mediterranean basin, and it now appears certain that Muslim craftsmen were directly involved in the execution of the most refined works.

Following the destruction of the original bronze doors of the main portals in a disastrous fire that broke out in 1595, all that remains to testify to the genius of Bonanno Pisano are the twenty-four panels of the "Porta di San Ranieri," representing *Scenes from the New Testament* (1180). The interior is filled with masterpieces too, but for

the sake of brevity we will limit ourselves to mentioning the remains of Tino di Camaino's monumental tomb of Emperor Henry VII, once located in the apse; the mosaic of the apsidal conch depicting *Christ in Majesty between the Virgin and Saint John the Evangelist*; and the pulpit executed by Giovanni Pisano at the beginning of the 14th cent. as a replacement for Guglielmo's previous pulpit.

The work of the architect

Diotisalvi, the baptistery was built from 1152 onward. Nicola and Giovanni Pisano also contributed to the exceptional creation, continuing work on the second tier of balconies, left incomplete, and producing an evocative gallery of marble busts, human heads and allegorical figures, most of them now replaced by copies. The building houses a precious baptismal font (1246) by Guido Bigarelli from Como and a pulpit by Nicola Pisano (1260).

But by far the most celebrated monument, or the one that has made the greatest impact on the popular imagination, is the bell tower. Known as the "Leaning Tower"

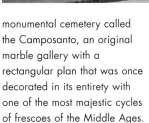

Top, Santa Maria della Spina; above, San Zeno (left) and San Paolo all'Orto; alongside, San Piero a Grado

owing to the curious tilt that it has had ever since it was built, it is by itself responsible for attracting the majority of tourists to the city. The unusual, circular structure, faced with marble and made up of six tiers of arcades, was commenced in 1172 by Gherardo di Gherardo, according to recent hypotheses, but was only completed after several interruptions in the second half of the 14th cent.

The square is closed on the northern side by the

monumental cemetery called the Camposanto, an original marble gallery with a rectangular plan that was once decorated in its entirety with one of the most majestic cycles of frescoes of the Middle Ages.

In the same style as the rest of the complex, although with hints of a new Gothic sensibility, it was built from 1277 onward. The initial architect was Giovanni di Simone, who also worked on the Leaning Tower, but the construction dragged on for a long time, tying up huge amounts of money and effort throughout the 15th cent. Damaged by the heavy bombing of 1944, the Camposanto has for decades been the object of a patient restoration, of which it is now possible to appreciate the results.

The exemplary character of the architectural language used in the "Campo dei Miracoli" was to exercise a powerful influence over subsequent religious architecture in the city. We will limit ourselves to singling out a few authentic gems like San Paolo a Ripa d'Arno, San Michele degli Scalzi, San Pierino, San Paolo all'Orto and the already Gothic San Michele in Borgo, Santa Caterina and Santa Maria della Spina. Another Pisan peculiarity is the widespread use of pottery bowls as an external decoration. Coming mostly from North Africa and

dating from between the end of the 10th cent. and the 12th, they were used to embellish the façades of many churches (San Zeno, San Sisto, Sant'Andrea Forisportam), although the most illustrious example is still the ancient basilica of San Piero a Grado.

The panorama of Pisan civil architecture is equally rich, even if time and constant human intervention have radically altered the appearance of the medieval city, which used to boast an exceptionally large number of tower-houses. Many of the finest buildings (Palazzo Toscanelli, Palazzo Agostini, Palazzo Lanfreducci and Palazzo Gambacorti, now the city hall) face onto the scenic embankments of the Arno, which have been remodeled several times and stripped of the numerous flights of steps and squares that were connected with the mercantile function performed by the river for centuries.

Not far from the river, on the site where the old Pisan magistracies used to be located and that is traditionally held to have originally been the Roman forum, extends the beautiful Piazza dei Cavalieri, one of the city's symbolic places. It is perhaps the most eloquent legacy of Pisa's Medici rulers, who established here the seat of the Order of St. Stephen, the powerful institution created (1561) by Cosimo I to combat Turkish and Barbary pirates in

the Mediterranean. Giorgio Vasari designed a complex of great stylistic coherence that was superimposed on the existing medieval buildings: it is made up of the Palazzo dei Cavalieri, with a rich graffito decoration, now the seat of the prestigious Scuola Normale Superiore, the church of Santo Stefano and the Palazzo dell'Orologio, or della Gherardesca, created out of the union of two preexisting towers.

Scientific and artistic collections are on show in the city's museums, of which the Museo Nazionale di San Matteo is perhaps the most significant. Housed in the evocative setting of a former Benedictine nunnery, it boasts one of the most extensive collections of medieval art in Europe. There is a particularly important group of painted crosses and statues from the 13th to 15th centuries, as well as collections of Islamic pottery bowls and illuminated codices.

The Museo dell'Opera del Duomo is the natural complement to a visit to the monuments in the Square of Miracles as it houses, for reasons of conservation, many of their external and internal sculptural decorations. Some of the best-known works are the bronze *Griffin* of Arab manufacture, once located on the cathedral's roof, a wooden *Christ* by a Burgundian artist of the 12th cent. and numerous sculptures by Nicola and Giovanni Pisano, Tino di Camaino and Nino Pisano.

A similar function is performed by the Museo delle Sinopie, housed in the former Spedale della Misericordia, built in 1258 by the architect of the Camposanto, Giovanni di Simone. The preliminary drawings of the great frescoes of the Camposanto damaged in the last war have been put on show here after restoration.

Francesco Traini, *Saint Dominic and Scenes from His Life*. Museo di San Matteo

Top left, Giunta Pisano, *Crucifix*; right, Masaccio, *Saint Paul*, detail. Museo di San Matteo

Facing page, Andrea and Nino Pisano, *Madonna del Latte*. Museo di San Matteo

The Lucchesia

The journey from Viareggio to Lucca is easy and pleasant. One might, for example, take S.S. 439 across Monte Quiesa, enjoying fine views and good food on the way.

There are, as we said, other ways of reaching Lucca. For example, we can follow the course of the Serchio, which means travelling the length of the Garfagnana. We mentioned just now that both from Aulla and from Massa one can get to the main town of the Garfagnana, Castelnuovo. The roads are very windy and narrow in parts, but the traveller is rewarded by majestic chestnut woods and staggering views of the Apuan Alps and the Apennines. Through country redolent with memories of the poet Giovanni Pascoli, especially at Castelvecchio, S.S. 445 leads to Barga, where there is a splendid cathedral in the Lombard Romanesque style, unfortunately remodelled several times and badly damaged in the earthquake of 1920, but now well restored so that its true nature is once again visible. Near Barga lovers of the Romanesque might at least take a trip to Gallicano to see the façade of the parish church of Sant'Iacopo. Nature-lovers, on the other hand, would do better to climb the road leading towards

The castle of Verrucole in the vicinity of San Romano in Garfagnana

Facing page, the gorge called the Orrido di Botri in Garfagnana

the Pania della Croce, at the foot of which is the Grotta del Vento (Cave of the Wind), with its forest of stalactites leading for more than a kilometer into the mountain.

Continuing towards Lucca, and near Fornaci di Barga, we find Loppia, in the vicinity of which we might visit the 10th-century parish church of Santa Maria. Further on, crossing to the right bank of the Serchio after the bridge of Calavorno, we can reach the Tuscan equivalent of the Grand

Canyon, the Orrido di Botri cut sheer between the mountains, with the Rio Pelago flowing in the bottom and high on its walls the nests of the golden eagle. Then, after Borgo a Mozzano, with its paper-works and its 15th- and 16th- century churches, there are other possible short deviations from S.S. 12 to visit the 13th-century Pieve di Santa Maria at Diecimo, and the two Romanesque parish churches at Brancoli, San Giorgio and San Lorenzo in Corte (11th-12th centuries). While in Borgo a Mozzano, folklore enthusiasts will not have

failed to cast an eye at the Ponte della Maddalena, which may have been built in the 14th cent., but which in local legend is called "The Devil's Bridge." What is more, he is said to have built it in a single night. In any case, devils and witches seem really at home in the Garfagnana and Lucchesia, among the Romanesque churches and the superb 16th- to 18th-century country houses built by the aristocracy of Lucca on the profits they made from the silk trade. These villas, which are worth a tour on their own, are scattered throughout the territory of Lucca in an area stretching in the north-west from the valley of the Freddana (tributary of the Serchio) and in an easterly direction more or less as far as Porcari, halfway between Lucca and Montecatini. Out of so many, perhaps the most worth a visit are Villa Torrigiani at Segromigno, Villa Mansi (now Villa Salom) at Piaggiori, and Villa Reale at Màrlia.

Arriving at Lucca through the Lunigiana or the Garfagnana are two good ways of doing so, unless of course one gets there straight from Florence, which is for obvious reasons the way taken by most tourists, in haste or in groups. Such a traveller will come along the Firenze-Mare motorway, which (we must admit) provides some wonderful glimpses as well as an almost infinite variety of detours towards the Prato area, or that of Pistoia, the baths of Montecatini and Monsummano, the Valdinievole with the little towns of Pescia and Collodi, and the delightful villages of Borgo a Buggiano and Montecarlo perched on the hilltops. (These were scarcely less than islands in times when between the Pescia and the Arno there was nothing but swamps, the only remainder of which is the marshy flatlands of Fucecchio).

But another interesting way of reaching the Lucchesia from the direction of Emilia is to take S.S. 12 (the Abetone Pass), through the snows which all the skiers in Tuscany

The Ponte del Diavolo, or "Devil's Bridge," at Borgo a Mozzano

 have made their first descents and mistakes on. Between one hairpin bend and the next you will come across towns such as Cutigliano and follow the upper reaches of the Lima as far as the vicinity of San Marcello Pistoiese. At this point there are three roads to choose from. Either you turn south-west and follow the S.S. 12 along the Lima valley, arriving at Borgo a Mozzano by way of Bagni di Lucca; or you take the 633 southwards over Monte Serra to the tourist centre of Marliana, and thence to Montecatini and the Valdinievole; or else you head due east, and then turn south for a tough drive along S.S. 66 across the Montagna Pistoiese. In this way you will be able to visit the towns of Gavinana and Maresca, and shortly before Pistoia you will cross the other noble road of the Pistoia mountains,

which is S.S. 64, headed for Bologna over the picturesque Passo della Collina and by way of the area between the Sambuca and Porretta Terme. The district is full of artificial lakes and mighty trees, which give it an air of being northern, perhaps in the Baltic, or even in Canada.

Top, Villa Mansi with a view of the park; right, Villa Torrigiani

Barga

Despite its small size and location on a steep slope, the city bears witness to the prosperity Barga enjoyed for centuries and to its importance as the local religious and cultural center. The two gates lead into a dense network of alleys, squares and streets lined with Renaissance buildings that all climb up toward the huge edifice of the cathedral on top of the hill.

The collegiate church of San Cristoforo, at the center of an area of level ground which offers a fine view of the Apuan Alps, was built in successive phases between the 11th and 14th cent. on the site of an earlier church. The façade in Longobard Romanesque style, which corresponded to the flank of the original building, is surmounted on the left by a massive bell tower. In the middle is set the main portal with a lintel carved in bas-relief flanked by two lions. The interior has a basilican plan with a nave and two aisles and its dimensions and precious furnishings reflect the

importance attained by the building in the years spanning the 13 and 14 centuries as the seat of the pontifical vicar. The presbytery is enclosed by plutei of polychrome marble in which

Top, bas-relief of the cathedral portal with scene of love feast; above, *Saints Roch, Julian and Anthony of Egypt*, detail showing Barga. Museo di Villa Guinigi, Lucca

Exterior and interior of the cathedral and, on facing page, the pulpit

The most interesting of the buildings in the historic center, which include many churches and palaces with façades in the Florentine style, are the 16th-cent. Palazzo Comunale with the Loggia del Mercato, the conservatory of Santa Elisabetta with a precious Della Robbian terracotta altarpiece and the 18th-cent. Teatro dell'Accademia dei Differenti. The latter, recently restored, is used to stage events connected with the Barga Opera Festival, which every year draws lovers of "bel canto" from all over Europe.

A few kilometers away, on a hill overlooking the city, is the Villa di Castelvecchio, the last home (now turned into a museum) of the poet Giovanni Pascoli, who wrote some of his most famous works here.

is set a richly carved 13th-cent. pulpit. Other works of significance include a 15th-cent. *Painted Cross*, the work of the so-called "Master of Barga"; a gigantic 13th-cent. wooden statue of *Saint Christopher*; and several Della Robbian majolica decorations in the chapel of the Sacrament.

Next to the cathedral stands the Palazzo Pretorio with a 14th-cent. portico. It houses Museo Civico, with archeological finds documenting settlements in the vicinity of Barga since prehistoric times.

Lucca

A favorable location on the plain, at the foot of the first spurs of the Apennines, and an abundance of water seem to have been the reasons for the foundation of the city by the Romans (180 BC), with the name of Luca. According to some interpretations that link it to the Celtic-Ligurian root *luk* ("swampy place"), the Latin name may in fact refer to the presence of the Serchio River (known as Auser in antiquity) which, in the absence of suitable regulation, used to pour its waters into the Luccan plain, turning it into a marsh. Whatever the origin of the name, it is certain that the history of the city is closely bound up with that of the river, the object of constant attention and works of hydraulic engineering. The city's bishop, St. Frigidian, is even credited with a miraculous deviation of the river's course.

Lucca acquired great political importance in the Longobard period, when the region was made a duchy (570) and the city became its capital, with its own mint. Its role was further increased by the opening of a new stretch of the Via Romea or Francigena – the great route of pilgrimage followed by the faithful of Northern Europe on their way to Rome – on which Lucca became a major halting place. Subsequent Frankish rule did not alter the balance that had been attained: Lucca, a flourishing city that already boasted a large number of churches, retained its supremacy throughout the early Middle Ages, only threatened from the 11th cent. onward by the emerging power of Pisa. Nor did Matilda of Canossa's decision to transfer the seat of the marquisate of Tuscany to Florence represent an obstacle to its economic growth, favored by the granting of imperial privileges.

On the eve of the age of free communes, and now limited in its political and territorial ambitions, Lucca shared with Florence, Pisa and Siena a position of dominance in the region. But unlike these cities – again confirming the peculiarity of its own history – it was able to maintain its independence from Florence for centuries, and did not lose it until the arrival of French troops in 1799 and its definitive annexation by the Grand Duchy of Tuscany (1847).

There were two basic pillars on which the city built its wealth: manufacturing activity, centering first on wool and then on silk, and banking. In fact the existence of a rich merchant class favored the growth of the "entrepreneurial" sector and at the same time allowed it to expand into the principal markets of Europe. It is a fact that toward the end of the 14th cent. and the beginning of the 15th some Luccan merchants were even in a position to lend money to sovereigns. The city also established flourishing commercial colonies in France and Flanders. From this point of view, the seigniorial rule of Paolo Guinigi (1400-30) turned out to be particularly favorable, giving a considerable boost to economic activity in the city.

An oasis of prosperity but one that was later to experience moments of social tension, culminating in the "revolt of the ragamuffins," the silk workers who did the most humble jobs, in 1531-32 and religious unrest linked to the Protestant Reformation (perhaps spread through frequent contacts with the Flemish world), which resulted in the exile of many members of the merchant families to Calvinist Geneva, where they founded a flourishing Luccan colony.

The progressive closure of the ruling oligarchy to outsiders in the 17th cent. was accompanied by the decline of the silk industry and a crisis in the banking families, including the ruinous collapse of the Buonvisi. The city's economy reacted to this difficult situation by falling back on the agricultural sector, into which the capital once invested in areas considered more profitable now began to flow. The most obvious result, and one that was destined to have a lasting effect on the landscape, was the construction of a whole series of villas with the aim of reorganizing farming

Top, Amico Aspertini, *The Diverting of the Course of the Serchio*. San Frediano

Alongside, San Michele in Foro with, on facing page, a detail of the façade

in the countryside. These were not just places of amusement and entertainment for the old merchant and banking classes, who sought confirmation of their social status in the magnificence of the architecture and the sumptuous symmetries of "Italian-style" gardens, but true farms engaged in improvement of the land and the exploitation of primary products like oil, wine or spelt, which were to constitute an important part of the Luccan economy even in the centuries to come. The over 300 country houses still in existence, although set in an environmental context that has changed profoundly, still represent a unique architectural and scenic heritage.

Still ringed by its massive walls, Lucca jealously guards the traces of its past, the great tradition of commerce and civic pride that is reflected in the quality of the urban fabric, studded with noble palaces and an exceptionally high number of churches, on which every

era has left its own mark.

Testifying to a moment of great vitality in the city's economy, the Romanesque religious architecture is unmistakable. The evident influence of Pisan culture was fused with the tradition of the Po Valley, introduced by craftsmen arriving in Lucca from the north along the Via

Francigena. Out of this came a style of great refinement, which found its most complete expression in the cathedral of San Martino and in the churches of San Michele in Forum, San Giusto and Santa Maria Forisportam.

The cathedral, founded according to tradition by St. Frigidian in the 6th cent., was reconstructed in the 11th cent. at the behest of Bishop Anselmo da Baggio (the future Pope Alexander II). Little remains of this building: the façade we see now, with its extraordinary portico of three arches, was added at the end of the 12th cent. by Guidetto da Como. Decorated by sculptors of various geographical and cultural origins, it is an architectural blend of great interest in which the language of Lombardy and Ravenna

coexists with that of Tuscan origin, represented here by Nicola Pisano.

The Gothic interior was extensively rebuilt in the second half of the 14th cent. and at the beginning of the 15th. The numerous outstanding works of sculpture and painting that it contains include a 13th-cent.

Top left, the cathedral of San Martino with a detail of the façade and the sculptural group representing *Saint Martin and the Beggar*

Facing page, Jacopo della Quercia, *Sarcophagus of Ilaria del Carretto,* **detail. Cathedral**

Exterior and interior of San Frediano with a view of the chapel of Sant'Agostino

group representing *Saint Martin and the Beggar* (replaced on the exterior by a copy); the *Sarcophagus of Ilaria del Carretto* by Jacopo della Quercia, unanimously regarded as one of his masterpieces; the panel by Domenico Ghirlandaio depicting the *Madonna and Child with Saints*; Matteo Civitali's *Altar of San Regolo*; the Tempietto del Volto Santo, with an ancient wooden *Cross* that is the object of particular devotion.

The nearby church of Santi Giovanni e Reparata, with an adjoining baptistery, used to perform the function of cathedral, but perhaps the best-known building in the city, or at least the one most representative of Luccan religious architecture, is San Michele in Forum. Erected at the center of the ancient Roman forum around the 8th cent., it was completely reconstructed from the second half of the 11th cent. onward, once again on the orders of Bishop Anselmo. It is characterized by a refined façade set on blind arches of the Pisan type and concluded by four tiers of small loggias decorated in bas-relief or inlay by the same stonecutter who had worked on the cathedral. The three statues set on the gable – with *Saint*

Michael in the middle – accentuate the verticality of the whole.

Given the impossibility of describing the whole of the city's immense heritage of religious architecture, we will confine our attention to the basilica of San Frediano, with its great mosaic on the façade depicting the *Ascension of Christ*. The origins of the building are traced back directly to the Irish bishop and saint Frigidian (called Frediano in Italian), whose most famous deed, the deviation of the course of the river Serchio, is

represented by Amico Aspertini in the fresco of the chapel of Sant'Agostino. In the evocative interior, it is possible to admire the Romanesque baptismal font by Master Roberto, a marble polyptych by Jacopo della

Quercia, and part of a Cosmatesque floor in the presbyterial zone.

It is still possible to make out the many different strata that have been laid down in the urban fabric, starting with the traces of the Roman city evident in the regular grid laid out around the *cardo maximus* (now Via Fillungo and Via Cenami) and the *decumanus* (Via San Paolino and Via Santa Croce). The Piazza dell'Anfiteatro, formerly Piazza del Mercato, unequivocally

Top, the Piazza dell'Anfiteatro; above, the Ducal Palace and, right, Palazzo Guinigi with its characteristic tower

Alongside, Palazzo Moriconi-Pfanner

Much of Lucca's rich artistic heritage is on view in the city's museums. The Museo Nazionale di Villa Guinigi, housed in the former residence of Paolo Guinigi, contains archeological finds made in the area and examples of Luccan figurative culture. These include fragments of architectural and sculptural decorations from religious buildings and sculptures and paintings covering a span of time stretching from the end of the 13th cent. to the beginning of the 18th cent.

Top, Anonymous artist from Lucca, *Madonna and Child with Two Saints*. Museo di Villa Guinigi; above, Filippino Lippi, *Saints Roch, Sebastian, Jerome and Helen*. San Michele in Foro

Top right, Mabuse, *Madonna of the Cherries* and, Luca Giordano, *Saint Sebastian*. Museo di Palazzo Mansi

reveals its origins as a Roman amphitheater, retaining its elliptical shape and several structural elements that are still visible at the back of the buildings now surrounding it.

There are numerous medieval tower-houses and noble palaces

in the historic center, from the 13th-cent. Torre delle Ore to the elegant brick palaces of the Guinigi family with their characteristic tower surmounted by Holm oaks; from Palazzo Bernardini to Palazzo Pretorio, both of which may have been designed by Matteo Civitali; and from Palazzo Moriconi-Pfanner, with its "French-style" garden, to the Ducal Palace (now Palazzo della Provincia). This last, designed by Bartolomeo Ammannati (1578) and enlarged in the 18th cent.

with the addition of monumental features, became the residence of Napoleon's sister at the time of French rule and as such was subjected to numerous alterations inside, as was the surrounding area, cleared of buildings and transformed into a square.

The 19th cent. also left a significant mark on the city, including the transformation of the great ring of walls, built between the 16th and 17th cent. to defend the city, into a promenade and public garden.

The Museo Nazionale di Palazzo Mansi provides an interesting opportunity to visit a noble palace in which the furnishings of the *piano nobile* have been preserved intact. It houses a collection of paintings (including works by Pontormo, Bronzino, Beccafumi and Luca Giordano) sent by Leopold II of Lorraine following the entry of Lucca into the Grand Duchy of Tuscany.

There is an important collection of sacred furnishings and vestments in the Museo della Cattedrale.

Domenico Beccafumi, *The Moderation of Scipio* and, on facing page, Jacopo Pontormo, *Portrait of Youth*, detail. Museo di Palazzo Mansi

Montecatini

An ancient settlement of Roman origin on the summit of a steep hill that expanded in the early medieval period around the parish church of San Pietro a Neure, Montecatini entered history at the beginning of the 11th cent. as a fief of the lords of Maona.

According to an age-old legend that has now become a tradition, the name Mons Catilinae derives from that of Catiline, the famous Roman politician who took refuge here after the fall of Fiesole and whose presence was to lead to the town's destruction. In reality history seems to suggest that, on the one hand, the area was settled in the remote past, a fact confirmed by researches in the field, and on the other, the whole of the Valdinievole was a borderland disputed by various feudal lords and therefore a zone of military conflict.

Wrested from a long period of rule by Lucca following a bloody siege that contemporary chroniclers described as an extraordinary feat of arms, Montecatini became a possession of the Florentine republic in the fourth decade of the 14th cent., although its position remained very precarious. Cosimo I's destruction (1554) of all its fortifications, which had become a refuge for French troops under the command of Piero Strozzi, was the final episode in a troubled history. From then on the spa town situated on the plain beneath, just a few kilometers from the

ancient castle, was to experience a slow but steady rise.

The hot springs located at the foot of Montecatini hill have been known since antiquity, but it was only in the Middle Ages that the depurative and curative properties of the water were discovered by the physician Ugolino da Montecatini (14th cent.). The Tettuccio Baths were open as far back as 1370, but Florence's subsequent decision to raise the level of the water in the Fucecchio marshes to encourage fishing, with the consequent flooding of the whole area, set back the development of the mineral spa for a long time. However, it was given a decisive boost in the second half of the 18th cent. under the Lorraine, who promoted the drainage of the plain and the exploitation of the springs.

Montecatini's international reputation, which has made it one of the most elegant and best-organized spas in Italy, is a recent development. In fact the most interesting establishments and hotels date from the first few decades of the 20th cent., and are surrounded by houses built in the art nouveau style of the period. Subsequent urban redevelopment and the expansion that has taken place in recent decades have not altered the character of the town, whose strong points are the vivacity of its social life and the large number of parks and gardens.

The Tettuccio Baths are the oldest and most representative in Montecatini, although the existing establishment, designed

The "tree-shaped" room designed by Paolo Portoghesi for the Tettuccio Baths

by Ugo Giovannozzi, was built in the early 1920s. The architect decided to preserve the previous façade, from the time of Grand Duke Leopold, reconstructing it inside the building, where it is also possible to admire the lavish decoration by Galileo Chini and Basilio Cascella and a reception room designed by Paolo Portoghesi.

The Excelsior Baths were built in 1915 in a Neo-Renaissance style to which a questionable structure of concrete and glass was added in 1968, while there are Byzantine and medieval reminiscences in the architecture of the Tamerici Baths.

Galileo Chini has left traces more or less everywhere, frescoing the reception room of the Grand Hotel & la Pace and designing its windows, decorating the interiors of the eclectic Palazzo Comunale and

leaving a fine composition inspired by Klimt in the *Spring*, in the art academy named after Dino Scalabrino.

Not far from Montecatini, in the midst of a landscape filled with watercourses and forests, is set the small burg of Collodi, one of the many ancient castles of the Valdinievole long disputed between Lucca and Florence. Its now international fame stems from the Florentine

writer Carlo Lorenzini who, under the pseudonym of Collodi, the birthplace of his mother, created the extraordinary figure of the puppet Pinocchio. A beautiful garden, laid out in the middle of the last century by Pietro Porcinai, celebrates the fable with a picturesque route lined with sculptures by celebrated artists.

The ascent to the burg is dominated by the elegant Villa Garzoni, built in a baroque style in the 17th cent. Its charm is linked to the fascinating garden designed by Ottaviano Diodati, laid out around scenic flights of steps and embellished with statues and fountains.

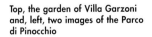

Top, the garden of Villa Garzoni and, left, two images of the Parco di Pinocchio

Pistoia

A Roman colony, used as a military stronghold against the Ligurian tribes living in the nearby Apennines, it developed like many other ancient centers in relation to the road network. In fact the opening of a new stretch of the Via Cassia (the important consular road that linked Rome with the Etruscan cities of the interior and Lunigiana), from which branched off the roads across the Apennines leading to the great centers of the Po Valley, made it a junction of primary importance. However, the whole of the territory was settled in the remote past and there are traces that can be dated back to the Etruscan era in Pistoia itself. Recent archeological investigations carried out in the area of the cathedral have revealed the exceptional continuity of the urban strata, bringing to light materials that span more than twenty centuries of history.

An episcopal see between the 4th and 5th cent., it played a role of some importance at the time of the barbarian invasions, putting up a long resistance to the advance of the Longobards, who later made it the seat of a chamberlain. Indeed it was in the Longobard period that Pistoia experienced a period of political and economic vigor that was reflected in the minting of its own gold coin and the raising of a ring of walls. Carolingian rule did not erode the prosperity that had been attained and the city saw the establishment of a precocious communal system (early 12th cent.). It gave itself a charter (1177), that is generally considered one of the oldest in Italy.

The city's economic success certainly stemmed from its position in the road system, but the abundant supply of water in the area and the timber of the nearby mountains also played a strategic role in the emergence of important manufacturing activities (wool, paper, wood) that still flourish today. Nor should we forget the smelting of iron ore from Elba, brought to Pistoia by waterborne transport, an activity already under way in the Etruscan period and elevated under the Medici to the status of a true industry.

However, this precocious "industrial" vocation – something that is still confirmed

today by the existence of engineering companies, operating alongside an important nursery-gardening sector – was not matched by an adequate political stability and the city that may have gone through its "golden age" in the 13th cent., with flourishing

Top, the Piazza del Duomo with the cathedral of San Zeno and the Palazzo Comunale and, below, a detail of the cathedral porch decorated by Andrea della Robbia

Left, the *Altar of San Jacopo*. Cathedral

Facing page, the baptistery of San Giovanni in Corte

The façade of Sant'Andrea with the lintel of the central portal decorated with the *Journey of the Magi* by Gruamonte

banks and splendid churches and palaces, became the scene of fierce internal conflict. On top of these came the designs of the nearby cities of Pisa, Lucca and Florence, which conquered it in turn until it lost all its political influence and came under the sway of Florence, which annexed it permanently in 1530.

The scenic Piazza del Duomo, which had reached its present size in the early 14th cent. following the demolition of the buildings that stood between the cathedral and the baptistery, has for centuries performed the function of the center of religious and civil life, and the monument that best embodies its role as a symbol of the community and hub of the city's memories is the cathedral of San Zeno. While its origins are uncertain, we do know that it was rebuilt after several calamitous events and renovated many times. The exterior dates from the second half of the 13th cent. and is in a Romanesque style of the Pisan-Luccan type, common to several of the city's other religious buildings, although altered by the later portico, decorated by Andrea della

Robbia with enameled terracotta coffers on the tunnel vault and a lunette in bas-relief on the central portal.

The interior has been affected by incessant alterations, although some restorations carried out in the middle of the 20th cent. have attempted to bring it back to its original Romanesque character. Its nave and aisles are thronged with masterpieces, including the *Monument to Cino da Pistoia*, a Gothic sculpture attributed to the Sienese artist Giovanni di Agostino; the *Cross* painted by Coppo di Marcovaldo in collaboration with his son Salerno; the panel depicting the *Madonna and Child between Saints John the Baptist and Donatus* (1475-80), always admired and recently identified as the work of Lorenzo di Credi; and the *Altar of Saint James*, one of the finest examples of the silversmith's craft in Italy. Made out of silver with enamels and precious stones (1287-1456), it is Pistoia's homage to the apostle James, elected its patron saint after the arrival of a venerated relic in the city.

Although a local tradition claims the imposing campanile

to have been a Longobard watchtower, it is in reality a structure dating from the 12th-13th cent. embellished with balconies in marble of two different colors. The adjacent baptistery of San Giovanni in Corte was built in the 14th cent. and has Gothic features. It is located in the area once occupied by the buildings that represented Longobard political power, of which another memory survives in the nearby Piazza della Sala, where the palace of the chamberlain used to stand. The baptistery, on an octagonal plan and faced with black and white marble, has refined portals and contains a

precious baptismal font (1226), made by Lanfranco da Como for a preexisting church.

Travelers in the past have remarked on the quantity and quality of the sculptures, or the carved decorations, which appear to be a distinctive trait of religious architecture in Pistoia but can only be hinted at in the small amount of space

available. The most interesting buildings date from the Romanesque period and are contemporary with the cathedral: Sant'Andrea, San Bartolomeo in Pantano, San Pier Maggiore and San Giovanni Fuorcivitas, all with lintels carved in relief (many of them the work of Gruamonte) and pulpits of great value, of which

Top left, San Pietro

Right, exterior and interior of San Bartolomeo in Pantano with, top, Guido da Como's pulpit

The north flank of San Giovanni Fuorcivitas and, bottom, Luca della Robbia's *Visitation*

Facing page, Bernardino Detti, *Madonna della Pergola*, detail. Museo Civico

the most famous is perhaps the one executed by Giovanni Pisano in Sant'Andrea.

It is also worth mentioning San Paolo, San Francesco, San Domenico and the later basilica of the Madonna dell'Umiltà, filled with ornaments and devotional objects, whose "powerful" impact on the city's skyline is due to the imposing dome built in the second half of the 16th cent. by Giorgio Vasari.

The city's finest example of civil architecture is the Palazzo del Comune, built along simple and elegant lines out of sandstone from the end of the 13th cent. onward. Inside there are frescoed rooms, along with the ancient chapel of Sant'Agata and the Museo Civico. Transferred here in 1982, its collection consists chiefly of paintings and sculptures (from the 13th to the 19th cent.) taken

from lay confraternities and religious congregations in Pistoia.

The Palazzo del Podestà or Palazzo Pretorio, seat of the law courts, is to a large extent a 19th-cent. reconstruction of the former residence of the podestà, the city's chief magistrate in medieval times. The Palazzo dei Vescovi adjoining the cathedral is more interesting. Built between the end of the 10th cent. and the 11th, it was enlarged and renovated several times to adapt it to new requirements. Having lost its original function as the bishop's residence some time ago, it has now regained its Gothic appearance following restoration in the 20th cent. and houses the Museo della Cattedrale with its rich Treasure of St. James.

The Museo Diocesano has recently been installed in the nearby Palazzo Rospigliosi, where the family's furnishings and large collection of

paintings are also on display.

Not far away we find Pistoia's oldest charitable institution, the Ospedale del Ceppo. Founded in the 13th cent:, it gave assistance to the sick and needy for centuries, especially during the outbreak of plague in 1348. In the first half of the 16th cent., as part of a renovation of the building, a portico in the Brunelleschian manner was added to the façade. It is decorated with glazed terracottas from the Della Robbia workshop, including the celebrated frieze with *Works of Charity* by Santi Buglioni.

To complete the picture of the city's museums, we must mention the former monastery of Sant'Antonio Abate, splendidly frescoed in the 14th and 15th cent., which now houses the center named after Marino Marini, the important 20th-cent. sculptor who was born in Pistoia.

The Apennine Roads

It is a little sad, this story of the mountain roads and the Apennine passes. We admit that a lot of roads are narrow, pot-holed, steep, a mass of bends, and even quite dangerous, particularly by night or in the winter. But if you flash through Tuscany by way of the Autostrada del Sole, which gives the traveller no time even to realize that there is such a place as the wonderful Mugello on his left, and that plummets down to Prato leaving unnoticed the Monti della Calvana to the right, and the massif which culminates in Monte Morello to the left, well then, this is a region that has been violated without being possessed, and ruined without enjoyment.

What are the alternatives then? For anyone with the time, and the ability to stay calm at the wheel of his car, they are many and various. Let us start from Bologna, and assume that the charms of the Autostrada are no longer so ravishing as once they were. One could take S.S. 325 from Castiglion de' Pepoli to Montepiano, with possible excursions of interest to the 16th-century sanctuary at Boccadirio and the artificial lake of Brasimone. Thereafter one could make one's way down the valley of the Bisenzio, through Vernio and Vaiano (with its 11th-13th century church of San Salvatore) as far as Prato. From here (wishing to avoid the Autostrada) we may reach Florence by way of the Sesto road along the south of Monte Morello, or else by way of Campi, Brozzi and Quaracchi, which follows the course of the Arno and is in fact the lovely "Via Pistoiese" that leads to Poggio a Caiano with its fine Medici villa and to Carmignano, famous for its red wines.

But another way to come from Bologna is by S.S. 65, which leaves Emilia just south of Monghidoro (at Filigara we still see the old customs buildings once at the borders of the Papal States and the grand duchy), crosses the passes of the Raticosa and the Futa, and then falls steeply through the Mugello, touching on the upper reaches of the Sieve and passing near Barberino, which has the fine 15th-century monastery of Bosco ai Frati, the Medici villa of Cafaggiolo and the castle of Trebbio. Once over the Passo di Pratolino and past the splendid park of Villa Demidoff (once a Medici estate) S.S. 65, at least for the Florentines, becomes "Via Bolognese" and arrives in what by now is the centre of Florence at Piazza della Libertà (formerly Piazza San Gallo).

Shortly after passing the castle of Trebbio, the traveller on his way to Florence from the Futa joins up with S.S. 503.

Top, Giambologna, fountain of the *Apennines*. Villa Demidoff, Pratolino

Jacopo Pontormo, *Visitation*. San Michele, Carmignano

This is the road from Firenzuola and the area of "Romagna Toscana" corresponding to the upper valley of the Santerno. It has by now crossed the Passo del Giogo and come down through Scarperia, the Florentine *terra nova* that boasts such a fine Town Hall, and San Piero a Sieve, where there is an impressive Medici fortress.

Through the upper valley of the Santerno one can also reach the Mugello if one comes from Imola. But, either from Imola or Faenza, another route into Tuscany is through the valley of the Sènio by way of Castagno (birthplace of the famous painter, Andrea del Castagno, 1423-57), past Badia di Susinana and Palazzuolo and over the pass of the Sambuca. Shortly after that the road joins the one coming down from the Val di Làmone through the important town of Marradi. From this point we have no trouble in reaching Borgo San Lorenzo, the historic centre of the Mugello. This is the meeting point of the roads coming over from Romagna, by way of San Benedetto, the pass of the Muraglione and the towns of Viccho and Dicomano. San Benedetto dell'Alpe is mentioned by Dante, with its waterfall which he compares with the river of blood falling into the 8th Circle of Hell.

Top, two views of the castle of Trebbio; right, the Medici villa of Cafaggiolo

Prato

The second largest city in Tuscany by number of inhabitants, Prato has for centuries been a center of great economic dynamism and cultural vivacity.

In spite of the fact that it is now an industrial city with large areas of modern construction, fruit of the rapid urban growth triggered by the boom in the textile sector, Prato has ancient origins and still has buildings from the medieval era and the Renaissance that are on a par with the best known and most appreciated monuments in the region.

The remains of a mosaic floor uncovered in the church of San Fabiano, variously dated to some time between the 7th and 10th cent., seem to be the oldest vestiges to have survived, but the origins of the city are still not completely clear. It has been suggested that there were Etruscan settlements in the area, followed by the formation of a village in the Roman era, with the probable name of Cornius. Then came a long period of silence, interrupted in the 10th cent. by the first reference in the documents, establishing the existence of a hamlet called Borgo al Cornio in the vicinity of the parish church of Santo Stefano (the area of the present cathedral) and close to a castle of the counts Alberti di Vernio, with which it was later fused to create the built-up area we see today. Its favorable geographical location in the shelter of the foothills of the

Top left, Fra Paolino and Domenico Sogliani (attrib.), *The Virgin Interceding to Stop the Contagion of the City of Prato*, detail of the city. Oratory of San Sebastiano; below, the Castello dell'Imperatore

Castello dell'Imperatore, or "Emperor's Castle." Built between 1240 and 1250 by the Sicilian architect Riccardo da Lentini for Frederick of Antioch, the son of Emperor Frederick II, it bears witness to a period of support for the Hohenstaufen in the commune's policies.

In the middle of the 14th cent. Prato would be militarily

annexed by Florence, although not without having first paid a considerable sum of money to the queen of Naples, Joan of Anjou, whose protection the city enjoyed. From that time on its fate was linked with Florence's, although it did retain a limited administrative autonomy.

Perhaps the most evident trait of the city's subsequent history would be its ability to maintain a constant openness to new ideas and a high level of economic enterprise that allowed it to grow and modernize, bringing in more up-to-date techniques of textile production alongside the traditional industries of wool and the reclamation of old cloth.

Apennines, on the right bank of the Bisenzio River (which long provided the motive power necessary to the development of its industrial activities), at the intersection of two important lines of communication, favored Prato's early conquest of a preeminent position in the area.

Between the 12th and 13th cent., in fact, the city set itself up as a free commune and exercised its jurisdiction over the Bisenzio valley as well. The progressive increase in population was accompanied by the construction of a new ring of walls. This was followed in the 14th cent. by another which was to represent the limit of urban expansion up until the beginning of the last century. Some of the most representative buildings were erected over the course of the 13th cent., and it was around these that the city began to construct its history and identity, commencing with the cathedral and the distinctive

Left, exterior and interior of the cathedral with, bottom, the chapel of the Sacro Cingolo and the pulpit of Mino da Fiesole and Antonio Rossellino

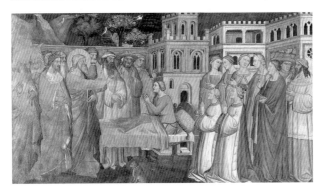

A good place to commence a visit to the city is Piazza del Duomo, the area of the first urban settlement and the location of Prato's most representative monument, the cathedral of Santo Stefano. Generally considered one of the finest examples of Tuscan Romanesque, the building is a successful blend of architectural styles of different cultural origin: the Lombard one, attributable to the Master Guido (perhaps the same man as the Guidetto da Como who worked on Lucca Cathedral) who was summoned to complete the church at the beginning of the 13th cent., the Pisan one evident in the use of two colors in the facing – where *alberese* limestone from quarries in the nearby Monti della Calvana alternates with green serpentine – and

elements of Florentine taste that are still perceptible in the cloister. The slender structure of the 13th-cent. bell tower is balanced by the airy grace of the external pulpit at the corner, conceived and executed (1428-38) by Michelozzo and Donatello, with the assistance of distinguished collaborators,

Ludovico Buti, *Portrait of Francesco Datini*. Palazzo Comunale

Facing page, Filippo Lippi, *Funeral of Saint Stephen*, detail. Cathedral

From the top, Filippo Lippi, *The Feast of Herod*; Andrea di Giusto, *Marriage of the Virgin*. Cathedral;

Niccolò di Pietro Gerini, *The Miracle of Saint Matthew*. San Francesco

Top on both pages, Bernardo Daddi, *Scenes of the Holy Girdle;* above left, Andrea di Giusto, *Polyptych,* right, Filippo Lippi and workshop, *Annunciation* and *Madonna della Cintola.* Museo Civico

Bottom left, Filippo Lippi and workshop, *Madonna del Ceppo;* below, Battistello Caracciolo, *Noli me tangere.* Museo Civico

152

for the display of the relic of the Holy Girdle to the faithful.

The nave and two aisles of the Romanesque interior, concluded by the broad 14th-cent. transept, echo the stylistic unity of the exterior. Separated by columns of green serpentine crowned with refined capitals, they contain art treasures of exceptional value, including the frescoes executed by Filippo Lippi in the chancel and the paintings of Paolo Uccello and Andrea di Giusto in the chapel of the Assunta, while the precious Marian relic of the Holy Girdle (significantly, in a city with an ancient association with the wool industry, a belt made out of goat's wool) is housed in a chapel frescoed by Agnolo Gaddi.

Onto the square in front, where the buildings of the civil authorities once stood (13th cent.) but were later demolished, now face later palaces, such as the Palazzo Vescovile housing the Museo dell'Opera del Duomo. Recently enlarged and renovated, it contains works from various places in the diocese as well as the original panels of Donatello's pulpit, put on show after careful restoration.

In the historic part of the city are also to be found the places of worship (San Francesco, San Domenico, Sant'Agostino, Spirito Santo) built by the great mendicant orders, who arrived in the city over the course of the 13th cent., but the most interesting church is undoubtedly Santa Maria dei Carceri, an authentic Renaissance jewel designed by Giuliano da Sangallo.

Little remains of the original structure of the Palazzo del Comune, which now has the neoclassical appearance bestowed on it by the architect Giuseppe Valentini, unlike the nearby Palazzo Pretorio, which has retained its medieval form. Since the beginning of the last century the latter has housed the Museo Civico, a collection of mostly Gothic and Renaissance paintings that comprises pictures by Bernardo Daddi, Giovanni da Milano, Filippo Lippi and his son Filippino, who was born in Prato.

But perhaps the building that best symbolizes the character of the city is Palazzo Datini, whose name conjures up the memory of an extraordinary figure, a merchant and writer (the first to introduce into Europe the bill of exchange, used for centuries in the Iranian world), whose business and private papers have been an invaluable source of information about the society of the time. Its rooms, decorated with frescoes painted at the end of the 14th cent. by Niccolò di Pietro Gerini and his workshop, are now home to the State Archives.

The interest shown by the Prato business community in innovation and experimentation is apparent in the cultural sphere as well, where it supports interesting avant-garde theatrical performances and has created the Luigi Pecci exhibition center, a point of reference for contemporary art in Tuscany.

The large sculpture by Henry Moore in Piazza San Marco; below, the Centro per l'Arte Contemporanea "Luigi Pecci"

Scarperia

With the defeat of the Ubaldini, the family that held fief over the upper Mugello valley, Florence commenced construction of a *terra nuova* or colony on the Tuscan side of the Apennines in 1306, with the aim of maintaining control over the territories it had annexed but not yet completely tamed.

Fundamental to the growth and development of Scarperia was its position along the road leading to the pass known as the Giogo, indispensable to Florence for the control of communications across the Apennines. For this reason Scarperia was made the seat of a vicariate in 1415, with judicial and administrative authority over the entire Mugello, and it was on this occasion that the castle was enlarged, assuming an appearance similar to the one it has today.

The town long continued to benefit from its position of obligatory transit, the fertility of the surrounding countryside, and the proceeds of a flourishing handicrafts industry, well known since the 15th cent. and hinging on the manufacture of knives and cutting tools, which made it a sort of Tuscan Sheffield.

The opening of the Futa road, which could be used by carts, in the middle of the 18th cent., and the consequent shift of the commercial route to the west led to the slow but inexorable decline of Scarperia and the neighboring villages.

Not many traces of the original 14th-cent. town survive

today, as it was struck by a powerful earthquake around the middle of the 16th cent. (1542) and rebuilt over the following decades. However, the linear plan typical of centers laid out to serve the function of a military garrison is still visible. The ancient longitudinal axis of development coincides with the modern Via Roma, onto which opens the main square, dominated by the Palazzo dei Vicari. This is unquestionably Scarperia's most symbolic construction, with its tall, battlemented tower and façade adorned with coats of arms (some of them produced by the Della Robbia workshop) of the men who succeeded one another in the post of vicar.

In the entrance hall, it too decorated with heraldic insignia, there are two frescoes from the beginning of the 15th cent. depicting the *Incredulity of Saint Thomas* and the *Madonna Enthroned with Saints*, including St. Barnabas, the patron of Scarperia, holding an effigy of the palace.

In front of the palace stands the church of Santi Iacopo e Filippo, extensively rebuilt in the last two centuries, while it was in the nearby chapel of the Madonna di Piazza, containing a fine panel by Jacopo del Casentino, that the vicars used to swear loyalty to the republic.

A memory of the ancient knife-making industry remains today in the Center for Research and Documentation of the Craft of Cutting Tools, set up in 1987. The museum aims to couple an understanding of the objects themselves with that of the places and techniques of their manufacture, through guided tours of the 19th-cent. Bottega del Coltellinaio, or "Knife-Maker's Workshop," where the traditional instruments of the ancient craft are preserved and practical demonstrations put on.

Not far from the town stands the ancient parish church of Santa Maria a Fagna with an 18th-century façade and a precious 13th-century baptismal font.

Top, the "Knife-Maker's Workshop"; left, the Palazzo dei Vicari

Below, the baptismal font of Santa Maria a Fagna with detail of an inlaid panel on the facing page

The "Heart" of Tuscany

We have travelled all the principal roads entering Tuscany across the Apennines from the north-west to the north-east, approaching that "heart" of the region contained by a very irregular triangle with its base on the seashore of Pisa and Versilia and angles at the cities of Viareggio, Livorno and Florence. It is

on this core that the system of motorways converges, together with the *superstrade* connecting the "capital" with the industrial and maritime city of Livorno and the residential area of Versilia, while along its irregular sides we find the principal and most active towns in Tuscany: Lucca, Pistoia and Prato, linked by the Firenze-Mare motorway, and Pontedera, Santa Croce sull'Arno and Empoli along the historic and in some ways glorious road down the left hand side of the Lower Arno, the "Tosco-Romagnola," now replaced by the *superstrada* for Livorno.

This heart of Tuscany was once a watery place, dotted with marshes, grooved by canals (some of which are still there), and travelled by barges and lighters. Once past the

crest of Monte Albano, which runs south-east from Serravalle (halfway between Pistoia and Montecatini) to meet the Arno near Capraia, and Montelupo right opposite, above the meeting of the Pesa and Arno, we reach what was once the great marsh between the Pescia and Arno, stretching west as far as Monte Pisano. Now there are only a few stretches – pathetic but still beautiful – near Fucecchio and Bientina. It was an area of waterways, which even the reclamation carried out under Peter Leopold left as they were, since transport by barge was cheaper and safer than by road. The place-names are often reminders of this ancient land of waters. We need only mention Altopascio, the "High Pass" where the great bell of the Hospitallers, known as "La Smarrita" (the Lost One) would ring out to guide travellers wandering on the heath. Or we might think of Scala (port of call), or Isola (island) between Empoli and the ancient administrative centre and imperial stronghold of San Miniato. These names are derived from docks and customs posts. If we come from Florence, once past Lastra and Signa, the eye is caught by the pools of the Gonfolina, mentioned by Leonardo da Vinci, but they are remnants of a landscape that no longer exists. Between the Autostrada Firenze-Mare and the lower Valdarno today we have the most densely populated zone of Tuscany, and alas the one in which the countryside has been most spoilt and the environment most polluted. It is the area devoted to industry, the "islands" of the leather trade, furniture and so on. Here more than elsewhere the traveller should keep a firm hold on the thread of memory and history. In monuments and settlements still wholly or partly intact, in ancient routes now "gutted" by super-highways, and in the place-names, he will be able to find traces of a past that will continue to exist as long as we are able to discern its remains.

The town of Vinci with the church
of Santa Croce and the castle
of the counts Guidi

Facing page, top, Bicci di Lorenzo,
Saint Nicholas of Tolentino
Protecting Empoli from the Plague,
detail. Museo della Collegiata;
bottom, Piazza Farinata degli
Uberti with the collegiate church

Empoli

The name Empoli (*Emporium*) recalls the ancient function of a river port on the Arno that the town already had back in the Etrusco-Roman era. With its close ties to the river, Empoli was an important halting place in the network of water and land communications between Florence and Pisa. The profound crisis that overtook the Roman world and undermined its political and economic system certainly affected the port as well, but did not put paid to it: despite a reduction in the volume of traffic and the population, Empoli survived and a few documents datable to the 8th cent. refer to it as a castle in the vicinity of the locality now known as Empoli Vecchio. However, the actual formation of a burg around the parish church of Sant'Andrea dates from the beginning of the 12th cent.

A fief of the counts Guidi, the town was soon forced to submit to the Florentine republic (1182), which wanted to extend its sphere of influence as far as the river Elsa, and the whole of its subsequent history unfolded in  the shadow of Florence.

Its obvious function as a western bulwark against the republic's enemies meant that particular attention was paid to its system of defense, which was promptly repaired following a destructive flood of the Arno (1333) and then completely rebuilt in the second half of the 15th cent. At the

war have greatly altered the town, which now has the appearance of a bustling industrial and commercial center, although one that is filled with works of art.

The heart of the town is the beautiful Piazza Farinata degli Uberti, adorned with a marble fountain from the beginning of the 19th cent. Onto it face the

Masolino, *Man of Sorrows*, detail, Museo della Collegiata; right, *Saint Ivo and His Wards*, Santo Stefano

same time, however, its central position on routes of communication and supply exposed it to other dangers. This explains the ferocity displayed by the imperial troops sent to Tuscany to restore the Medici to power in their siege and conquest of Empoli, put to the fire and sword by the mercenary forces of Vitellozzo Vitelli.

The destruction of part of the walls and the gates over the course of the 19th cent. and the damage caused during the last

Left, interior of Santo Stefano; right, Bernardo Rossellino, *Annunciation*, Museo della Collegiata

most important historic buildings, commencing with the Romanesque collegiate church of Sant'Andrea. Significantly dedicated to the patron saint of sailors, St. Andrew, it is thought to have been built on the site of a pagan temple. The building we see today is the fruit of a radical intervention at the beginning of the 18th cent., which also affected part of the fine façade of green and white marble, perhaps derived from the more famous models of San Miniato and the Florence Baptistery.

Many of the works that adorned the altars have been transferred to the adjoining Museo della Collegiata, one of the oldest in the region and one of the most important of its minor institutions. Alongside a significant collection of sculptures by Tino da Camaino, Mino da Fiesole and Bernardo and Antonio Rossellino,

it houses Della Robbian terracottas and paintings by Masolino, Agnolo Gaddi, Lorenzo Monaco, Filippo Lippi and Francesco Botticini.

The nearby Palazzo Ghibellino, which lost its original lines when it was rebuilt in the 16th cent., is important for its value as a historical testimony: former residence of the counts Guidi, it was the location in 1260 for the celebrated Ghibelline "parliament" referred to by Dante, at which Farinata degli Uberti fought to avoid the destruction of Florence after the battle of Montaperti.

Not far from the collegiate church stands the church of Santo Stefano, erected by the Augustinians from 1367 onward and completed in the early decades of the 15th cent. Over the course of repeated renovations, unfortunately, an important cycle by Masolino has been lost: all that remains today are two frescoes (*Saint Ivo and His Pupils, Madonna and Child*) and a number of *sinopie* with episodes from the Legend of the Cross.

In the nearby, ancient locality of Pontorme, which has now become a suburb of Empoli, it is possible to see two panels by Pontormo depicting *Saint Michael* and *Saint John the Evangelist* in San Michele Arcangelo. Recently restored and placed on the altar of the Crocefisso, they represent a fitting tribute paid by the celebrated painter to his birthplace.

Top, Filippo Lippi, *Madonna Enthroned with Angels and Saints*; left, Francesco Botticini, *Annunciation*. Museo della Collegiata

Right, Jacopo Pontormo, *Saint John the Evangelist*. San Michele Arcangelo

Seeing the Cities of Tuscany

So far we have said little about the cities, and we seem to see the crafty reader already lurking in ambush for the incautious author. For, to tell the truth, to deal with the history, landscape and economy of Tuscany in a few dozen pages is easy enough, and to describe roads and mountain passes, and mention churches and castles, is child's play. But giants of art and history such as Pisa and Lucca are hard to get round, and who on earth could deal in a few lines with Florence, about which whole libraries have been written?

Let me say at once that all guide-books – and I repeat that this is no such thing – no sooner turn to the big cities than they commit an error, if not a fraud: they make a calculation of the length of the visit in terms of hours or days. What does it mean to say that for Florence we need a week, while for Pisa three days is enough and for Pistoia only one? The problem of visiting cities can never be reduced to the number of churches and museums to be seen and the number of miles of footslogging involved. Everything depends on how one looks at a city, and what one asks of it. I know some scrupulous visitors, born travellers, who never go and see a historical monument or join a queue in front of a museum, but walk about the ancient town- centres apparently in a daydream, drinking in the atmosphere, dawdling in the cafés, or merely window-shopping. And then I know others who never leave a place without having counted every altar-piece and minutely scrutinized every fresco. A lifetime might be too short to get to know a city, while on the other hand a lightning glimpse, the

Ambrogio Lorenzetti,
*Effects of Good Government
in the City*, detail.
Palazzo Pubblico, Siena

space of an afternoon, might be enough. How can one say that the "right" amount of time to spend in front of Botticelli's *Primavera* is half-an-hour? Or that the Campo dei Miracoli at Pisa takes half a day? And then, what demands does one make of a city? To visit Florence thinking of the Divine Comedy and Foscolo's *Sepolcri* is not at all the same thing as to wander through its streets and squares thinking of Fattori and the painters of the Macchiaioli movement. Pistoia and Lucca make a completely different impression depending on whether one is a hunter of specimens of Romanesque architecture or an investigator of what remains of the Tuscany of Pinocchio. And before advising you to make a stop at Montecatini Terme (I advise a visit to Montecatini Alto in any case) I would have to find out not so much about the state of your liver and intestines (which are treated in those "Baths") as the level of your knowledge of the writings of D'Annunzio and Decadent literature, according to which you will find the town marvellous, insignificant or intolerable. Or else, what do you expect from a city such as Prato? Lovely memorials of the Middle Ages and the Renaissance, such as the 13th-century Castello dell'Imperatore or the 15th-century church of the Madonna delle Carceri? Or the sprawling open, faintly vulgar town full of rag-merchants fond of mutton and sweet rusks with almonds in them? Or else the capital of the "Industrial miracle," along with Biella and Reggio Emilia the city with the highest per capita income in Italy?

However, there is no answer to all these questions. Every town, whether it be one's birthplace or somewhere else, answers to a secret code, a spiritual gesture, a unique page in the book of life. One can know every stone of it, or never have seen it except through the medium of pictures and films, of words one has read or heard. A city resembles nothing but itself, and very often this changes from one visit to another. For this reason there are cities I will never tire of seeing, and others (equally dear to my heart) that I never wish to clap eyes on again.

From Florence to Arezzo through the Casentino

So one leaves Florence, and where does one go? I myself was born and bred on the south bank of the Arno, in the district of San Frediano, so for me the quickest way out would be Porta Romana and then the so-called "Via Senese" out past the Certosa (Charterhouse). From there on we either take the "Volterrana," which cuts across Valdipesa and Valdelsa, or else aim southwards towards Poggibonsi. Here we join the route of the old Via Francigena as far as Siena (though now, alas,

everyone roars down the *superstrada*). Coming from Florence, Volterra could well be the springboard for discovering the Maremma, while Siena would fulfil the same function for the Grossetano and the region of Monte Amiata. The fact is, however, that when I was a lad in the mid-fifties very few young people were lucky enough to have anything grander than a bicycle; and in any case, as far as I was concerned, I was a lone camper, given to taking buses and then getting around on foot. So for me the question

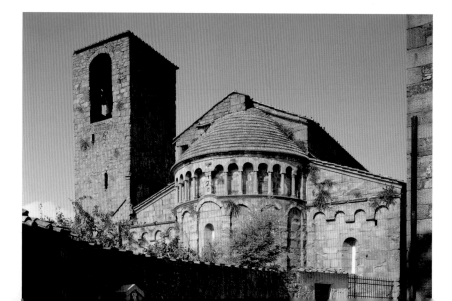

Facing page, top, a view of the monastery of Vallombrosa today and detail of its representation by Giovanni Stradano in a fresco in the Villa di Parugiano, near Prato

Above, capitals of the parish church of San Pietro a Gropina illustrated on facing page

Right, the ancient ambo of San Pietro a Gropina, probably from the Longobard era

The parish church of San Pietro di Romena with detail of the capitals

The castle of Romena and, right, the palace of the counts Guidi at Poppi

Bottom, the castle of Porciano

of "getting out of Florence" meant taking a bus as far as Pontassieve, so one sees that the journey eastwards was the one I enjoyed most. Then there came a wondrous climb up the S.S. 70, which in fact I still know every bend of, and every yard of wall. And up and up I went through places with magical names (Diacceto, Fonte all'Orso) until I reached the Passo della Consuma, the gateway to the Pratomagno. After that I might take the road south through the firwoods as far as Vallombrosa and its great monastery, its vivarium and its tame deer, up to the barren Secchieta that rises to over 1300 metres, and then come down through Saltino and Reggello into the upper Arno valley. Or

I could go on (still on the S.S. 70) past Romena with the ruins of its castle and its abbey, towards Castel San Niccolò and Strada, with the road running alongside the plain of Campaldino before arriving at Poppi and Bibbiena. When I was at school, to read Dante was to find myself climbing those roads again, breathing the resinous air of those woods, drinking the icy water of those springs. I well knew the castle of the Counts of Romena, where Maestro Adamo was persuaded to falsify the coinage, thus earning a truly uncomfortable place in hell. I had explored the banks of the Archiano where Buonconte di Montefeltro met his end (*Purgatorio* V), and was by no means unacquainted with the storms that arise

so suddenly in those parts (according to Dante the Devil raised a furious storm, such was his anger at being cheated of Buonconte's soul ...). I learnt to love old stories from *Novelle della Nonna* (Grandmother's Tales) by Emma Perodi, a sort of Casentino equivalent of the Brothers Grimm.

Anyway, this road (S.S. 70) is truly the gateway to the world of wonders. After Castel San Niccolò and before reaching Poppi (coming from Florence) we turn sharp left for Pratovecchio, for Stia, for the incredible fortress of Porciano near which, so legend has it, there lies buried a golden bell that is worth the rest of the Casentino put together. From there we may continue along a road of fearful beauty as far as the Passo della Calla, where it crosses into Romagna, or turn towards Monte Falterona and the source of the Arno. Otherwise, from Poppi it is easy to reach the hermitage of Camaldoli, in the midst of solemn forests, and from there go on to Badia Prataglia and the Passo dei Mandrioli, a few kilometers from Bagno di Romagna. Or again – and this is the route I particularly think

of as "mine" – from Bibbiena along the S.S. 208 to the Franciscan sanctuary of La Verna, the mountain where St. Francis received the stigmata, from which a steep climb through the forest takes one to the peak called "La Penna" at 1283 metres. From here we can gaze upon the Apennines and over Romagna, with Monte Falterona on one side and on the other Monte Fumaiolo, source of the Tiber.

Such is the Casentino: technically the region of the high reaches of the Arno, including the Alpe di Catenaia and stretching as far as the threshold of Arezzo and the edge of the Tiber valley. But for me it is the place most beloved of my soul, containing all the scents and flavours of my childhood and boyhood, the age at which choices and preferences are established for ever, and never change. And – since we know that only fools imagine that history is not made up of ifs and buts – I am perfectly certain that if I had been born a little further from the mountain of St. Francis, or the river of Buonconte da Montefeltro, my whole life would have been quite different.

**The sanctuary of La Verna
and its representation by Domenico
Ghirlandaio in a fresco in the
Florentine church of Santa Trinita**

Bibbiena

Today Bibbiena is an active economic center of the Casentino, whose offshoots extend right to the foot of the elevation on which its oldest part is perched.

Like many other Tuscan towns, it is of Etruscan origin, but no trace of that civilization remains and the earliest vestiges all date from after 1289, the year of the battle of Campaldino and the consequent destruction of Bibbiena by the Florentine Guelphs.

In the 14th cent. it became a fief of the powerful Tarlati family of Arezzo. After a long and turbulent period, during which it was occupied several times, it was definitively annexed by Florence.

The center of modern Bibbiena still has the appearance of a Renaissance town, embellished with fine aristocratic homes and churches.

The palace that stands out for its dimensions and architectural style is the one that used to be owned by Cardinal Bernardo Dovizi, powerful secretary to Leo X, the pope portrayed by Raphael in a famous picture in the Galleria Palatina (Florence). Dovizi was the author of a play, *La Calandria*, that was often performed in the 16th cent.

Opposite the palace stands the complex of San Lorenzo, consisting of the 15th-cent. church and a porticoed cloister of later date. Inside are two large Della Robbian altarpieces donated to the friars by Cardinal Dovizi himself.

In the upper part of the old town we find the parish church of Santi Ippolito e Donato, containing several interesting panels including a triptych by Bicci di Lorenzo and a beautiful *Madonna and Child* by Arcangelo di Cola da Camerino. Not far off is the oratory of San Francesco, a refined example of baroque architecture that has few parallels elsewhere in the region.

Luca della Robbia the Younger, *Adoration of the Shepherds.* San Lorenzo

Bicci di Lorenzo, *Madonna Enthroned with Saints* with two scenes from the predella. Santi Ippolito e Donato

Arezzo

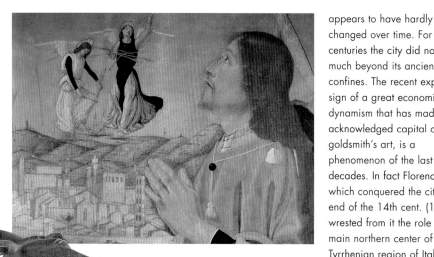

Arezzo first appears in history as the most important Etruscan center of the northern part of the region, known to the Romans as Arretium. Situated in the shelter of the Apennines and close to the sources of the Arno and the Tiber, at the intersection of different geographical areas, the city has come under a variety of cultural influences.

The origins of Arezzo's name, like the names of numerous minor centers in its province, date from at least the second millennium BC. This reflects a cultural continuity unique in Italy and in Europe, stretching back beyond the Etruscan civilization of which Arezzo was a wealthy *polis* famous for its pottery and production of metal. "Arretine" pots made their way throughout the classical world and beyond, reaching as far as India.

Its characteristic fan-shaped layout, opening onto the western side of the hill on which stands the cathedral, appears to have hardly changed over time. For centuries the city did not grow much beyond its ancient confines. The recent expansion, sign of a great economic dynamism that has made it the acknowledged capital of the goldsmith's art, is a phenomenon of the last few decades. In fact Florence, which conquered the city at the end of the 14th cent. (1384), wrested from it the role of the main northern center of the Tyrrhenian region of Italy. The submission to Florence came at the end of a period of frenzied struggle that was marked by the battle of Campaldino (near Poppi) in 1289, made famous by Dante Alighieri who was an exile in the Casentino, and then by quarrels between the city's factions that saw the predominance of the powerful Tarlati family.

There followed a long period of decline, reflected in a marked drop in population and a progressive impoverishment of the city's art and culture. It was at this time, between 1549 and 1568, that alterations were made to the medieval walls, which were fortified on the orders of Cosimo I de' Medici, who showed a great interest in the defensive system of the new state. The Fortezza Medicea on the top of the hill also dates from this period. It was during the work of

fortification that the two greatest masterpieces of Etruscan bronze sculpture to be found in Arezzo came to light, the *Minerva* and the *Chimera*, both now in the Museo Archeologico of Florence.

The main street, the picturesque Corso Italia, once known as the Via del Borgo Maestro, runs right through the city. It is lined by the most interesting architectural features of the entire urban fabric.

The main square, or Piazza Grande, once the city's forum, is dignified by the Loggia built by Giorgio Vasari, the grand-ducal architect *par excellence* and a native of Arezzo. In front of it stands the Palazzo della Fraternìta dei Laici, commenced in the 14th cent. by Baldino di Cino and Niccolò di Francesco and finished two centuries later.

At the highest point of the

Top, Bartolomeo della Gatta, *Saint Roch Interceding on Behalf of the City of Arezzo*, detail of the city. Museo d'Arte Medievale e Moderna

Above, bronze group from the end of the 5th cent. BC representing the *Plowman of Arezzo*. Museo Etrusco di Villa Giulia, Rome; below, *bronzes* from the 6th cent. BC. Museo Archeologico, Arezzo

Left, bronze from the first half of the 4th cent. BC representing *The Chimera*, detail. Museo Archeologico, Florence

city, the ancient Poggio di San Donato, stands the cathedral, built from 1277 onward on the site of the Benedictine church of San Pietro Maggiore on the initiative of Bishop Guglielmino degli Ubertini. The imposing building we see today, however, is the culmination of a long process of construction that lasted right up until the beginning of the 16th cent., while the façade dates from the 20th. The splendid stained-glass windows by the Frenchman Guillaume de Marcillat, who also built the flight of steps leading up to the building, date from 1530. Among the works of art it contains it is worth singling out the *Tomb of Pope Gregory X*; the *Tomb of Saint Donatus*, the work of Sienese

and Florentine craftsmen; the *Cenotaph of Bishop Tarlati* by Agostino di Giovanni and Agnolo di Ventura; and Piero della Francesca's fresco of *Mary Magdalene*.

Adjoining the cathedral is the Museo Diocesano di Arte Sacra, whose treasures include several wooden crucifixes from the cathedral and works by local painters.

The noblest building in the city for its antiquity and for the history to which it bears witness is the parish church of Santa Maria. Known simply as the Pieve, its front faces onto the Corso and its apse onto Piazza Grande. The façade, of the Pisan-Luccan type, dates from the beginning of the 13th cent. (1216), although the building

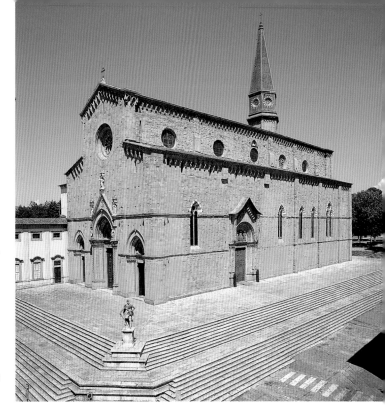

has not escaped heavy-handed alterations and subsequent restorations right up to the last century. The sculptural reliefs of great quality are the work of anonymous artists, although the

The cathedral and, bottom, the *Tomb of Saint Donatus*

name of a certain Marchionne has been put forward for the architrave and lunette of the main portal. The suggestive interior in the Romanesque style houses a marble bas-relief representing the *Epiphany* and the celebrated polyptych with the *Madonna and Saints* painted (1320) by Pietro Lorenzetti for Bishop Tarlati.

The large church of San Domenico dates from the 13th cent. It was commenced in 1275 and Vasari claims it to be the work of Nicola Pisano. Inside there are a number of significant frescoes of the 14th-century Arezzo school, but by far the most important work, and one of the finest in the city, is an early *Crucifix* by Cimabue (*c.* 1260), recently restored.

The most frequently visited of Arezzo's churches is without doubt San Francesco, in the square of the same name, thanks to the famous cycle of paintings by Piero della Francesca, now again visible in their original splendor after patient restoration work.

Begun in the 13th cent., the church was completed by Fra Giovanni da Pistoia the following century. The long

Exterior and interior of the "Pieve"
with detail of the polyptych of
Pietro Lorenzetti depicting the
Madonna and Child with Saints

Facing page, view of the left-hand
aisle of the cathedral and detail
of Piero della Francesca's
Mary Magdalene

Cimabue, *Crucifix*. San Domenico

nave was enriched over the course of the 14th and 15th cent. by numerous chapels, tabernacles and wall paintings of considerable artistic quality commissioned by the city's wealthy families. One of these, the Bacci, entrusted (1457) Bicci di Lorenzo with the task of frescoing the Main Chapel, or choir, with the *Legend of the True Cross*, an undertaking that, on Bicci's death, was continued and completed by Piero. The cycle of frescoes is unanimously regarded as one of the masterpieces of European Renaissance painting.

Among Arezzo's many other churches it is worth mentioning Santa Maria in Gradi, Santissima Annunziata, the Badia and, just outside the city walls, Santa Maria delle Grazie, characterized by an

extremely elegant Renaissance colonnade (1478-82) by Benedetto da Maiano.

Arezzo also boasts a number of remarkable civil monuments. The Palazzo del Podestà or Palazzo Pretorio of the 14th-15th cent., now the seat of the Biblioteca Civica; the towered and battlemented Palazzo Comunale, formerly Palazzo dei Priori, dating from 1333 but with subsequent alterations right up to the radical restorations of the 20th cent.; the Casa del Petrarca, the house in which the poet Petrarch was born, built between the 15th and 16th cent. and now the seat of the Accademia Petrarca di Lettere, Arti e Scienze. The eclectic Giorgio Vasari, painter, architect and writer, was also born in Arezzo in 1511. He bought a house in Borgo di San Vito (Via XX Settembre), that has

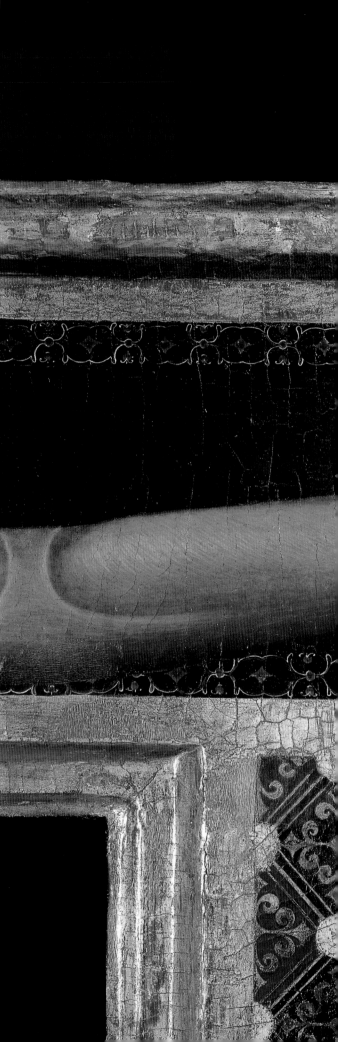

Piazza Grande with the apse of the "Pieve" and the Palazzo della Fraternita dei Laici

Left, medieval houses on Piazza Grande and a view of the Palazzo Comunale on Piazza della Libertà

now been turned into a museum and an archive of precious documents from the time.

Next to the ruins of the Roman amphitheater stands the Museo Archeologico, housing interesting finds from the Etrusco-Roman period. Finally, the Palazzo Bruni-Ciocchi, a building in elegant renaissance style also known as the Palazzo della Dogana, houses the Museo Statale di Arte Medievale e Moderna: it contains important collections of majolica ware, paintings and sculptures testifying to the vitality of the city's art.

Arezzo is today a city of goldsmiths and antiquarians. The monthly Antique Fair is the most important in Italy. The revival of the medieval tradition of the "Giostra del Saracino," lastly, attracts numerous tourists from Italy and from abroad.

Andrea di Nerio, *Annunciation.* Museo Diocesano

Right, Bartolomeo della Gatta, *Saint Roch in front of the Palazzo della Fraternita dei Laici.* Museo d'Arte Medievale e Moderna

Facing page, the Cappella Maggiore in San Francesco with Piero della Francesca's *Scenes from the Legend of the True Cross*

175

Valtiberina and Valdichiana

There are several ways of getting to Arezzo. Of course there is the Autostrada del Sole, which passes through the Valdarno and (from Incisa on) runs parallel to the S.S. 69. This latter route is far more advisable for anyone who has the time or the wish to look around the upper Valdarno, where the river is cleaner and – between Levane and Ponte a Buriano – is inclined to dawdle in twists and turns and pools. Or you can get to Arezzo by the splendid S.S. 70, which also (after Bibbiena) follows the higher reaches of the Arno.

The "Aretino," or area of Arezzo, is usually underrated by travellers in Tuscany.

They pay visits to Arezzo itself, and perhaps Anghiari, Monterchi and San Sepolcro on account of Piero della Francesca, but rarely venture east of the *superstrada* that crosses the Val Tiberina on its way over from Ravenna. In other words no one ever goes to that extraordinary enclave of Tuscany overlooked by the Alpe della Luna and wedged in between Romagna, the Marche and Umbria. This is a real "borderland" which provides a meeting-place for the Florentine *pietra serena*, the red brick of Umbria, and the

Two views of Anghiari and, on facing page, Piero della Francesca, *Madonna del Parto*, detail. Monterchi

pale pink or pinky-grey brick of Romagna and the Marche. It is a region where the harshness of the Apennines, as well as the cuisine, already, has the flavour of the Adriatic.

Certainly, setting out from Arezzo, the tourist less accustomed to leaving the beaten track, or more short of time, might be more attracted southwards, towards the (now reclaimed) lands of the Valdichiana, of Castiglion Fiorentino, and above all the beautiful, mystical town of Cortona, from where he will have a unique view over Lake Trasimeno, and over the southern Sienese lands as far as the hills of Sinalunga, Torrita and Chianciano. In Cortona he will visit the Palazzo Comunale, the Palazzo Pretorio, the Etruscan Museum, the Duomo and the Diocesan Museum which has Fra Angelico's *Annunciation*. If he has any breath left in his body he will clamber up to the high town, and the acropolis now occupied by the Neo-Gothic sanctuary of Santa Margherita.

Not far from the town he will admire the abbey of Farneta, partly ruined; dating from the 9th-10th centuries, this is the oldest early Romanesque church in the Aretino, while its crypt is one of the most incredible in the whole

Top, the Chiana Valley from Cortona looking toward Lake Trasimeno; left, the Madonna del Calcinaio

Two views of Castiglion Fiorentino;
bottom, the castle of Montecchio
Vesponi

of Christendom. But before getting to Cortona and immersing himself in its wonders, our traveller will have done well to spare at least a glance at Castiglion Fiorentino (well-preserved mediaeval centre, with some interesting Renaissance buildings), and at the castle of Montecchio Vesponi, once the feudal property of the 14th-century English military adventurer (*condottiero*) Sir John Hawkwood, known in Italy as Giovanni Acuto. If our traveller is a crafty one he will be led to suspect that it is just a trifle too mediaeval to be true, with all those battlements and turrets. It could have been copied from a fresco by Lorenzetti, and yet... this time it is not a Neo-Gothic folly.

Sansepolcro

Tradition has it that two pilgrims on their way back from the Holy Land in the early decades of the 10th cent. stopped over in the upper valley of the Tiber, where, on divine instructions, they built a chapel to house the holy relics they had brought from Jerusalem. The Borgo del Santo Sepolcro, or "Burg of the Holy Sepulcher," also known as "New Jerusalem," grew up around this chapel.

More reliable documentary references tell us of the existence, shortly after the year 1000, of a Benedictine monastery dedicated to the Holy Sepulcher that formed the nucleus of the city.

In 1269 Sansepolcro became a free commune but was soon forced to defend its freedom against Perugia and Arezzo, perhaps as a consequence of its excellent position on the fringes of a fertile valley watered by the Tiber. Its checkered history as an independent entity was brought to an end when it was sold (1441) by Pope Eugenius IV to

Piero della Francesca, *Polyptych of the Misericordia* and detail on facing page. Museo Civico

Top left, Anonymous artist from the first half of the 16th cent., *Pilgrimage of the Company of the Crucifix to Loreto*, detail with Sansepolcro. Museo Civico

Top right, the cathedral and, above, the Palazzo delle Laudi

Florence, and from then on it was part of the Florentine state.

The Medici, and Cosimo I in particular, took steps to reinforce the defensive walls, which were equipped with embrasures by Buontalenti and the fortress designed by Giuliano da Sangallo. But Medicean rule also resulted in a frenzy of building that enriched the city with monumental townhouses that can still be seen today. Sansepolcro has come down to our own time with its appearance virtually unchanged, as is only fitting for the birthplace of Piero della Francesca, Matteo di Giovanni, Santi di Tito and the mathematician Luca Pacioli.

Above, Piero della Francesca, *Saint Julian*; left, *Resurrection* and, below, detail. Museo Civico

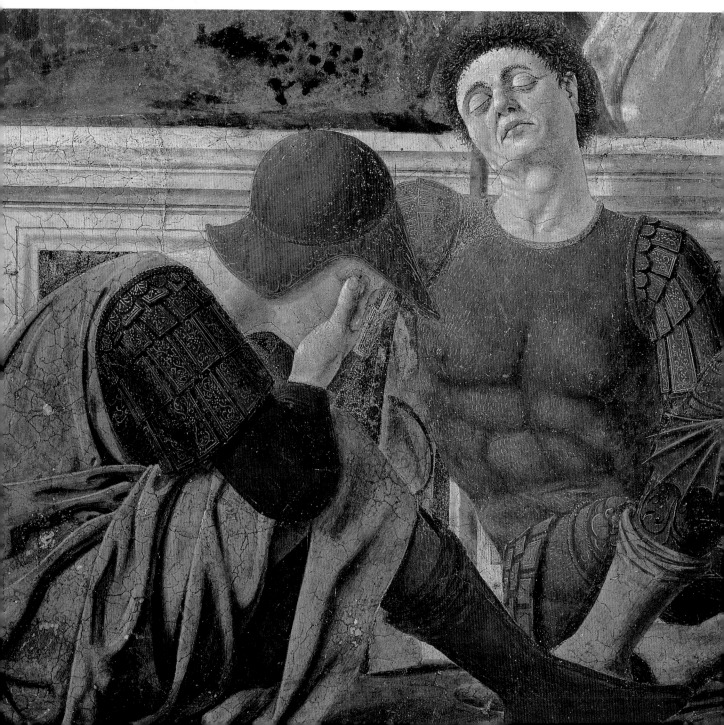

The Romanesque-Gothic cathedral is the result of a series of reconstructions that lasted right up until the restoration work carried out last century, so that nothing remains of the original 11th-cent. abbey. The interior of the church is still 13th-cent. in style. It houses fine works by Bartolomeo della Gatta., Perugino and Santi di Tito. The *Holy Face*, an ancient wooden crucifix of Oriental origin and uncertain date, is particularly attractive. Next to the cathedral stands the Palazzo delle Laudi, with a Mannerist façade from the end of the 16th cent., which was once the seat of the confraternity of the same name and today houses the city hall.

Only the exterior of the church of San Francesco with its squat campanile retains the appearance of its mendicant origins (late 13th cent.), as the interior was completely rebuilt in the 18th cent. The adjoining monastery was the home of the great mathematician Luca Pacioli, pupil of Piero della Francesca.

Of the many other religious buildings located inside the city walls, it is worth mentioning Santa Chiara, the former church of the Augustinian monastery that has now been restored and is used as an auditorium; Santa Maria delle Grazie, with an interesting carved ceiling from the end of the 16th cent.; San Rocco and the oratory of the Compagnia del Crocifisso underneath, frescoed with *Scenes from the Passion*; and San Lorenzo which houses Rosso Fiorentino's

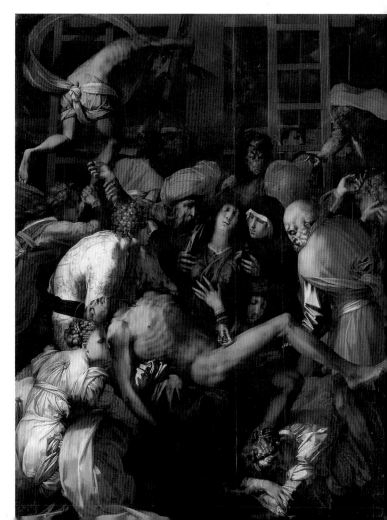

Jacopo Pontormo, *Saint Quentin*. Museo Civico; below, Rosso Fiorentino, *Deposition*. San Lorenzo

dramatic *Deposition*.

A fine example of 15th-cent. architecture that has subsequently been restructured is the Casa di Piero della Francesca, home of the painter and today seat of the foundation for Renaissance studies and research of the same name. Those masterpieces of the great artist still present in Sansepolcro (*Madonna della Misericordia, Resurrection, Saint Julian*) can be seen instead in the important Museo Civico situated in the old (13th-14th cent.) Palazzo Comunale. They are flanked by works by Matteo di Giovanni, Luca Signorelli, Santi di Tito, Pontormo and Raffaellino del Colle.

Matteo di Giovanni, *Assumption of the Virgin*. Church of the Servites; left, scene from the predella with the *Dance of Salome*. Museo Civico

Cortona

An old tradition makes Cortona the most ancient city in Italy, contemporary with Troy. And in fact archeologists have been making incredible finds in Cortona for centuries.

An ancient center of the Umbrians, from the 8th cent. BC onward it was one of the most important Etruscan *poleis*, whose growth was rooted in the flourishing agriculture of the Val di Chiana below. In fact the burial mounds of the wealthy families of Cortona, known popularly as "melons," have yielded artistic and

historical treasures of enormous value. Subsequently entering the orbit of Rome (mid-5th cent. BC) and becoming its ally, Cortona continued to prosper up until the time of the barbarian invasions.

It did not experience a revival until many centuries later, when it managed to shake off the influence of Perugia and set itself up as a free commune at the beginning

Top, Francesco Signorelli, *Madonna with Saints*, detail with Cortona. Museo dell'Accademia Etrusca

The Palazzo Comunale; right, Via Jannelli with overhanging medieval houses

of the 13th cent. After a few decades, however, it was occupied by the forces of Arezzo. With the aid of Siena, it eventually broke away from the influence of the bishops of Arezzo, becoming an independent episcopal see and then a signoria of the Casali family until it was acquired by Florence in 1411. From that moment on the city's historical and political destiny, apart from a few brief interludes, was closely bound up with that of the Grand Duchy of Tuscany.

Fortunately Cortona was

spared from bombing in 1944 and this fact, combined with its geographical location on a steep spur of the Alta di San Egidio, has preserved the city from unchecked development, contributing to the conservation of its rich urban fabric studded with austere townhouses and religious buildings. There are also numerous works of art left by some of its most illustrious citizens, among whom it is sufficient to recall Luca Signorelli, Pietro da Cortona and, in more recent times, Gino Severini.

The cathedral, which dominates the Piazza del Duomo, was built on the ruins of a Romanesque parish church of the 11th-13th cent., of which some remains can still be seen on the façade. Under the portico on the right-hand side, added in the 16th cent., there

is a portal carved by Cristofanello, while the left-hand side abuts onto the Etruscan walls. Taken as a whole, it is the noblest and oldest place of worship in Cortona. The interior, filled with works of art, is characterized by the tunnel vault of the nave and the stone columns reminiscent of Brunelleschi.

In front of the cathedral stands the Museo Diocesano, part of which is housed in the ancient church of Il Gesù and the frescoed oratory underneath. The museum displays church ornaments and vestments and paintings from the cathedral and various churches in the diocese. The best-known work is Fra Angelico's *Annunciation*. In addition, there are important panels by Pietro Lorenzetti, Sassetta, Bartolomeo della Gatta and Luca Signorelli and a precious Roman sarcophagus representing *The Battle between Dionysus and the Amazons*.

The city's other principal museum is the Accademia Etrusca, established by a group of archeologists in 1727 and founded on the donation of the

The courtyard of Palazzo Casali; below, views of the Biblioteca dell'Accademia Etrusca and one of the rooms in the library

abbé Baldelli's collection. Over time the Accademia has been enriched by bequests and donations and today boasts a large number of Etruscan and Roman antiquities, old medals and paintings from the 12th to 18th century, as well as the Saletta Severini with works donated by the artist. It has become a cultural point of reference of more than local significance. The academy is housed in the Palazzo Casali, the former residence of the lords of Cortona: dating from the 13th-14th cent., it has a Mannerist façade built at the beginning of the 17th.

Among the city's numerous churches it is worth singling out San Domenico, San Francesco and San Nicolò, along with the basilica of Santa Margherita: in a dominant position, the latter is celebrated as the place where the venerated St. Margaret of Cortona underwent her dramatic conversion, but in reality was constructed in a neo-medieval style in the middle of the 19th cent. on the site of an oratory where the saint had died. But the most evocative religious building is undoubtedly Santa Maria delle Grazie, or del Calcinaio, located just outside the city and

notable for its harmonious simplicity. Built in the Renaissance manner by Francesco di Giorgio Martini, its purity of line and sobriety of decoration are derived from the teachings of Leon Battista Alberti and Brunelleschi.

From its illustrious past, Cortona also preserves sections of the massive ring of Etruscan walls: dating from the 4th-5th cent. BC and extending for about three kilometers, the walls were partially rebuilt in the 13th cent. after the destruction wrought by Arezzo and culminate in the Fortezza del Girifalco, erected in the middle of the 16th cent. by Cosimo I for defensive purposes.

A tour of the city's archeological sites cannot fail to include a visit to the Etruscan necropolises located near the hamlet of Camucìa, where two large tumuli known as the "Meloni del Sodo" can be seen. One of them still has its altar with sculptural decorations. Not far away, but from a later period, stands the tomb called the Tanella di Pitagora.

Above, Luca Signorelli, *Adoration of the Shepherds.* Museo dell'Accademia Etrusca; top right, Pietro Lorenzetti, *Crucifix.* Museo Diocesano

Left, Bartolomeo della Gatta, *Assumption;* below, Roman sarcophagus from the 2nd cent. AD with the *Combat between Dionysus and the Amazons.* Museo Diocesano

Facing page, Fra Angelico, *Annunciation,* detail. Museo Diocesano

The Volterrano and the Coast

From Cortona and the Valdichiana one might be tempt- ed to make one's way towards the Valdorcia, Monte Amiata and even Siena. Historically speaking, this would be a plausible itinerary, for Arezzo and Siena fought until the late Middle Ages (first battles of words over the borders of dioceses, and then good hearty stuff with swords) to establish their respective areas of influence in this zone, where there is a strong flavour of nearby Umbria and northern Lazio. But "official" history and tourist brochures gang up lawlessly to link the name of Siena with that of Florence, and with their two bones of contention, Valdel- sa and Chianti. And we intend to follow their example.

But not before turning our eyes yet again to the south-west, if we start out from Florence. I am a Florentine who lives on the Porta Romana side of the city, and I of- ten have to go to Siena. Well sometimes, when I get to Galluzzo, I take the right fork at the signpost for Volterra and the detour along the fierce bends of the Gore (night- mare of the amateur cyclists of the "Tour of Tuscany"). Even leaving aside its memories of the Etruscans, and in- deed of Gabriele d'Annunzio, Volterra is one of the most beautiful cities in the whole of Tuscany, and this road is the most superb way of getting there.

As usual, of course, there is the short cut for the tourist

Panorama of the cliffs in the vicinity of Volterra

Facing page, top, the Romanesque parish church of San Giovanni at Campiglia Marittima; bottom, the gulf of Baratti from Populonia

in a hurry. From Florence one can take the *superstrada* for Siena and pull off at Colle di Val d'Elsa (the upper town of which is well worth a leisurely visit) and then take the S.S. 68. Along this we might think of making a few stops or detour, for example at the 15th-century church of Santa Maria delle Grazie, at Casole d'Elsa, at Mensano (with its fine church of San Giovanni Battista), at Radicondoli, and at San Donato di San Gimignano, with its 11th-12th century Romanesque parish church. The road then rises to Volterra, and on its way down offers an extraordinary panorama of cliffs and eroded steeps all the way to the sea.

Dominated by the vast bulk of its fortress, Volterra boasts a number of fine mediaeval monuments, such as the Palazzo dei Priori, the Duomo, the Baptistery, the 13th-century church of San Francesco, and many "tower-houses" of the kind so characteristic of the factious family rivalries of the Middle Ages. There are also Roman remains such as the Baths and the Theatre, and the Guarnacci Museum with its famous collection of Eruscan artefacts.

Once we reach Saline di Volterra we many take various roads towards the coast. The most direct is certainly the S.S. 68, which follows the valley of the Cecina and af-

retains a certain rough-hewn charm. But it would be wiser to turn south after Saline di Volterra and follow the windy S.S. 439 to Follonica, the seaside resort in the exact centre of the gulf named after it, which ends with the two promontories of Piombino to the north and Punta Ala to the south. This S.S. 439 is a bit of a grind to drive, but is lovely, and will take the traveller through the Colline Metallifere with their woods and their mines (some of which are still working) and the towns of Pomarance with its Etruscan associations and Larderello with its borax-bearing fumaroles. Short-

ter a few dozen kilometers leads to the town of that name at the mouth of the river. It is a seaside resort of some importance, immediately south of the cliff of the Livornese, with its rocky coast and the beaches (once fashionable) of Calafuria, Quercianella and Castiglioncello. The sandy coast to the south of Castiglioncello, where we find Vada, Cecina itself, Bibbona, San Vincenzo and Riva degli Etruschi, is perhaps a little less sought-after, and in the last few years has lost much of its wild "Maremman" quality. All the same, the road that forks left from the S.S. 68 at Ponteginori, and joins the Via Aurelia after the town of Bibbona (with its sanctuary dedicated to the Virgin) still

ly before reaching the coast, in a landscape full of folds and wrinkles, we come to Massa Marittima, with a splendid Romanesque cathedral set in an irregularly-shaped piazza that creates an impressive scenario. This town, which has a wealth of mediaeval associations, is the "historic capital" of the Tuscan mining zone. But if our traveller, on arriving in the heart of the Colline Metallifere, should discover that he is panting to get to the sea, then he can turn right after Lardarello and reach the Tyrrhenian at Castagneto Carducci, skirting the hills and pinewoods that once belonged to the noble Pisan Gherardesca clan and (if he has had an Italian education) sip-

Top, the picturesque cloister of the abbey of Torri

The abbey of San Galgano and, on facing page, a view of the transept

ping at memories of the poet Carducci, who celebrated a Maremma that perhaps no longer exists.

Another way of getting to Follonica from Colle di Val d'Elsa, or even from Siena, is to pass through the valley of the Merse. This river, which rises in the Colline Metallifere not far from Montieri, joins the right hand side of the Ombrone after a truly tortuous course through a landscape that is sometimes barren, sometimes gladdened with evergreen scrub and fields of wheat. From Colle we come by way of the S.S. 541, which follows the river Elsa for a while and then turns south as far as Le Cetine. From there, bearing right in a south-westerly direction, we get to the impressive Gothic ruins of the abbey of San Galgano and the nearby chapel of Montesiepi, where one can see the sword which (according to the legend) this saint thrust into a rock at the moment of his conversion. From San Galgano we may take the route via Prata (S.S. 441) to Massa Marittima, or else continue south towards Grosseto through Roccastrada and Montepescali. Rather grim towns, these, closed in on themselves in a barren, isolated landscape. They have an air of

southern Italy, and few of those scattered farms and tiny villages that go to make up what we think of as the "classic" landscape of Tuscany.

These are the roads that lead to the coast, and inevitably "flow" at various points into the Via Aurelia. Here, at least if we are south of the Piombino promontory, we breath the aroma of what is left of the Maremma, in the "oases" created by the nature reserves of the Monti dell'Uccellina, the lagoon of Orbetello that links the coastline to Monte Argentario, and the Lago di Burano which is the last protected remnant of the ancient marshes, and

Top left, the coast in the vicinity of the tower of Calafuria near Livorno; right, aerial view of the island of Giannutri

Castiglione della Pescaia with its harbor-canal

the borderland between the Maremma of Tuscany and of Lazio. In the Maremma there is a hard, bitter quarrel going on between tourism and nature, suspended as it were between open warfare and symbiosis; but it does seem that in the last few years the tourist trade has become more aware and the property speculators more mature, so that they realize that the "development" of the Tyrrhenian shoreline also means the preservation of nature, rather than its destruction.

From Livorno there are ferries to Gorgona, Capraia and Elba. From Piombino they run to Elba whence (from Porto Azzurro) we can also reach Pianosa. Boats run from Porto Santo Stefano to Giglio and Giannutri. There are no services to the uninhabited "Formiche di Grosseto," which lie out to sea opposite the Monti dell'Uccellina, and none for Montecristo, which has been turned into a nature reserve. It is indeed a pleasure to make a cruise through that world of islands in the Tuscan archipelago. It is a world of light, an archaic world, suspended between the fine wines of Elba and the water-shortage in Giannutri, and in which the Mediterranean still seems intact, and clean, glorying in a light and colour that are still "Homeric."

Volterra

For centuries Volterra has dominated the vast and bleak landscape of the *balze*, or "crags," from the top of the massive elevation that divides the valleys of the Era and the Cecina, a long way from major routes of

communication and yet no less important for that.

The wealth of the Etruscan city of Velathri stemmed essentially from the riches of the earth on which it stood (copper, salt, alabaster quarries), rather than from the fertility of the countryside, and from the ability to trade its products through control of the ports of Populonia and Vada Volaterrana (now San Gaetano di Vada). We know too that in the 7th cent. BC Volterra had attained a position of great importance in the Etruscan confederation of twelve cities known as the Dodecapolis and extended its sway from the Arno to

Vetulonia and Roselle and from Arezzo and Chiusi to the Island of Elba. Its urban agglomeration, enclosed by a massive ring of walls stretching for over seven kilometers, had a population of around 25,000, a number that it would never again be capable of reaching.

Inevitably, as for the rest of

Above, the keeps of the Fortezza Medicea; left, the tower-houses of the Buomparenti

Bottom, Piazza dei Priori

when, with the defeat of the Longobards and the alliance between the Church and the Carolingian empire, the bishops began to assume a political role of primary importance (9th-10th cent.), clashing first with the nobility and subsequently with the emerging class of "burghers," who had organized themselves into a free commune. The growing need for defense

against the appetite of outsiders was met with a new ring of walls, partly built onto the earlier Etruscan-Roman ones, from which the beautiful gate known as the "Arco Etrusco" has survived. The walls were constructed over the course of the 13th cent. and have come down to us intact. The imposing fortress that greets visitors arriving from the east is to a great extent a legacy of Medici

rule, built by Lorenzo the Magnificent between 1472 and 1475 onto the preexisting bastion.

From the second half of the 14th cent. Volterra entered more or less covertly into the orbit of Florence, submitting completely in 1472.

Signs of a revival in the Volterran economy would come in the 19th cent. under the Lorraine, but it is only in the last

Etruria, decline set in at Volterra too and its capitulation, according to the historian Titus Livius, came in 298 BC following the defeat that the Romans inflicted on its inhabitants. The city became part of the Italic Confederation with the Latin name of Volaterrae and did not obtain Roman citizenship until 90 BC.

This was followed by the dark centuries of the barbarian invasions, which wrought havoc and destruction until the time

few decades that Volterra has gained a new lease of life thanks to the widespread interest in Tuscan centers of the minor arts. From this point of view the city has all the necessary requisites: a well-preserved urban fabric, with several first-rate museums, set in a landscape of great charm.

The focal point of life in the city today is still Piazza dei Priori, where the principal medieval buildings are concentrated, commencing with Palazzo dei Priori, constructed between 1208 and 1254 and considered the oldest city hall in Tuscany. On the opposite side of the square stands a complex of buildings of 13th-cent. origin, much restored, which make up the Palazzo Pretorio, the former residence

The exterior and the interior of the cathedral

Right, the baptistery

of the Capitano del Popolo, or commander of the local militia. Other interesting buildings such as those of the Monte Pio, the Palazzo Incontri and the Palazzo Vescovile, partly reconstructed in their original medieval style, complete the perimeter of the square.

Alongside the Palazzo dei Priori stretches the flank of the cathedral, constructed out of black and white marble in the Pisan style, while its front faces

Wooden group representing the *Deposition*. Cathedral

Votive bronze of the 3rd cent. BC called the *Shadow of the Evening*. Museo Guarnacci

onto Piazza San Giovanni. Dedicated to Our Lady of the Assumption, it was built in 1120 on the site of an early Christian church and then renovated around the middle of the 13th cent. as part of the work of enlargement attributed by Vasari to Nicola Pisano. The interior, restructured in the 16th cent., is embellished with various works of art, including a wooden *Deposition* of the 13th cent. and a pulpit reassembled in the 17th cent. out of ancient panels.

In front of the cathedral stands the octagonal Baptistery, which may date from the 11th cent. but was certainly subjected to modifications later (end of the 13th cent.), when its façade was clad with white and green marble. It houses a

fine baptismal font carved by Andrea Sansovino in 1502.

Among the numerous religious buildings it is worth singling out San Francesco, with the attached chapel of the Croce di Giorno, frescoed in its entirety with the *Legend of the Holy Cross* by Cenni di Francesco (1410), and San Girolamo, built in the middle of the 15th cent., perhaps to a design by Michelozzo. The abbey of Santi Giusto e Clemente, constructed outside the city around 1030, was first damaged by an earthquake (1846) and then affected by the erosion that is inexorably eating into the sides of the hill on which Volterra stands and that has molded the surrounding landscape into the so-called *balze*.

The prestigious civic museums are entrusted with the task of preserving the memory of the city's past. In the first place the Museo Guarnacci, which is

one of the oldest museums in Europe, created in 1761 by the abbé Guarnacci, a scholar who donated to the city the archeological collection he had assembled over years of study and research, along with the over 50,000 volumes in his library. Subsequent acquisitions and excavations have augmented the materials on show today in the museum's thirty-eight rooms, which include an unrivalled collection of cinerary urns in tufa, terracotta and alabaster.

The Museo Diocesano is located in the Palazzo Vescovile, while the Pinacoteca Civica occupies the rooms of the beautiful Palazzo Minucci-Solaini, traditionally attributed to Antonio da Sangallo the Elder.

Top, gold earrings from the 4th-3rd cent. BC.; right, 3rd-cent. bronze mirror with the *Dioscuri*. Museo Guarnacci

Below, small Etruscan urn from the 2nd cent. BC with lid carved in the shape of a woman, representing *Actaeon Devoured by His Dogs*. Museo Guarnacci

Among the many pictures that offer an exhaustive survey of Tuscan painting from the 13th to the 17th cent., the large panel by Rosso Fiorentino depicting the *Deposition from the Cross* takes pride of place.

Abutting onto the eastern side of the medieval walls are the imposing remains of the theater (end of 1st cent. BC) and the later baths (4th cent. AD), the only surviving relics of the great Roman city.

Top left, Rosso Fiorentino, *Madonna Enthroned between Two Saints.* Museo Diocesano; right, Domenico Ghirlandaio, *The Redeemer and Saints.* Pinacoteca Civica

Above, Benvenuto di Giovanni, predella with the *Marriage of the Virgin.* Pinacoteca Civica

From the left, Pieter de Witte, *Deposition;* Rosso Fiorentino, *Deposition from the Cross* and detail on facing page. Pinacoteca Civica

Massa Marittima

In the 19th cent. there was a saying in the Maremma: "*Massa, saluta e passa*," ("Massa, say hello and move on.") In previous centuries, in fact, malaria had progressively depopulated the city until it had no more than a few hundred inhabitants in the last years of Medici rule. Revival came under the Lorraine, who promoted major works of reclamation throughout the area, as well as providing incentives for the mining industry. And yet the site on which it stands, protected from the frequent Saracen raids from the sea, had been coveted since ancient times for its valuable mineral deposits. Remains of an important settlement from the Etruscan period linked to mining activity

The cathedral of San Cerbone

were found in the early decades of the 20th cent. We know too that Massa Marittima acquired increasing importance in the Longobard era, in parallel to the decline of the ancient Etruscan maritime centers of Vetulonia and Populonia. In particular, it was the destruction of the latter by Saracen pirates that favored Massa's promotion to an episcopal see before the year 1000.

Coming under the political influence of Pisa over the course of the 12th cent., it was able to proclaim itself a free city in 1225, going so far as to coin its own money in the most flourishing period of its

Right, the baptismal font

Below, Goro di Gregorio, *Tomb of Saint Cerbo* with details of the decoration

economy. It also drew up the first mining charter in Europe. However, the city was unable to stand up to Siena, which in 1337 subjugated it definitively. Under Sienese rule, Massa saw the enlargement of the Palazzo Comunale and the completion of the walls with the Cassero or keep, but entered a phase of economic decline to which an outbreak of the plague (1348), malaria and the cessation of mining activity contributed.

As its inhabitants proudly affirm today, the city's finest monument is the historic center as a whole. It is divided into two distinct parts, Massa Vecchia, of Romanesque character, which grew up around the symbols of religious and civil power, and Massa

Nuova, higher up and corresponding to the establishment of the commune and the phase of demographic expansion.

The heart of the city is the beautiful Piazza Garibaldi, onto which face the most significant medieval buildings: above all, set in a

The Palazzo Comunale and, right, the Palazzo Pretorio

scenographic position at the top of a tall flight of steps, the cathedral of San Cerbone. The saint to whom it is dedicated – scenes from his life are carved on the lintel of the main portal – is linked to the presence of bishops from Populonia, where the cult of St. Cerbo was closely bound up with the history of the city. We do not know who was responsible for such refined architecture, but it is logical to think that the monumental complex is the result of several phases of construction, commencing in the first half of the 13th cent., or perhaps even in the 12th. The interior is divided into a nave and two aisles by travertine columns with elegantly carved capitals, and houses works of great value. For brevity, we will limit ourselves to mentioning the great baptismal font by Giroldo da Como (1267), completed much later with a tabernacle; the marble urn by the Sienese sculptor Goro di Gregorio known as the *Tomb of Saint*

Cerbo; the *Cross* painted by Segna di Bonaventura; and the *Madonna delle Grazie*, a large but mutilated panel painted on the back with *Scenes from the Passion* and perhaps executed in Duccio di Buoninsegna's workshop around 1316.

Opposite the cathedral stands the Palazzo del Podestà, dating from the early decades of the 13th cent. Its travertine façade is adorned with coats of arms that are still engraved with the city's ancient linear unit of

measurement, the *passo* (equal to 60 cm). It houses the civic archeological collections and paintings taken from places of worship, including Ambrogio Lorenzetti's large panel with the *Maestà*, formerly in Sant'Agostino.

The other buildings on the square are the small but elegant palace of the counts of Biserno with its tall battlemented tower, and the Palazzo Comunale, a building in travertine of vast proportions

that was created by uniting various houses dating from the 13th and 14th centuries.

Memories of the ancient activity of mining, which was so closely bound up with the birth and development of Massa, are preserved in the museum on Via Corridoni, where the techniques that have been used to exploit the deposits since ancient times are illustrated.

Ambrogio Lorenzetti, *Maestà*. Museo Civico

Facing page, Goro di Gregorio, *Tomb of Saint Cerbo*, detail. Cathedral

Populonia

Tomb of the Funeral Beds

A small 15th-cent. burg set on top of a bluff above the sea, surrounded by the dense maquis that has covered the entire promontory for centuries: this is how the Etruscan Pupluna, the city that was the most important center of iron smelting in Etruria during the Hellenistic era, presents itself to the visitor today.

Mentioned quite frequently in the ancient sources, Populonia seems to have prospered up until the age of imperial Rome, before being destroyed first by the Longobards and then razed to the ground, in 809, by corsairs from Mauritania.

Archeological excavations that were commenced in sporadic fashion in the 19th cent., pursued more systematically in the 20th and are still under way have revealed the existence of an exceptionally large settlement, located not just in the vicinity of the acropolis, where the burg now stands – and traces of the city walls can still be seen – but also lower down, close to the harbor and along the edge of the bay, where most of the industrial activities were concentrated.

The extraordinary mineral wealth of the nearby Island of Elba, abounding in iron and copper, and the hills around Campiglia, rich in deposits of lead, provided the raw material for smelting. Contrary to what might be expected, at least as

far as Elba is concerned, this was not done *in situ* but at Populonia.

Recent excavations have uncovered a sort of industrial district laid out according to a rational urban plan in the zone of Poggio alla Porcareccia, close to the landing area for boats. However, the destruction of the district at the beginning of the 3rd cent. BC did not signify an abandonment of metalworking, as is demonstrated by the iron Populonia supplied to fit out the fleet for Publius Cornelius Scipio's expedition to Africa (205 BC). By this time, the city may have entered into federation with Rome.

The importance attained by

Circular tomb; right, tomb in the shape of an aedicule

Two views of the Rocca di San Silvestro

Populonia, and the fact that it was the only large Etruscan city located directly on the sea, favored the establishment of strong connections with other peoples of the Mediterranean. Evidence for this comes from the objects found in tombs, which include goblets and containers for balsam from Eastern Greece, materials from Corinth and rare examples of Phoenician pottery, while it is known that bucchero ware was produced in Populonia itself and from there distributed fairly widely in Northern Etruria.

Most of the materials found in the excavations, and which have been fortunate enough to escape the clutches of the illegal antique market, are now on display at the Museo Archeologico in Florence, although a fairly interesting

Museo Etrusco has recently been set up in the nearby town of Piombino.

The need to protect this important archeological heritage while making it accessible to the public has led to the creation of a system of parks in the Val di Cornia. This links together (under the common denominator of the ancient metallurgical industry) the Parco Archeominerario di San Silvestro and the Parco Archeologico di Baratti e Populonia. The former, situated between San Vincenzo and Campiglia, takes its name from the medieval burg of San Silvestro, now destroyed, where the mining activity begun in Etruscan times was still being carried out between the 10th and 14th cent. The second offers guided tours of the

Etruscan necropolises (of San Cerbone, the Porcareccia and the Grotte), along with visits to some of the large burial mounds, such as the Tomb of the Flabella and the Tomb of the Chariots.

Livorno

Bernardino Poccetti, *View of Livorno Harbor*, **detail. Palazzo Pitti, Florence**

The difficulties presented by the local environment must have hampered the formation and initial development of what by the end of the 18th cent. had become the city with the second largest number of inhabitants in Tuscany, a position it long held before "abdicating" in favor of Prato over the last decade.

Situated on the southern edge of the vast plain of the Arno River, exposed to frequent raids from the sea and to the problems of a territory that consisted largely of ponds and marshes, Livorno was for a long time not much more than a small landing place. Archeological investigations seem to confirm this, revealing the existence of scanty settlements on the site but a more significant human presence to the south, near the town of Castiglioncello, where excavations in the 19th cent. brought to light an interesting necropolis (4th-1st cent. BC).

Between the 10th and 11th cent. Livorno became a *castrum*, and by the 12th cent., defended by the tower known as "Matilda's keep," it was already a structure of support for the nearby harbor of Pisa. The latter's defeat at Meloria (1284) exposed Livorno to the reprisals of the Genoese, but did not threaten its existence. On the contrary, the republic of Pisa encouraged people to

The Fortezza Nuova; below, the Fortezza Vecchia

A view of the Venezia Nuova quarter; right, the Cisternone constructed by Pasquale Poccianti to store water

move to the area through a policy of tax exemptions.

In addition, the progressive silting up of the bay into which the Arno flowed, and on which Pisa harbor was located, favored the development of Livorno as a port, situated on the open sea.

After a brief period of rule by Genoa (1408-21), when it became the seat of a vicariate, Livorno was bought for a 100.000 gold florins by Florence, allowing the landlocked city to fulfill its

Ulvi Liegi, *Livorno Synagogue.* Museo Civico Giovanni Fattori; right, Piazzale Mascagni

desire for an outlet to the sea. The reconstruction of the system of defense and the building of the Fortezza Vecchia to a design by Antonio da Sangallo the Elder, in the early 16th cent., reveal the extent of Florentine interest in Livorno. This continued under Cosimo I and above all his son Francesco, who is in fact regarded as the city's founder, having planned the enlargement of its harbor and radically altered its appearance with the help of the architect Bernardo Buontalenti.

The ordinances issued by Ferdinando I at the beginning of the 1590s, and in particular those of 1593 known as the Livornine Laws, set the city on a course of unstoppable growth, giving it the cosmopolitan and tolerant character which was to remain its distinctive cultural trait. Building on a policy of privileges and tax exemptions commenced long before and then revived by Grand Duke Cosimo, Ferdinando gave a special status to ethnic groups traditionally discriminated against in the Christian West (Turks, Jews, Moors), offering them numerous concessions: above all, the dropping of any criminal cases against them and the freedom to profess their religion and follow their own customs. Alongside "Europeans" from England, the Netherlands, Germany, Spain and Portugal (it was at this time the city acquired its English name,

Top, Eugenio Cecconi, *Rag Pickers in Livorno*; above, Giovanni Fattori, *Assault at Madonna della Scoperta.* **Museo Civico Giovanni Fattori**

"Leghorn"), colonies of Armenians and Turks settled in Livorno and the Jewish community, still the largest in the region, soon assumed a leading role.

On the eve of the 19th cent. foreigners had no difficulty in describing Livorno as a city of modern appearance, with broad streets and fine squares, a sort of international "enclave" within a state whose cultural horizons were much more limited. It has retained many of these characteristics, although the urban fabric has been heavily damaged by bombing in the war and by a hasty reconstruction.

It is possible to find a few traces of the older part of the city in the picturesque quarter of Venezia Nuova, recently restored. This was built in the 17th cent. near the old burg, between the Fortezza Nuova and the Fortezza Vecchia. which incorporates older fortified structures. It is an imposing landmark in the modern fabric and overlooks the central Piazza Micheli, where there is another structure dear to the people of Livorno, the *Monument to Ferdinando I*, better known as the "Quattro Mori," or "Four Moors," for its four statues of Barbary pirates in chains carved by Pietro Tacca.

There are fewer religious buildings than in most Tuscan centers, given Livorno's recent origin, but they reflect the freedom of worship long enjoyed by the city: the church of the Dutch and German congregation, the Greek Orthodox cemetery, the synagogue (rebuilt after partial destruction in the last war) and the church of San Gregorio or of the Armenians, of which only the façade survives today.

The cathedral of San Francesco was erected between 1594 and 1606 by Alessandro Pieroni. Faithfully rebuilt after the war, it houses works by Passignano, Ligozzi, Empoli and Curradi. In addition to the Jewish Museum, opened in the early 1990s, there is the Museo Civico Giovanni Fattori. Located in Villa Mimbelli since 1994, it displays works by 19th- and 20th-cent. artists from Livorno, including many paintings by Giovanni Fattori.

Above, Matteo Vittorio Corcos, *Portrait of Yorick*; facing page, Giovanni Fattori, *Portrait of the Artist's Wife.* **Museo Civico Giovanni Fattori**

Giovanni Fattori, *The Rotunda of Palmieri.* **Galleria d'Arte Moderna, Florence**

The Valdelsa and Chianti

North of Volterra, and immediately west of the famous Valdelsa, there is a Tuscany in a "minor key" that is rather off the beaten track. It is more or less the area of the roughly parallel valleys of the Egola and the Era, both of them left-hand tributaries of the Arno, joining it respectively at Santa Croce sull'Arno and Pontedera. One can claim that nowadays the part of the Valdelsa north of Poggibonsi is rather neglected as well.

From Ponte a Elsa, immediately south-west of Empoli, and Poggibonsi runs the route of the S.S. 429, which brushes that of the ancient Via Francigena; but not many tourists take it. Of the towns it runs through, Certaldo is something of a tourist centre, being the birthplace of Giovanni Boccaccio, while Castelfiorentino is scarcely visited at all. Empoli itself deserves a special mention if only as a kind of Tuscan "mini-Parma," a centre for music-lovers and in-

veterate Verdi fans. But to the south of Empoli and San Miniato there are a mass of places worth visiting. Lovely Montespertoli, for example, or Gambassi with the nearby Pieve a Chianni, Montaione with its monastery of San Vivaldo near which in the 15th and 16th centuries the Franciscans built a kind of "Holy Mountain" based on the idea of a Jerusalem. There is also the area between Peccioli and Castelfalfi, where the countryside is almost untouched, suspended between the raw landscape of the

Volterrano and the essence of the Pisan seacoast. This last effect is given by the Maritime pines, which grow here although we are still some way from the the sea.

The spread of the suburbs and the tendency to take the most "direct" routes to places has in effect made both Tuscans and tourists deaf to the appeal of small towns just outside the city, to the local fairs, which at one time were picnic spots. The Florentines of today no longer go to San Martino la Palma, to Pieve a Giogoli, to San Casciano in Val di Pesa (where – at Sant'Andrea in Percussina – they would find the house where Niccolò Machiavelli lived in exile). Nor do they often visit Impruneta, which for centuries on end was the most famous Marian shrine in the whole of Tuscany. From here, we reach the Valdelsa at Poggibonsi, with its Medici castle above it, and the Franciscan monastery of San Lucchese. People usually leave the *superstrada* at this point to visit the towers and churches of San Gimignano.

This is indeed worth doing, but it is easy, to forget that in the immediate neighbourhood there is the lovely parish church of Cellole and a fascinating mediaeval "Pompeii," by which we mean the incredible sprawling ruins of Castelvecchio, now almost entirely overgrown.

But a traveller who does not wish to get to Siena by

pp. 210-11, the abbey of Passignano

Top, Certaldo Alto; left, the parish church of Santa Maria at Chianni

Facing page, views of the Sienese part of Chianti

the *superstrada*, can still take the S.S. 222, which leads into the Chianti hills through Greve and Castellina. Or at a certain point (shortly after Panzano) he could fork left into more rugged landscape, to Radda, Gaiole, the Badia a Coltibuono, and the ruins of the castle of Montegrossi, the original home of the powerful feudal family of the Ricasoli. Here we find ourselves on the watershed of the range of the Chianti hills (which incidentally rise to some 3000 feet). Descending into the Valdarno towards the east, we find the important towns of Figline, San Giovanni and Montevarchi.

Colle di Val d'Elsa

The fortunes of Colle, an ancient Etruscan settlement on the banks of the river Elsa, can be ascribed to its favorable geographical position at the heart of a territory long inhabited by human beings, dominated by centers of primary importance such as Siena, Volterra and Florence, and where the nearby passage of the Via Francigena, a road of "European" significance, favored the circulation of people and ideas. Then the proximity of a watercourse like the Elsa constituted an indispensable prerequisite for the emergence, as far back as the 11th and 12th centuries, of activities of an "industrial" character, linked to the production of wool and paper. This last was destined to have a

long life and to make Colle one of the main centers of papermaking in the 18th and 19th cent. The later (mid-14th cent.) industry of glassmaking, on the other hand, still flourishes in the city, which holds an exposition of its

artistic products in September every year and has recently dedicated a museum to glass.

The urban development of the last few decades has not cancelled out the characteristic division of the built-up area into three parts, corresponding to

Above, Giovanni di Cristofano and Francesco di Andrea, *The Surrender of Colle Val d'Elsa*. State Archives, Siena

Left, Palazzo Campana; right, the Palazzo dei Priori

different phases of construction: Colle Bassa (the lower part of the city where most of the new building has taken place), grown up around the ancient church of Santa Maria della Spugna (10th cent.); the Castello, laid out on the top of the hill, on the site of Piticciano Castle; and the Borgo, protected by a ring of walls that has partially survived and whose entrance is marked by the distinctive round towers of the imposing Porta Nuova.

The life of Colle Bassa today centers on the 19th-cent. Piazza Arnolfo di Cambio, named after the great architect and sculptor who was born here in the 13th cent. (c. 1245). In fact the city abounds in memories of his existence. Hidden amid the folds of a rapidly growing urban fabric, which has transformed and swallowed up everything, stand a few fine buildings that are also reminders of an ancient industrial past, but the best preserved section, rich in valuable works of art and architecture, coincides with the upper part of the city. Our tour begins, almost as if it were a

gateway, at the beautiful Palazzo Campana (1539) designed in the Mannerist style by Giuliano di Baccio d'Agnolo. Beyond it rises the gentle slope of Via del Castello – lined with ancient tower-houses and elegant Renaissance palaces – leading up to Piazza del Duomo. Onto Via del Castello faces the 14th-cent. Palazzo Pretorio, now the seat of the Museo Archeologico (a selection of materials organized into sequences that stretch from protohistoric times to the Middle Ages) dedicated to the great archeologist Ranuccio Bianchi Bandinelli.

The cathedral of Santi Alberto e Marziale was commenced in

1603 on the site of the old parish church of San Salvatore, whose remains are incorporated into the left flank. The new construction was prompted by the elevation of Colle to the status of an episcopal see, and consequently a city, with a papal bull of 1592. The present neoclassical façade is the work of the Sienese architect Agostino Fantastici; the interior presents a sort of repertoire of 17th-cent. painting.

There are also numerous buildings worthy of interest

Piazza Duomo with the Palazzo Pretorio

Left, Taddeo di Bartolo, *Madonna and Child.* Sant'Agostino; below, Volterran *kelebai* from the 4th cent. BC. Museo Archeologico Bianchi Bandinelli

(Palazzo Vescovile, Palazzo dei Priori) on the continuation of Via del Castello, including the 13th-cent. tower-house traditionally held to be the birthplace of Arnolfo, which concludes in the great Renaissance bastion of the "Baluardo," with an interesting view of the surroundings.

Certaldo

Though the name is of uncertain etymology, perhaps connected with the presence of extensive woods of turkey oak (*Quercus cerris*), Certaldo has remote Etrusco-Roman origins, as the archeological finds made at Poggio del Boccaccio and Poggio delle Fate testify.

However, its name is universally linked with Giovanni Boccaccio, author of the *Decameron*, who according to an old tradition was born there around 1313. In fact the writer spent the last years of his life in Certaldo (he died in 1375), and the town is filled with memories of his presence, starting with the house in which he lived. This has been almost entirely rebuilt (1947) following the damage caused during the last war and today houses a study center with a specialized library.

The present town is divided into in two distinct parts: Certaldo Basso or Borgo, and Certaldo Alto or Castello. The lower section, which developed later (13th-14th cent.) along the route of the Via Francigena, is now the economic and residential heart; the upper part, huddled around the elegant Palazzo Pretorio, a true civic icon that was once the home of Certaldo's rulers, the counts Alberti, has preserved intact its character of medieval burg.

It is traversed in its entirety by Via Boccaccio, the most important street lined with the warm colors of buildings constructed largely out of brick. Along its route or in the immediate vicinity, in fact, are located the palaces and churches that bear witness to the town's history and culture, commencing with the monastic complex of Santi Jacopo e Filippo (12th-13th cent.) and its handsome asymmetrical cloister with a double order of columns. Recently made the seat of the Museo di Arte Sacra, displaying important works of local origin, it houses Boccaccio's cenotaph and relics of the Blessed Giulia, who lived here in a cell: the extraordinary figure of a "hermit saint," she belonged to a tradition that was strong in the Valdelsa and whose most illustrious model was that of St. Verdiana of Castelfiorentino (12th cent.).

Meliore, *Madonna and Child*. Museo di Arte Sacra

Left, Giovan Francesco Rustici, *Bust of Giovanni Boccaccio*. Santi Jacopo e Filippo

The Palazzo Pretorio, formerly a symbol of civil authority, recalls the long-ago times when Certaldo was the most important center of the Valdelsa, before its decline with the advent of the Lorraine. All that remains of the original residence of the counts Alberti is the keep, while the rest of the building was reconstructed in the 15th cent. Of particular interest are the courtyard with painted and sculpted coats of arms and the rooms on the *piano nobile* decorated by Pier Francesco Fiorentino. Adjoining Palazzo Pretorio, and by now an integral part of it, is the ancient church of Santi Tommaso e Prospero. It now houses the reassembled Tabernacolo dei Giustiziati, once located on the banks of the river Agliena in a chapel close to the place of execution for those condemned to death. The important cycle of frescoes with *Scenes from the Passion* was painted by Benozzo Gozzoli and collaborators (1466-67).

Benozzo Gozzoli and workshop, *Deposition of Christ from the Cross*, detail. Santi Tommaso e Prospero

The Palazzo Pretorio

San Gimignano

The town has been dubbed the "Manhattan of Tuscany," with the evident intention of drawing a parallel between its incredible stone towers and the skyscrapers of New York.

Yet San Gimignano is a unique place that does not easily bear comparison with anywhere else, a sort of cameo set in the most "typical" Tuscan landscape which has aroused the wonder of countless travelers in the past.

In the remote past, as is often the case with Tuscan centers, it seems to have been an Etruscan settlement, something to which the numerous tombs found in the vicinity also attest. Its entry into more recent history, on the other hand, came in the early Middle Ages and appears to have been linked to its location on the Via Francigena, the important road used by pilgrims on their way to Rome and Jerusalem. The first to leave a record of his stay there was Sigeric, archbishop of Canterbury, on his way back from Rome toward the end of

Bottom left, the Palazzo del Podestà; right, the Palazzo del Popolo with the collegiate church

Facing page, Piazza della Cisterna

the 10th cent., but the very road that had made the town's fortune led to its freezing in time when the route went into decline and was then abandoned.

San Gimignano reached the peak of its splendor when it became a free commune and with the rise of a class of aristocrats whose wealth derived from trading the produce of the fertile countryside (saffron in particular), but the continual strife between the town's factions, especially the bitter struggle between the Guelph Ardinghelli and Ghibelline Salvucci, combined with the devastating effects of the plague (1348), resulted in its economic decline and spontaneous submission to Florence in 1351.

Today, on the contrary, San Gimignano is one of the biggest tourist attractions in Tuscany, an indispensable stop on any tour of the region, with effects that are undoubtedly positive for its economy but with the ever present threat of an irreversible alteration of the miraculous equilibrium between human intervention and natural setting. This is where the challenge for the future lies: moving into the new millennium without losing a heritage that has been built up with patience over centuries.

Visitors usually enter the town through the most beautiful of the gates, that of San Giovanni, and then follow the street of the same name, lined with churches, towers and palaces, to Piazza della Cisterna (its name derives from the ancient cistern built by the commune in

Interior of the collegiate church looking toward the right-hand aisle

1287): a sort of upside-down triangle, the square was once used to stage spectacles and tournaments and is surrounded by interesting medieval buildings and the twin towers of the powerful family Ardinghelli.

A short walk takes you to the equally picturesque Piazza del Duomo, dominated from the top of a flight of steps by the collegiate church of Santa Maria Assunta. The Palazzo del Podestà with its imposing tower called the "Torre della Rognosa" and the Palazzo del Popolo also face onto the square.

The collegiate church, with a sober stone façade, was built in the second half of the 12th

From the top, Bartolo di Fredi, *The Earthquake in Job's House*, *Joseph's Dream*, *Abraham and Lot Go Their Separate Ways*, *The Destruction of Job's Army*. Collegiate church

cent. on the site of an ancient parish church of more modest dimensions and with a different orientation. The interior, by contrast, offers a stunning sight, its walls and ceilings entirely covered with frescoes painted by Sienese and Florentine artists, including Lippo and Federigo Memmi, Taddeo di Bartolo, Bartolo di Fredi and Domenico Ghirlandaio.

Since the middle of the 19th cent. the Palazzo del Popolo, flanked by the tall tower known as the "Torre Grossa" and now the seat of the municipality, has housed the important Museo Civico, a collection of paintings from the Florentine and Sienese schools reflecting the role of a meeting point between the two cultural areas that San Gimignano played in the past.

The building has an artistic significance of its own, quite apart from the museum, and some of its rooms bear witness to the town's previous political and economic importance, especially the Sala del Consiglio where Lippo Memmi painted a magnificent *Maestà* in 1317.

Following Via San Matteo, a lively and beautiful street, you will come in succession to the Palazzo della Cancelleria, the church of San Bartolo, the Pesciolini tower-house and the Palazzo Tinacci, before reaching the church of Sant'Agostino on the square of the same name. The imposing building (1280) with its simple brick architecture conceals, like the collegiate church, a rich interior on which Lippo Memmi, Bartolo di Fredi (frescoes with *Scenes from the Life of the Virgin*) and Benozzo Gozzoli, who painted the celebrated *Scenes from the Life of Saint Augustine* in the Cappela Maggiore, have all left their mark. There is also an outstanding marble altar by Benedetto da Maiano in the chapel of San Bartolo.

Left, Benozzo Gozzoli, *The School at Tagaste*. Sant'Agostino

Facing page, Domenico Ghirlandaio, *Annunciation of Her Death to Saint Fina*, detail. Collegiate church

In and around Siena

The great centre of the south of Tuscany is Siena. Every country has its southlands, its "southern question," its loyalists and its lovers (unless, as in England, it is the other way round, and there is a "northern question"). From Siena down, the landscape is more harsh and bare, the soil more severe and stinting, the colours darker and less merciful. The network of roads down here has a wider mesh, and the settlements are further apart. We more rarely see those little clusters of houses which "humanize" the landscape of Chianti or the Valdelsa. South of Siena grazing gets the better of farming, while industry is confined to mining. In the Senese the summer is more scorching, the winter is more bitter, and the wind more cutting.

Cor tibi magis Sena pandit, we read inscribed on Porta Camollia, gateway to Siena: "Siena opens her heart even wider to you." This is true, on condition that we manage to find the way in. Because to anyone visiting Siena for the first time the city is a labyrinth surrounding the Piazza del Campo, a spiral of concentric and intersecting streets in which the stranger loses his way at once. Churches and palaces, tower-houses and warehouses all look the same, and if you pass twice in front of the same building there is a risk that you won't recognize it – unless, of course, it happens to be Palazzo Tolomei or Palazzo Salimbeni. Siena changes with the seasons and with the light at different times of day, and its face of pale red brick and brown-gold or

iron-grey travertine is always different. It appears warm and welcoming, but it retains something of enigma and mystery, of a hermetic emblem no less hard to interpret than the esoteric symbols inlaid in the floor of its wonderful cathedral.

The Sienese have been this way for centuries: coarse and courageous, proud of their background and given to flights of greatness and of braggartry. In the Middle Ages they lost their battle against the bankers of Florence be-

Chapel of the Madonna di Vitaleta
in Val d'Orcia
The countryside to the south
of Siena

dral dedicated to the Virgin Mary was planned to be merely the transept of another, truly gigantic construction. A shell, or sketch, of what would have been the walls, still looms over the city. They were "people full of vanity" who were thought (Dante, *Inferno* XXIX) to have introduced the use of the costly clove into their cooking, and who could boast of gangs of gilded youths who amused themselves by quite literally throwing money away (gold florins in this case). Just look at the gorgeous sweetmeats they still know how to make from the finest honey, the most flavourful dried fruits, the most fragrant almond paste. Compare them with the scrawny glory of Florentine confectionery, the flat cake made with a fistful of flour and a powdering of icing sugar. The centuries-old rivalry between Siena and Florence can all be summed up in this: it is the clash between the proud generosity and extravagance of the people who created the Piazza del Campo and the suspicious stinginess of the men who created capitalism.

cause they had no gold coinage and because they had backed the wrong horse – the Ghibelline party supporting the Empire. They lost once more, against the wool manufacturers of Florence, because they were short of water, which is indispensable in the making of textiles. In exchange for this, they "thought big." Their enormous cathe-

Isolated, defeated and subjugated, Siena has become a wonderful historical fossil, and when it really comes down to it, in the debased Tuscany of today, she is the winner. Go and see the Palio and attempt to understand it. If you do, then you will realize that you have not seen a game, or a festival, but something truly unique in anthropology, the secret and hidden (well, perhaps not so hidden) motive force of a city. In it are the courage, ferocity, pride, thirst for adventure and love of hazard of one of the greatest and most glorious peoples on the face of the earth.

There are two ways of leaving Siena towards the south. One can take the S.S. 223, which follows the Merse valley for a while on its way to Civitella, Paganico and the ruins of Roselle (which are worth the short detour involved), and finally arrives in Grosseto. From there we can pay visits to Vetulonia, Castiglion della Pescaia (as stern as a Spanish fortress in the Carribbean), and the lovely Maremma of Grosseto. Otherwise we may take the S.S. 2, the Via Cassia. A few miles down this road and we find ourselves in a lunar landscape, with the horizon dominated by the bulk of Monte Amiata. Here we cross the Val d'Arbia and arrive at Buonconvento at the point where this river flows into the Ombrone. The Arbia, incidentally, is the river said by Dante to have been "dyed red" in 1260, when the Sienese Ghibellines defeated the Guelphs of Florence at Monta-

perti (*Inferno* X, in the episode of Farinata degli Uberti).

To return to Buonconvento, famous because the emperor Henry VII died there in 1313, the town forms a rectangle surrounded by fine 14th-century walls. From here we advise at least two detours. First and foremost, if we take the S.S. 451 in a north-easterly direction we pass through the barren landscape of the "Crete," with its colours that vary from pale grey to ochre to sulphur yellow and finally to the dark "burnt Siena," and arrive at the abbey of Monteoliveto Maggiore, the "mother-house" of the Olivetan Order, which was founded in the 14th cent. by a group of Sienese aristocrats as a reformed branch of the great Benedictine Order. Several times remodelled between the 14th and 19th centuries, dominating the landscape with its impressive red-brick bulk, the monastery still preserves the precious cloister with paintings by Signorelli and Sodoma.

After Monteoliveto the tourist who likes to see only the

Facing page, the parish church of San Giovanni Battista at Ponte allo Spino (top) and the villa of Cetinale in the environs of Sovicille

**The Crete near Vescona
The cloister of the abbey of Monteoliveto Maggiore**

which can mature and improve for as much as forty years) and its homemade pasta known as "pici." About ten kilometers south of Montalcino we get to the Benedictine abbey of Sant'Antimo, maybe the most beautiful and certainly the most touching of all the Romanesque churches in Tuscany. It is no longer in service, as it were, but luckily still in a good state of preservation. The onyx decorations from the nearby quarries of Castelnuovo give it a uniquely iridescent look. This visit will take as much time as you care to give it, from half a day to weeks on end. Many years ago I happened to camp nearby with a bunch of young friends, and for day after day we never tired of simply gazing at it. Even now, to go back there is to revisit something eternal in one's life, a time of unsullied happiness and a memory that brings only comfort.

But it is time to get back on the Via Cassia, and head south towards the Val d'Orcia. The historic chief town of the valley is San Quirico d'Orcia, in which the tourist who thinks of himself more as a true "traveller" would do well to spend some time; not only to look at it really thoroughly, but to make it his base for two long but exquisite excursions,

essential – and thinks he knows what it is – can turn and retrace his steps and go on down the Via Cassia. His wiser and more patient colleague, however, will not let slip the opportunity of pushing a little further north, as far as Asciano (where he will find a delightful little museum containing a 14th-century panel of the Madonna that was one of the great loves of my adolescence). Or else he can turn south and follow secondary and justifiably dusty roads (dust forms part of the fascination of the "Crete") as far as Lucignano, a lovely little town on account of its oval shape – typical of what in Tuscany is called a "castle," or in other words a fortified village – and also for the view over the neighbouring Valdichiana and for the magnificent "Albero di San Francesco," the most extraordinary silver-gilt reliquary in the whole Gothic art of Siena, or of Italy.

We return to Buonconvento and prepare for the second "compulsory" trip. We take another "secondary" road to Montalcino, the last heroic bulwark of Sienese freedom against the tyranny of the Medici, with its fine Palazzo Comunale, its mighty fortress, its superb red wine (Brunello,

The collegiate church of San Quirico d'Orcia with detail of the lateral portal from the second half of the 13th cent.

Right, Piazza del Popolo with the Palazzo dei Priori at Montalcino

one to south-eastern Tuscany, the other to the area of Monte Amiata.

But San Quirico should not be neglected in itself. In many respects it is a typically "Sienese" town, with its winding streets and brick-built towers with the purest lines. Of special interest is the splendid Romanesque collegiate church (the ancient Pieve di Osenna, dedicated to Saints Quirico and Giulitta), which can boast a genuine masterpiece in its Roman portal decorated with monsters and other figures. There is also the great Palazzo Chigi, a vast building of the late 17th cent. that appears to have been designed for a city such as Rome, and which here – enormous, isolated, almost frightening – is so disproportionate as to give one a certain enigmatic delight. Finally there are the Orti Leonini, the large 16th-century gardens.

The S.S. 146, which heads east from San Quirico d'Orcia, is the best road to take if you want to enjoy the south-east of the "Senese." After 10 kilometers or so you reach Pienza, the model town built in brick and travertine by order of Pope Pius II, who as a member of the family of the local lords (the Piccolomini) was born there. At that time it was called Corsignano, and was only re-named Pienza after him.

As it is today the town can be considered from a number of points of view. One of these is certainly the Utopian Renaissance notion of the "ideal city," with straight streets and perfect proportions, and all based on Neo-Platonic models. But as it is so small it is more of a toy town, the whim of a Humanist overlord who became pope, translated into four streets forming a cross around the serene and perfect piazza, with the cathe-

Two views of the abbey of
Sant'Antimo

dral built according to designs by Bernardo Rossellino, the Palazzo Piccolomini by the same architect (here clearly inspired by Alberti's Palazzo Rucellai in Florence), and the Palazzo Comunale weighed down by restorations carried out in this century. And as a background to the piazza, behind the church, the mass of Monte Amiata completes the scenic effect. A little down from the town the serene and simple parish church of Corsignano (11th-12th centuries) reminds the visitor of the mediaeval nature of the place. Still travelling east from Pienza we get to Montepulciano, which can boast splendid 14th- to 16th-century buildings in the town centre, such as the church of Sant'Agostino (by Michelozzo), the late-Renaissance Palazzo Avignonesi (attributed to Vignola), and the 16th- to17th-century cathedral. The central piazza possesses a rare harmony, even though it is surrounded by buildings from various periods. We need hardly add that it would be madness to leave Pienza without a little store of "pecorino" cheeses, both fresh and matured, mild or piquant according to taste; or to leave Montepulciano without a reserve of the celebrated local wine, the "Vino Nobile" which – according to Dr. Francesco Redi, physician to the archduke and a great enologist – is the "king of all wines."

Enriched by these delights of the palate we continue towards the place where those who enjoy them to excess are fated to end up: Chianciano Terme, a famous hydrothera-

The Italian-style garden of Palazzo Piccolomini at Pienza

The rectory of San Biagio at Montepulciano, built to a design by Antonio da Sangallo the Elder

Facing page, the fortified castle of Spedaletto

peutic centre and a pleasant town, though perhaps too much the watering and holiday place that flourished most brillianty in the Thirties. Of this it still bears the traces in the Fascist architecture of the public buildings and the bourgeois taste for little private villas. Our route lies through Chianciano if we want to get to the lovely town of Chiusi, with its mediaeval Duomo (6th-12th century, but very much altered in the 12th), the National Etruscan Museum and the Etruscan tombs scattered outside the town. We advise you to take a glimpse at the two lakes of Chiusi and Montepulciano to the north of the necropolis area.

Any one itinerary is debatable. A short while back we crossed the Valdichiana, coming from Arezzo. It would certainly have been logical from there, having visited Cortona with its Etruscan museum and associations, to have reached Chiusi by following the Chiana or else the S.S. 71 which runs beside Lake Trasimeno. Another possible choice, and certainly an interesting one, would be to get to Chiusi by striking east-south-east from Siena, which would open up to us more of the Sienese Valdichiana. Anyone preferring this solution should leave Siena by the S.S. 326 or 438, which in any case join up after about thirty kilometers near Rapolano Terme, another of the watering places in the Sienese country that repays a visit. From that point the S.S. 326 leads to Sinalunga, a fine town full of art and industry, and to Torrita, where the brick is redder and the geraniums more magnificent than elsewhere. You see them everywhere, in flower-pots set in iron hoops outside the windows, according to a system common throughout Central Italy, but especially flourishing around Siena. And from there a brief detour northwards will bring you to the agricultural centre of Foiano della Chiana. Either by state road or the motorway it is easy to get from Torrita to Chiusi, whence one may head south for Cetona and for the spas of San Casciano.

Siena

According to more or less fanciful legends Siena was founded by the Gaulish tribe of the Senones, or by the sons of Remus, the twins Aschius and Senius, who fled Rome to escape the wrath of their uncle Romulus. This belief was the reason for the adoption of the Capitoline she-wolf as the city's emblem in medieval times. In reality archeologists have demonstrated the existence of fairly small Etruscan settlements in the area, not capable in themselves of giving rise to a true urban center. This evidently did not occur until the Roman era, when the city became a military colony with the name of Sena Julia.

However, its importance must have been limited as it was only rarely mentioned by ancient historians. Its subsequent history is also shrouded in silence up until the Longobard period, when the city, which had become an episcopal see in the 5th cent., began to expand its sphere of influence (7th cent.) at the expense of the diocese of Arezzo. At the root of this phase of expansion of Siena lay the displacement of the important line of communication between Northern Europe and the city of Rome, the famous Via Francigena that was to play such a part in the history of many Tuscan towns and cities.

Expanding in step with its

Sienese artist of the 16th-17th cent., *The Blessed Ambrogio Sansedoni*, detail with the Palazzo Pubblico. Siena

The Palazzo Pubblico

economic growth the city developed in a tripartite pattern, determined by the topography of the site, which had existed ever since the early Middle Ages, when the city was already split into the three distinct sections of Castelvecchio, Castel Montone

and Castello del
Poggio Malavolti. This
was to continue in the
communal era with a
division into the *terzi*
or "thirds" of Città,
Camollia and San Martino.
And as the city grew, the ring
of walls was expanded,
through a series of additions
rather than a more radical
rebuilding.

In the early decades of the
12th cent. Siena organized
itself as a commune and carried

on with its policy of
expansion, which
sometimes brought it
into conflict with
Florence. However, the
government's loyalty to
Emperor Frederick I earned it
his support against the growing
pretensions to temporal power
on the part of the bishops and
allowed it to attain full

autonomy (1167). The
subsequent disputes between
Guelphs and Ghibellines would
only be calmed with the
establishment of the government
of the Nove ("Nine") in1287,
made possible by the alliance
of the nine most important
Guelph families.

The stability of this rule,
which was to last beyond the

middle of the 14th cent.,
coincided with the golden
period in the history of Siena in
which artists of the caliber of
Duccio, Simone Martini and the
Lorenzetti brothers were active.

**Top, the Sala del Mappamondo in
the Palazzo Pubblico with Simone
Martini's** *Maestà*

Ambrogio Lorenzetti, *The Effects of
Good Government.* **Palazzo Pubblico**

At this time the city was enriched with splendid private and public buildings and took on the Gothic forms it still has today. The flourishing economy was fueled by commercial and manufacturing activities – in particular the production of wool – and the city's role as a great financial center (up until at least the end of the 13th cent.) where the Tolomei, Piccolomini, Buonsignori and Chigi families operated as bankers.

The terrible outbreak of the plague in 1348, combined with the effects of the failure of several banking institutions, brought this positive period to an abrupt end and reintroduced instability into the city, which was shaken by frequent uprisings. After the brief interlude of rule by Gian Galeazzo Visconti (1399-1404), Siena recovered its freedom but was increasingly racked by internal unrest and squeezed by Florentine territorial designs. Eventually it succumbed to Cosimo I de' Medici, the last of the major Tuscan cities to hold out, in the April of 1555. Annexed to the grand duchy four years later, it retained its republican institutions (although they were progressively stripped of meaning) and kept up a cultural life of its own centered on the academies (Rozzi, Intronati and Fisiocritici) and the university, the ancient *studium* which had been created at the beginning of the 13th cent.

The cathedral of Santa Maria Assunta with detail of the façade

The civic pride and consciousness that represent the guiding thread running through the entire history of Siena also provide the foundation for its urban fabric, dominated by two great symbolic monuments: the cathedral of the Assunta, an imposing structure on the top of the hill of Santa Maria that the city for a while had plans to enlarge still further in order to make it one of the biggest churches in the Christian world; and the elegant Palazzo Pubblico, a highly successful model of civil architecture, in the shadow of the soaring Torre del Mangia whose profile constitutes, along with the campanile of the cathedral, Siena's most distinctive landmark and a constant point of reference for travelers as they approach the city.

Nicola Pisano and assistants, pulpit;
left, Francesco di Giorgio Martini,
angel holding candle. Cathedral

**Below, view of the transept
of the cathedral**

**pp. 238-9, Matteo di Giovanni,
Slaughter of the Innocents.
Floor of the cathedral**

Standing on the site of a previous church, the cathedral was built in the 12th cent. and consecrated in 1179. It was subsequently greatly altered and enlarged until it attained its present proportions. The oldest parts of the building we see today date from the 13th cent. and represent a fairly rare example of Romanesque architecture in a largely Gothic city. It is impossible to list all the treasures it contains: we will confine ourselves to drawing attention to the octagonal pulpit, constructed between 1265 and 1268 by Nicola Pisano with Arnolfo di Cambio and other collaborators; the floor of inlaid marble, divided up into fifty-six panels of great iconographic coherence, on which the city's most significant artists worked from the 13th to the 19th cent.; the chapel of San Giovanni Battista; the Piccolomini Altar, carved by Andrea Bregno and adorned with some early sculptures by Michelangelo; and the Libreria Piccolomini with its famous cycle of frescoes painted at the beginning of the 16th cent. by Pinturicchio.

The adjoining baptistery of San Giovanni Battista, in the Sienese Gothic style, is located

on a lower level and faces onto the small square of the same name, reached by a steep flight of steps built in the middle of the 15th cent. It houses important frescoes by Vecchietta and Benvenuto di Giovanni and a precious baptismal font on which Sienese and Florentine artists collaborated (Giovanni di Turino, Lorenzo Ghiberti, Donatello, Jacopo della Quercia).

The Palazzo Pubblico stands

on the edge of the celebrated Piazza del Campo, the hub of city life today as in the past, when it was used along with the area beneath as a marketplace. Later it was given its characteristic shell shape and, by the middle of the 14th cent., split into nine segments paved in brick and provided with a fountain that was renamed Fonte Gaia or the "Gay Fountain" for the welcome it received from the population. The fountain we see today is actually a 19th-cent. copy by Tito Sarrocchi, while the original carved by Jacopo della Quercia in 1419 is now in Santa Maria della Scala.

The city hall known as the Palazzo Pubblico was erected under the government of the Nove and was intended to serve as a symbol of their

authority. Commenced at the end of the 13th cent. and completed several decades later, it was a harmonious structure destined to influence subsequent civil architecture with its elegant three-light windows divided by slender mullions and with the presence

Top left, the oratory of the Madonna del Rosario; above, Palazzo Piccolomini and Palazzo Chigi Saracini

Bottom, the Fonte Gaia

of the characteristic Sienese arch of Oriental derivation. The extremely tall tower was begun in 1325 and finished between 1338 and 1348 by Francesco and Muccio di Rinaldo.

The interior, much of it now a museum, is a sort of compendium of the great Sienese painting of the 14th cent., although there are also paintings and frescoes from later periods. In the Sala del Mappamondo is located the *Maestà* painted by Simone Martini between 1312 and 1315, surrounded by an

elegant frame. Opposite it is the mysterious portrait of a knight, known as *Guidoriccio da Fogliano*, that has long divided the critics over the identity of its author, generally considered to have been Simone Martini himself. In the adjoining Sala del Pace, it was Ambrogio Lorenzetti who left his own masterpiece in the wall paintings known as the *Good Government* and *Bad Government*, a sort of "political manifesto" of the rule of the Nove that set out on the one hand to demonstrate the authority and benevolence of its

own influence and on the other to warn against the devastating effects of tyranny.

It is impossible to describe here all the interesting works of civil architecture, but we cannot fail to mention the Palazzi Tolomei, Chigi Saracini, Sansedoni, Buonsignori (seat of the Pinacoteca Nazionale) and Piccolomini.

Lack of space again requires us to make a drastic selection of the city's religious buildings, even though they represent an important chapter in its history. We must, however, draw attention to the great basilica of San Domenico, of 13th-cent. origin but expanded and continually altered right up to the radical interventions carried out in the middle of the 20th cent. It is a sort of treasure chest of works of art, filled with memories linked to the figure of St. Catherine.

The basilica of Santa Maria dei Servi, in a position overlooking the city, was begun in the 13th cent. and constructed over the course of several centuries. The interior

Bernardino Mei, *Ghismunda*. Pinacoteca Nazionale

Paolo di Giovanni Fei, *Nativity of the Virgin*. Pinacoteca Nazionale

Left, Donatello, *Madonna del Perdono*. Museo dell'Opera del Duomo

is decorated with frescoes by Pietro Lorenzetti and important panels by Matteo di Giovanni, Francesco Vanni and Rutilio Manetti. Significant examples of the work of the Lorenzetti brothers can also be seen in San Francesco and Sant'Agostino. The latter has been turned into a museum and

Sano di Pietro, *Saint George and the Dragon*. Museo Diocesano

Below, Sassetta, *Adoration of the Magi*. Collezione Chigi Saracini

Vincenzo Rustici, *Parade of the Contrade*. Florentine Galleries, on deposit in the Art Collection of Monte dei Paschi di Siena

is also used to stage exhibitions. A required stopping place on any tour of the city is undoubtedly the oratory of San Bernardino, erected on one of the sites chosen for his preaching by St. Bernardine (patron of the city of Siena along with Catherine). Recently the Museo Diocesano di Arte Sacra has been installed on the ground floor of the oratory. It displays works from various places in the diocese, including Ambrogio Lorenzetti's tender *Madonna del Latte*. In the chapel of Santa Maria degli Angeli on the upper floor we find the most important decorative complex of the 16th cent. in Siena, on which Sodoma, Domenico Beccafumi and Girolamo del Pacchia all worked.

Other important museums in the city include the Pinacoteca Nazionale, boasting a collection of high-quality works of the Sienese school from the 12th cent. to the 17th, and the Museo dell'Opera. Located in the spaces that were to have constituted the right hand aisle of the "new cathedral" that was never completed, it is a museum of extraordinary importance that now houses many of the sculptures, pictures and church ornaments and vestments linked to the history of the cathedral, among them the ten statues of *Sibyls* and *Prophets* carved by Giovanni Pisano for the façade, Donatello's *Madonna and Child* from the ancient Porta del Perdono and Duccio di Buoninsegna's great *Maestà* (1308-11).

The large complex of Santa Maria della Scala has recently been added to the city's

network of museums, in which it is supposed to perform the function of a "multipurpose cultural container." Located right in front of the flight of steps leading into the cathedral (whence the name, "St. Mary of the Stairs"), it was built, perhaps before the year 1000 (but first documented in 1090), as a hospice for pilgrims, paupers and abandoned children. Within a short space of time it developed into a true hospital, which it remained until late in the 20th cent. Its huge dimensions can be explained by the economic power it attained in the past through subsidies from the Sienese government, donations and charity. Today its original purpose is recalled by the large and evocative room known as the "Pellegrinaio," frescoed in the 15th cent. by Sienese artists, such as Domenico di Bartolo and Vecchietta.

The extensive collections of the Museo Archeologico Nazionale have also been transferred to Santa Maria della Scala.

The Palio

There is an abundance of festivals and contests in costume, as they say in Tuscany (i.e. in mediaeval dress), and some of them are fair enough. Let us avert our gaze from the football game in Florence, which dates back to the 16th cent. but has a rather spurious background and has never been a great hit with the citizenry. But other such occasions with a serious historical background and an impressive impact are the "Giostra del Saracino" at Arezzo, the "Giostra dell'Orso" at Pistoia, the "Gioco del Ponte" at Pisa, and a number of competitions in crossbow shooting between towns ranging from Massa Marittima to Borgo San Sepolcro.

But nothing, nothing at all, can be compared with the Palio of Siena, in which the entire life of the city comes together. The saying is that "The Palio goes on all year round," and the various sections into which the city is divided work tirelessly year in year out, investing capital, imagination and passion into this event.

As it is at the moment the Palio is run twice a year, on July 2nd (day of the Madonna di Provenzano) and August 16th, the day after the Assumption. In all the other towns in Italy the 2nd of July is one of the first days of the summer holidays, and the 16th is the day after the most important holiday of the year, known in Italy as Ferragosto. The towns and cities are empty. But Siena is cram-full, and feverish with excitement. The festivities commence three days before the one on which the Palio is held, with the drawing of lots to assign horses to ten of the seventeen Contrade still in existence. The climax of the festival, the race itself, consists of three circuits of the Piazza del Campo by the horses that have been chosen by lot, ridden bareback by jockeys hired for the occasion as in the ancient *palio alla lunga*, when the mounts used to belong to noblemen and rulers from all over Italy.

The contestants are the seven Contrade excluded from the previous Palio plus three others drawn by lot. The atmosphere just before the start is so dense it could be cut with a knife, and during the brief moments of the race itself the Piazza explodes.

The Palio lasts all year round, and it is a purely Sienese business, and strangers are tolerated as long as they create no disturbance. For the most important thing for non-Sienese to understand is that the Palio is intensely serious, the most serious thing there is. Anyone eager to grasp some of the atmosphere surrounding it cannot be content with watching the procession in splendid renaissance costumes which precedes the race. No, he must arrive at least the day before, be present at the dress rehearsal, see the blessing of the horses in the parish churches, and attempt to understand the plots and intrigues by which they try to get their own Contrada to win, or at least defeat their traditional enemies. For each Contrada has its allies, its enemies and its downright antagonists. Then, as he wanders around Siena after the Palio, our visitor will have a chance to hear the full-throated joy of the citizens of the winning Contrada and the rage of the losers. And the day ends with laughter and celebrations.

Unless one has grown up in the shadow of the Palio from childhood on it is impossible to understand the mechanisms of this "game" that twice a year splits families in half and changes the dearest friendships into ferocious antagonism. It is both the glory and the madness of the Sienese, who are most justifiably proud of it.

Pienza

Piazza Pio II with the cathedral
and Palazzo Piccolomini

The old settlement of Corsignano, born around the 9th cent. as a castle belonging to the abbey of San Salvatore on Monte Amiata and then rebuilt a few centuries later as a burg on the site where the cathedral now stands, changed its name to Pienza at the explicit behest of its most celebrated citizen, the Humanist Enea Silvio Piccolomini (1405-64), who was elected Pope Pius II in 1458. It was Piccolomini, on a visit to his birthplace in 1459, who had the idea of turning it into a sort of temporary residence of the papal court, a perfect location that would combine Humanistic notions of the ideal city and a worldly desire to link his own name to a memorable undertaking. The dream took shape over the space of just a few years (1459-64) and Pius II was able to make the town the seat of a bishop under the name of Pienza and to reside there for brief periods before meeting his death at Ancona, where he had gone to prepare a crusade for the reconquest of Constantinople.

With the disappearance of its creator, work on the city came to a halt and the "spotlight" that had played on it for such a short time went out. Pienza returned to its life as a country town linked to Siena and was burned and devastated on several occasions over the course of the political struggle between the papacy and the empire, and between Siena and Florence.

Today, like nearby Montepulciano and Montalcino, it attracts a considerable influx of tourists, who seem to flock there at all times of the year,

attracted by the perfection of an urban scenery that after many centuries has not ceased to astound and a natural setting that appears to mirror that perfection.

The architect called on by Pius II to realize his plans was the Florentine Bernardo Rosselli, called Rossellino, who had the great merit of adapting his creation to the preexisting structure. Thus the beautiful square, whose harmony is the result of the perfect relations that bind the constructions together, was inserted into the ancient medieval main street without altering it. The cathedral, Palazzo Piccolomini and Palazzo Borgia face onto it.

The cathedral, with a fine travertine façade and simple saddleback structure, stands on the site of the ancient parish church of Santa Maria, whose foundations have reemerged during restoration work. The apsidal part is set on a slope of clay that has caused problems of instability right from the beginning (a series of major restorations have been carried out over the course of the 20th cent.

The interior of the cathedral with the wooden choir and the baptismal font designed by Bernardo Rossellino

The courtyard of Palazzo Piccolomini; left, Piazza Pio II with the Palazzo Comunale and Palazzo Vescovile

Alberti's Palazzo Rucellai in Florence. It has an inner courtyard, providing access to the hanging garden onto which faces the beautiful three-story loggia.

The left-hand side of the square is closed by the Palazzo Vescovile, formerly Palazzo Borgia: in a limpid Renaissance style with fine windows in the form of Guelph crosses, it has recently been renovated to house the Museo della Cattedrale.

This boasts one of the most important collections in the Sienese region, enriched with works from churches in the vicinity that include panels by Pietro Lorenzetti, Ugolino di Nerio, Bartolo di Fredi, the Master of the Osservanza and Fra Bartolomeo. The most precious piece in the museum, however, is the *Pluvial of Pius II*, a work of English manufacture embroidered with a refined technique that was donated to the Piccolomini pope by Thomas Palaeologus.

About three kilometers from the city stands the 7th-cent. parish church of Corsignano, dedicated to Sts. Vitus and Modestus. Renovated several times over the centuries, its oldest parts include the cylindrical tower converted into a campanile and a small crypt. The refinement of the decoration of the two portals contrasts with the rough font inside, in which Pius II was baptized.

without finding a definitive solution to the problem). On the other hand, the disposition of the building answered in full to the scenographic requirements of the square, opening on the vast panorama of the Val d'Orcia, to which it acted as a backdrop. The luminous interior is adorned with important works that Pius II himself had

commissioned from Sienese artists, including paintings by Sano di Pietro, Vecchietta and Matteo di Giovanni.

Palazzo Piccolomini, built on the site of previous residences of the nobile family, is the work of Rossellino, who took his inspiration directly from

Vecchietta, *Madonna and Child with Saints*, detail of the lunette with the *Annunciation*; facing page, English manufacture, *Pluvial of Pius II*, detail. Museo della Cattedrale

Montepulciano

On the top of a hill between the Val di Chiana and the Val d'Orcia has stood for centuries, like an ancient icon, one of the most beautiful and celebrated cities in southern Tuscany: Montepulciano.

The small city first appears under the name of "Castello Politiano" – later transmuted into Puliciano – in documents dating from 714, but archeological finds have established the existence of Etruscan and then Roman settlements in the area.

Its elevated position, high above the marshes of the Val di Chiana, and strategic geographical location allowing it to exercise control over the southern areas of the region made it a bone of contention between the larger cities. Siena and Florence, in particular, made it the object of their designs over the course of centuries of struggle, in which it came alternatively under the sway of one or the other. However, it was its definitive passage to Florence (1511) and subsequent elevation to the status of episcopal see (1561) that brought about the urban development and architectural character that it has maintained to the present day.

The entry into a broader political sphere did not automatically translate into economic benefits for Montepulciano. On the contrary, it began to go into decline in the 15th cent. and it was only with the reclamation of the plain below – a process brought to a conclusion under the Lorraine, at the end of the 18th cent. – and the assumption of a more important role from the administrative standpoint that the city showed signs of revival.

Today it is an unrivalled magnet for tourists, with the

Detail of a 16th-cent. painting with view of Montepulciano. Collection of the Banca Popolare dell'Etruria

Bottom left, the Palazzo Comunale; right, Palazzo Bucelli with detail of an Etruscan urn set in the base

result that for much of the year its ancient streets are crowded with people from every part of the world, drawn by the fascination of its architecture and the wonderful balance between natural and constructed scenery that makes this part of Tuscany so unique.

Florentine architecture has certainly left a distinctive mark on Montepulciano, commencing with the spectacular Piazza Grande onto which faces the Palazzo Comunale, modeled on the Palazzo della Signoria in Florence, with a façade designed by Michelozzo. Not far away stands the cathedral of the Assunta (1594-1680), built on the site of an ancient parish church whose stubby bell tower still survives. The interior is a sort of treasure chest, containing among many other works Taddeo di Bartolo's monumental triptych of the *Assumption*, Giovanni

d'Agostino's baptismal font and the sepulchral monument of the Humanist Bartolomeo Aragazzi, by Michelozzo, divided into seven fragments that are now located at different points of the church.

Numerous religious buildings are scattered through the urban fabric, commencing with Sant'Agnese – built along with the adjoining convent by St. Agnes of Montepulciano herself and dedicated to her later – and continuing with Sant'Agostino and Santa Maria dei Servi. But by far the most fascinating building, San Biagio, is located just outside the city on the western slope of the ridge. It is one of Tuscany's authentic Renaissance gems. The work of Antonio da Sangallo the Elder, its luminous structure rises elegantly in the midst of the greenery, against the backdrop of the Sienese hills, as if it were the

materialization of a utopian dream.

The many noble houses that are crammed within the medieval walls face onto the three main streets that run parallel to the ridge. Via di Gracciano in particular offers a view of some of the finest

Palazzo del Monte Cantucci and, bottom, Palazzo Tarugi

buildings, such as Palazzo degli Avignonesi, Palazzo Cocconi (attributed to Antonio da Sangallo the Elder) and Palazzo Bucelli, famous for its cinerary urns and the Etruscan and Latin inscriptions walled into its base.

The Gothic Palazzo Neri Orselli, on the other hand, is Sienese in style. For several decades it has housed the Museo Civico and Pinacoteca Crociani. The latter, fruit of a bequest from the man it is named after, contains a collection of paintings from the Sienese and Florentine schools and an important group of Della Robbian terracottas.

Two more significant civic institutions are the Biblioteca Comunale (Palazzo Ricci) and the Teatro Poliziano, named after the great Humanist and poet Politian, a friend of Lorenzo the Magnificent, who was born here.

Top, Sant'Agostino with Michelozzo's façade

Left, Giovanni d'Agostino, baptismal font; right, Michelozzo, *The Virgin Blessing the Aragazzi Family.* Cathedral

Facing page, San Biagio

250

Chiusi

A city of ancient origin, Chiusi still has to reckon with a legendary past today. Its birth predates even the Etruscan era, as is indicated by traces of the Villanovian culture, but it was in the 6th-5th cent. BC that it reached its peak as a city of the Etruscan Dodecapolis with the name of Camars.

Its fame is linked to its king Lars Porsenna, who according to legend laid siege to Rome in 510 BC with the aim of restoring Tarquinius Superbus to the throne, but later Camars entered into alliance with Rome and became a military station with the name of Clusium. However, it never lost its importance, favored by a strategic position on the southern edge of the Val di Chiana and on the route of the Via Cassia.

A center for the spread of Christianity, as the catacombs

Exterior and interior of the cathedral with detail of a capital with a dosseret from late antiquity

of Santa Caterina and Santa Mustiola attest, it was occupied by the Goths and then the Longobards, who made it the seat of a large duchy.

The progressive transformation of the Val di Chiana into marshland, with the usual complements of malaria and depopulation, led to its decline around the 11th cent.

Paolozzi Cinerary Urn from the 7th cent. BC. Museo Archeologico

Sold to Siena by King Ladislas Durazzo of Naples, it remained a Sienese possession until 1556, when both cities were incorporated into the Grand Duchy of Tuscany.

Today the most significant testimonies of such a rich history are to be found in an archeological complex of great value that covers a vast area in the heart of a fascinating landscape still characterized by the cultivation of vines and olives.

Top left, 6th-cent. BC sphinx carved from *pietra fetida*; above, 5th-4th cent. BC pictorial decoration with two-horse chariot, from the Tomb of the Hill. Museo Archeologico

Among the most famous of the tombs, some of them closed to the public for reasons of conservation, are the Tomb of the Lion, the Bonci Casuccini Tomb, the Tomb of the Monkey and the Tomb of the Pilgrim.

Chiusi's most illustrious monument is the cathedral of San Secondiano, founded in the 6th cent. on the site of a preexisting basilica, rebuilt in the 12th cent. and massively restored at the end of the nineteenth. Inside it is subdivided into a nave and two aisles by columns of fine marble taken from ancient Roman buildings in the region of Chiusi. The Museo della Cattedrale in the adjoining episcopal complex houses twenty-one precious illuminated anthem books from the abbey of Monteoliveto Maggiore. Visitors to the museum can also enter the Labyrinth

of Porsenna, a suggestive underground route stretching for over 100 meters through tunnels carved out of the stone. Perhaps a work of hydraulic engineering, its name derives from an erroneous identification with the immense mausoleum of the Etruscan king described by Pliny the Elder.

Above, 5th-cent. BC bas-relief with musicians; below, lid of the urn of Larth Sentinates Caesa, from the Tomb of the Pilgrim. Museo Archeologico

The Museo Archeologico Nazionale, founded in 1870 and housed in an elegant building of the same period, displays a collection of cinerary urns, Canopic jars – vessels with lids sculpted into the form of the deceased's head – and sarcophagi from the nearby necropolises.

Monte Amiata

B ut let us return to San Quirico d'Orcia, for an itinerary that will take us south-south-west by the S.S. 323 and the roads branching off it towards Monte Amiata. From Castel del Piano one easily reaches the summit of the mountain at 1738 metres, with a superb panorama as far as the Tyrrhenian and Lakes Trasimeno and Bolsena. But I advise a proper visit to the whole of the massif, with its lovely chestnut forests and picturesque villages, such as Pian Castagnaio, as well as the summits of Monte Calvo (930 metres) and Monte Civitella (1107 metres). At Abbadia San Salvatore you will find what is left of the famous Benedictine abbey: dating back to the 8th cent., its abbot was, in the late Middle Ages, one of the most powerful overlords in the region. The church is Romanesque, but the delightful crypt goes back to the period of its foundation. Another noteworthy Romanesque church is that of Sante Fiora e Lucilla at Santa Fiora. From here we reach Arcidosso, and enter the area of "Lazzarettian" pilgrimages.

Beech wood on the slopes
of Monte Amiata

Facing page, Arcidosso with
the Rocca Aldobrandesca; bottom,
the church of the Benedictine
abbey at Abbadia San Salvatore

This is an interesting story not widely known outside Italy. The "Prophet of Amiata," Davide Lazzaretti, was a carter born in Arcidosso in 1834 and from 1868 to 1878 led a religious cult based on asceticism and penitence and marked by a strong tendency to millenarism (the expectation of "Christ the Leader and Judge"), as well as by generous if somewhat confused social ideals. With his great charisma he had a large following among the peasants and shepherds of Monte Amiata. His actions were foreign to any sort of violence, and he does not even seem to have toyed with Protestant ideas – indeed he had a deep reverence for the Virgin Mary. But he was condemned by the Church and awakened concern among the civil authorities, who were anxious about social unrest. On August 18, 1878, Lazzaretti, having proclaimed himself the Christ of the Second Coming, came down from his Sacred Mountain, the nearby Monte Labbro (1183 metres) at the head of a harmless procession of his followers. At the entrance to Arcidosso a platoon of Carabinieri mowed them down, killing the "Prophet" and many other innocent people. On the site of this slaughter there is now a Neo-Gothic chapel to commemorate this sad act of repression, one of many which the government of newly-united Italy perpetrated in Tuscany and elsewhere. On Monte Labbro, in an enclosure invaded by sheep, there is the modest sanctuary of the "Chiesa Giurisdavidica" founded by Lazzaretti. It is a narrow fissure in a rock. Plenty of followers of the cult remain in the area, and they even have a temple in Rome.

Towards Ancient Tuscia

We return northwards along the S.S. 323, visiting Seggiano, Castiglione d'Orcia (with the ruins of the castle of the mightiest feudal family of southern Tuscany, the Aldobrandeschi, lords of Santa Fiora) and Rocca d'Orcia, overlooked by other impressive ruins, those of the fortress at Tintinnano dei Salimbeni. Here we once more join the Via Cassia, which however it is better to leave about fifteen kilometers further south (at Bisarca) to fork left up the S.S. 478 to the volcanic rock of Radicofani, a town impressive in its solitude and dominated by a severe 13th-century fortress, rebuilt several times. At its foot is the 16th-century "Palazzo della Posta," a hostel and customs post at the borders of the grand duchy and the Papal States. The pass at Radicofani, mentioned by Boccaccio on account of the bandit Ghino di Tacco who terrorized it, was for centuries the place at which the Via Francigena left Tuscany.

Present-day administrative boundaries cut across an area that in fact has a deep-seated unity, and we suggest starting from Radicofani and continuing along the Cassia as far as Acquapendente, in the part of Tuscia which falls in Lazio. Here we should see the ancient church containing the late mediaeval votive chapel of the Holy Sepulchre. In this way we shall travel through the whole of the ancient feudal domain of the Farnese family: Grotte di

Castro, the west bank of the Lake of Bolsena, Ischia di Castro, Farnese itself, the ruins of the town of Castro, and then – using the S.S. 312 – the Etruscan necropolis of Vulci. Continuing south we meet the Via Aurelia at Montalto di Castro, whence after a few kilometers we find ourselves at the marvellous town of Tarquinia; we then go on to Tuscania, with its Etruscan remains and its incomparable mediaeval churches. In a word, what we have is the whole region of "Tuscia in Lazio" contained within a perimeter that follows the Via Cassia to the east of the Lake of Bolse-

The village of Radicofani

The Piazza del Pretorio at Sovana

 na, touches Montefiascone, arrives at Viterbo and then at Ventralla, from which the S.S.1bis takes us to Tarquinia. Whatever the administrative borders may be, if we do not visit this area we cannot understand southern Tuscany, which is closely united with it in history and landscape, quite apart from the fact that the "Etruscan Itinerary" that we started at Cortona and Chiusi must logically end at Tuscania, Tarquinia and Vulci.

Bas-relief on the portal of the cathedral and interior of Santa Maria Maggiore at Sovana

But for our visit to Tuscia we do not have to start from the line of the Cassia. We can also make a perfectly logical tour starting from Orbetello, which stands on the sandbar connecting the Argentario to the mainland. From there the Via Aurelia runs east-south-east past the ruins of the Etruscan city of Cosa above Ansedonia, crosses the reclaimed area of the Lake of Burano and travels on past Montalto di Castro. All the same, shortly after the lake, which we leave on our right because it is wedged in between the coast and the road, we will turn off and head for the pretty little town of Capalbio, with its mediaeval walls and its splendid cuisine typical of the Maremma. Going north from Capalbio we can link up with the Amiata tour we have just described. We will see Manciano, the sulphur baths of Saturnia (which can also be reached easily from Arcidosso and Santa Fiora), and further to the east Sovana, birthplace of Hildebrand, the 11th-century monk who became pope with the name of Gregory VII. It has the ruins of an Aldobrandeschi fortress and some lovely Romanesque churches. Further on, Pitigliano has the immense Orsini castle, and the tufa precipices honey-combed with caves that make one aware how close one is to Lazio. From Sovana a path leads down to an impressive Etruscan necropolis composed of tombs cut into the tufa cliffs, in a precipitous landscape as breath-taking as any in the region.

These are a few, and perhaps all too few, of the multitude of things one can see in Tuscany. I cannot even claim that they are the most important; and in any case, with the aid of guides and maps and asking questions when on the spot, everyone will be able to work out his own itinerary, choosing between what I have mentioned and what I

The "sunken street"
of San Sebastiano in
the environs of Sovana

have had to leave out for reasons of space. But this is "my" Tuscany, the Tuscany of my own experiences, and knowledge, memories, tastes and perhaps even manias both great and small. I do not so much admire as love this part of the world. Others may want to do things in a different way, and to "pick up" on different things. For my part I have tried to avoid making a museum of a world abounding in beauties and works of art, but one that should be taken as its own rhythms dictate, with an approach as free as is humanly possible, within which a traveller does not feel guilty if he misses a church or omits visiting a palace. The Tuscans are a frugal people, with a fund of antique avarice derived from their historical experiences, which have not always been easy. They are a people who hate surfeit and indigestion of any kind, art and culture included. The intelligent visitor will not gobble down the Romanesque and the Gothic, the hills and the seashores; he will select with care, taste with discretion, and enjoy a little at a time. With luck he will be able to put some things off until the next time – for there is always a next time – he comes to Tuscany.

The village of Sorano, perched spectacularly on a crag of tufa, with the Rocca Orsini (right)

Grosseto

The ascent of Grosseto seems to have begun with the progressive decline of the Etruscan and Roman city of Rusellae (Roselle), culminating in the transfer of the episcopal see to Grosseto (1138) by Pope Innocent II.

The first records of the city refer to a castle built around the 9th cent. near the mouth of the swampy Ombrone River, in a natural setting dominated by extensive forests, from which it derives its name (*grossetum* = large wood).

A fief of the powerful Aldobrandeschi family, counts of Maremma, it soon had to guard itself against the designs of the Sienese – interested in its position and its profits from the production of salt – who succeeded in annexing it definitively in 1336, having already demolished its walls in the past. For its role as an active Ghibelline stronghold in the Maremma, it had been previously, in the middle of the 13th cent. (1242-45), been chosen as the seat of the imperial vicar for Tuscany by Emperor Frederick II, who seems to have stayed in the city, surrounded by the usual pomp of his court of intellectuals.

The subsequent history of Grosseto, marred by epidemics, malaria and recurrent raids by Barbary pirates (far more frequent than is normally thought, the latter made a lasting impression on the popular memory), was played out in the shadow of Siena, fighting alongside it in the long and bloody war against Florence in which it would be the last to fall (1559).

Following the city's surrender, the Medici started work on draining the surrounding territory in an effort to improve the environmental conditions, but it was only under the

Top, Ilario Casolani, *Madonna and Child with Saints*, detail showing Grosseto. Museo Archeologico e d'Arte della Maremma

Right, the cloister of San Francesco; below, the cathedral with the Palazzo Comunale

Above, the portal on the right flank and the interior of the cathedral; below, Antonio Ghini, baptismal font

Lorraine (Peter Leopold and then Leopold II) that appreciable results were attained, although the work of reclamation was to continue right up until the middle of the 20th cent. More incisive were the results achieved by Cosimo I in the defense of the lands he had conquered through the construction of a coastal chain of lookout towers that can still be seen today, and the erection of new city walls which, in Grosseto as elsewhere, were also intended as a measure

against possible rebellion.

Designed and constructed (1593) by Baldassarre Lanci, a famous military engineer of the time, the walls have conditioned the urban development of the city, and even today, after the devastation wrought in the last war, represent one of the strongest marks of continuity with the past.

The cathedral, dedicated to the city's patron St. Lawrence, is Grosseto's principal monument and, in spite of

repeated alterations, the most interesting. The Neo-Gothic façade in white and red marble dates from around the middle of the 19th cent. and only the symbols of the Evangelists belong to the original construction of the late 13th. The interior, with a nave and two aisles, is also the result of a series of interventions and houses a baptismal font (1470) by Antonio Ghini, a 17th-cent. high altar in colored marble with a ciborium by Giovanni Antonio Mazzuoli and a panel

Top, Guido da Siena, *Last Judgment*; above, Ilario Casolani, *Madonna and Child with Saints*, left, Sassetta, *Madonna delle Ciliegie*. Museo Archeologico e d'Arte della Maremma

depicting the *Assumption* by Matteo di Giovanni.

The city's other important church, San Francesco, stands on the site previously occupied by a Benedictine monastery. Simple and essential in its lines as suits a building of the mendicant order, it is adorned with frescoes from various periods and a precious painted *Cross* attributed to Duccio di Buoninsegna or the Master of

Badia a Isola. The nearby San Pietro is the oldest church in Grosseto, and has a fine Romanesque apse.

The most important memories of the city and its region are preserved in the Museo Archeologico e d'Arte della Maremma, situated in the 19th-cent. building that used to be the Courthouse. In addition to a permanent display of finds made in the excavations of the

archeological area of Roselle, the museum houses objects from the Maremma region dating from prehistoric times up until the modern era. On the top story of the building, recently renovated and opened to the public, there is a collection of sacred art, made up of paintings, sculptures, illuminated codices and liturgical silverware.

Pitigliano

Pitigliano appears to the eyes of the unsuspecting traveler like a vision of another world. The tall bell tower of the cathedral, the great arches of the 16th-cent. aqueduct, the old houses, the palaces overhanging the cliff and the fortifications seem to emerge, like spontaneous growths, from the blocks of tufa, themselves pierced by a thousand openings that barely illuminate the entrances to caves. At the foot, vegetable gardens and vineyards appear to cradle the crag.

Pitigliano is perched on a wedge of tufa modeled over the ages by the Lente and Meleta torrents, a protected site where its ancient inhabitants felt safe from attack. Its origins are unknown, but it was definitely inhabited in the Etruscan and Roman eras, although not many traces of these settlements are left today. The most significant relics are in the south, at Porcarecce and Poggio Buco on the way to Manciano, where many tombs have been found, along with the remains of what may have been a

princely residence, and, to the north, at nearby Sovana with its rock tombs and "sunken streets" carved out of the rock.

In the 13th cent. Pitigliano belonged to the Aldobrandeschi of Sovana, and then, in the 14th, to the Orsini, who took over this area from its previous rulers and were responsible for the development of the burg, which they made their capital. From then on the destiny of Pitigliano was tied to the Orsini family, up until its extinction when, after a brief period of rule by Piero Strozzi, the city passed into the hands of the Medici.

The memory of the Orsini still survives today in the spectacular aqueduct which Gian Francesco had built to the design of Antonio da Sangallo the Younger to bring water to

the family palace. Added to over time, the Palazzo or Fortezza Orsini is now an amalgam of architectural styles. It houses the Museo Diocesano di Arte Sacra and Museo Civico Archeologico.

The cathedral of Santi Pietro e Paolo has a 16th-cent. structure with a baroque façade and high altar, but the oldest church, documented in the 13th cent., is Santa Maria, with a Renaissance façade built by Niccolò III Orsini. The church stands in the picturesque quarter of Capisotto, on the western edge of the crag, a dense network of tortuous alleys that

overlook the precipice, sometimes connected by nothing more than steps.

The existence of an ancient Jewish community in the ghetto, created in order to escape the taxes exacted by the papal state and further expanded following a bull of Pius IV (1569) which banned Jews from Rome, is attested by the synagogue. Neglected for decades, partly as a consequence of the depopulation of the ghetto, it was restored a few years ago and reopened for worship.

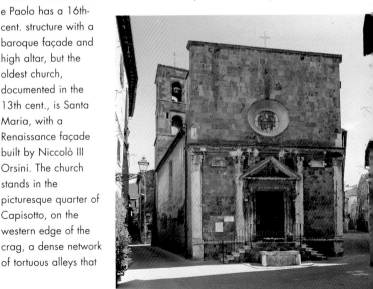

© 2003 SCALA Group S.p.A., Florence

This 2006 edition published by
Barnes & Noble, Inc.,
by arrangement with SCALA Group S.p.A.

Text by *Franco Cardini*

Monographic sections on towns and cities
compiled by the Scala editorial staff

Editing: Marilena Vecchi

Translation: *Patrick Creagh* (text)
Huw Evans (sections on the cities)

Photographs: Archivio Fotografico SCALA Group
(Bacherini, Grifoni, Lampredi, Lensini, Savorelli)
except pp. 16 b, 18, 25, 51, 62 b, 188 b,
192 b, 213 a, 225, 226 a, 227 a, 233, 242,
243, 247, 252 b, 254, 255 a, 256 a
(A. and F. Lensini); pp. 49, 105 a, 193
(Pubbliaerfoto/Aerocentro Varesino); pp. 80/81
(by permission of Dr. Luigi Zalum, Villa
Gamberaia); pp. 110, 111 (P. Savorelli)

The pictures on pp. 22b, 23, 28 a, 32 b, 35,
37, 41 and 123 have been reproduced by kind
permission of Bruno Giovannetti, to whom we
would like to express our particular gratitude

The images from the SCALA PICTURE LIBRARY
reproducing cultural assets that belong to the
Italian State are published with the permission of
the Ministry for Cultural Heritage and Activities

ISBN-13: 978-0-7607-7852-4
ISBN-10: 0-7607-7852-3

Printed and bound in China

3 5 7 9 10 8 6 4 2